robing
eviathan

Probing Leviathan

An Investigation of
Government in the
Economy

Edited by:
George Lermer

Contributors:
Thomas J. Courchene
Herbert Grubel
John L. Howard
Richard G. Lipsey
Rolf Mirus
W. T. Stanbury

Papers appearing in this volume were first presented at a conference sponsored by The School of Management, The University of Lethbridge, Lethbridge, Alberta, April 1 and 2, 1982. The School of Management gratefully acknowledges the financial support of the Burns Foods Endowment Fund.

Canadian Cataloguing in Publication Data

Main entry under title:

Probing Leviathan

Includes index.

1. Canada - Economic policy - 1971-   2. Canada - Economic conditions - 1971-   3. Government spending policy - Canada.   I. Lermer, George.   II. Fraser Institute (Vancouver, B.C.)
HC115.P762 1984   330.971   C84-091416-4

Printed in Canada.

CONTENTS

FOREWORD, Michael A. Walker   vii
PREFACE
GOVERNMENT AND THE MARKET ECONOMY,
George Lermer   ix

PART I
Chapter 1
CAN THE MARKET ECONOMY SURVIVE?
Richard G. Lipsey   3

I.   What the Market Economy Does   3
II.   The Case for the Market Economy   9
III.   The Case for Intervention   13
IV.   The Erosion of the Free Market   19
V.   The Future of the Market Economy   28
      Notes   35
      References   36

Chapter 2
THE CITIZEN AND THE STATE: A MARKET
    PERSPECTIVE, Thomas J. Courchene   39

I.   Introduction   39
II.   The Protected Society   41
      The drive for economic security and the interaction
         between citizen and the state   42
         Protectionism and the realities of the 1980s   46
         Federalism and the market system   49
III.   Conclusion   53
      Notes   54
      References   55

PART II
Chapter 3
THE COSTS OF CANADA'S SOCIAL INSURANCE
    PROGRAMS, Herbert Grubel   59

I.   Introduction   59
II.   Rationale for Public Insurance   62
III.   Some Facts About Welfare Spending   65
IV.   Moral Hazard   72

V.   Costs Through Changes in the Nature of Society
     and High Taxes   79
VI. Policy Conclusions   83
VII. Recommendations   83
     Notes   84
     References   85

Chapter 4
MEASURING LEVIATHAN: THE SIZE, SCOPE AND
GROWTH OF GOVERNMENTS IN CANADA, John
L. Howard and W. T. Stanbury   87

I.   Increasing Concern About the Role of Government   88
II. Summary of the Main Findings   91
III. Understanding Leviathan: Conclusions and Implications   94
     Notes   106
     References   108

Chapter 5
THE INVISIBLE ECONOMY: ITS DIMENSIONS AND
IMPLICATIONS, Rolf Mirus   113

I.   Introduction   113
II. Unobserved Economic Activity—An Attempt at
     Classification   114
III. Measurement of the Invisible Economy   116
IV. Causes of the Invisible Economy   122
V.   Implications and Policy Options   123
     Notes   125
     Bibliography   126

Appendix to Measuring Leviathan: The Size, Scope and Growth
of Governments in Canada, John L. Howard and
W. T. Stanbury   127

I.   Expenditures   128
II.   Public Employment   141
III. Tax Expenditures   144
IV.   Regulation   152
V.   Public Enterprises/Crown Corporations   160
VI.   Loans and Loan Guarantees   174
VII. Mixed Enterprises: Equity Ownership in Private
      Sector Firms   181
VIII. Chosen Instruments   188
IX.   Suasion   193
      Notes   199
      References   213

FOREWORD

Seldom in recent history has the role of government been more in question than at the present time. Mushrooming deficits have focused public attention on the spending and taxing of governments and caused widespread concern. The increasingly obvious burdens associated with government regulations have caused a reconsideration of their role in furthering the public interest. As well, there is growing recognition that the same human motives which have lead some to be cynical about the operation of the marketplace also operate in the public sector.

The purpose of this book is to probe different aspects of the government sector from a behavioural and quantitative point of view. The Institute is pleased to be able to publish the results of the enquiry, ably edited by Professor George Lermer. However, owing to the independence of the authors the views expressed by them do not necessarily reflect the views of the members, trustees, or funding agencies of The Fraser Institute.

Michael A. Walker
Director
The Fraser Institute

GEORGE LERMER

George Lermer is Professor, Director of the School of Management, and Acting Dean, Faculty of Professional Studies, the University of Lethbridge. He was awarded a B.Sc. by the Massachusetts Institute of Technology, and an M.A. and Ph.D. in economics by McGill University. He furthered his studies by spending one year at the Wharton School, University of Pennsylvania and another at the London School of Economics.

After twelve years of teaching at the University of British Columbia, Concordia University and the University of Waterloo, Professor Lermer joined the staff of the Economic Council of Canada. There he contributed to the Council's study, "Efficiency and Regulation" which dealt with Canada's banks and other desposit taking financial institutions.

In 1976, Professor Lermer became Director, Resources Branch, Consumer and Corporate Affairs Canada, where he was responsible for pursuing a number of major investigations and research studies into Canadian resource industries, including a detailed analysis of performance in the Canadian agriculture and food processing industries.

The joint author of a book on Canadian money and banking, Professor Lermer has also published articles in economic theory, the rationalizing of Canadian industry, the Canadian tariff structure, the efficiency of banks, and most recently, on regulation of industry. He served on the editorial board of the *Canadian Journal of Economics*.

Professor Lermer has consulted for a number of government agencies and private trade organizations, and has written studies on the Canadian machinery manufacturing industry and the socio-economic problems of communities suffering the loss of a major industry.

PREFACE

GOVERNMENT AND THE MARKET ECONOMY

Authority over economic decisions is rapidly being transferred from the private to the public sector. The conference, for which the papers in this volume were originally prepared, examined the speed and consequences of this transfer. The conference's objective, like this book's, was to acquaint a non-professional audience with a wide range of professional opinion and empirical findings about the decline of the market sector as an allocator of resources and about the prospects for the mixed economy. The conference addressed such questions as why government grows, why there is dissatisfaction with large government, and where the growth of government is likely to take us.

Growth of government intervention

During the post-war years, many professional economists, like a majority of academics, supported an expanded role for governments. Some argued from a strong commitment to Keynesian ideas about how government should manage an apparently unstable market economy. Their views were particularly influenced by the still vivid memories of the pre-war depression. Others argued for government intervention in order to deal with a feared secular stagnation of demand in rich economies, and the alleged undersupply of public goods like public transport, parks, and security. More recently, in response to growing criticism of the market's performance, government has undertaken to allocate those resources for which property rights are ill-defined or unenforceable, such as the right to harvest a fishing ground or to enjoy a pollution free environment.

The predilection of intellectuals towards a benevolent and rationally planned allocation of resources under government auspices is well known. George Stigler,[1] for instance, commented that, "The intellectual has never felt kindly towards the market place: to him it has always been a place of vulgar men and base motives." Indeed, Stigler's motive for writing was, "To persuade young intellectuals that they should re-examine the traditional hostility towards private enterprise." All the authors represented in this volume share Stigler's objective. Their concerns include not only the rapid expansion of government influence over the economy, but also the growing threat to the viability of the market sector of the mixed economy, and to our economic and social freedoms, posed by the concentration of economic power in the political arena. They remain pessimistic about the future for the Western democracies, discerning trends towards further expansion of the government sector. Nonetheless, all the essays end on one optimistic note, namely that the intellectual community at least can be persuaded to accept the arguments why government intervention so often fails to deliver on its promise, whereas the free market so often succeeds. All the authors remain optimistic that reason will prevail over the twin evils of centralization and politicization of economic life.

The essays provide not only a clear analysis of how government intervention has spread as it has, but also a clarion call to resist the growing role of government. They are reminiscent of the pessimism expressed by the late Professor Joseph Schumpeter,[2] who viewed capitalism as a condemned social system. For Schumpeter, this great engine of progress would inevitably be derailed by the intellectual's implacable hostility to capitalism, a hostility aggravated by the growing number of intellectuals, spawned by capitalism's success, who would share the intellectual's traditional anti-capitalist and anti-market bias. The authors share Milton Friedman's[3] belief that, "we shall be able to preserve and extend freedom... despite the economic powers already concentrated in Washington" (government).

Pressure for further intervention

Richard Lipsey and Tom Courchene, more explicitly than the other authors, share Schumpeter's pessimistic vision of the future of capitalism. In particular, Lipsey develops the theme that the entrenched level of government intervention will not easily be rolled back. According to Lipsey, unwillingness to face the consequences of the messages about the reality the market transmits is reflected in political intervention to eliminate windfall gains and to cushion windfall losses. Ironically, the already enormous impact of government policies and regulations reinforces the drive to still more intervention, as prices in private markets swing ever more wildly because normal market adjustments are postponed and frustrated, and because government so frequently, haphazardly, and abruptly, changes policy directions. As Lipsey eloquently puts it: "today's rulers pass laws seeking to suspend the actions of the market economy and end up executing it."

Pursuit of economic security

For Courchene it is the citizen's pursuit of economic security that foreshadows the doom of the enterprise system. In the long run, flexibility, nimbleness, adaption and entrepreneurship provide the only true security for society. In the short run, however, individuals and groups expect and receive from government protection from the apparently arbitrary and unjust market.

This natural instinct for self-protection is particularly pronounced in Canada. One possible explanation is the traditionally cyclical nature of an economy driven by exports of resources. Another is that Canadians demand more security from their governments than do Americans, for example, simply because they have learned to expect better results when approaching governments. Arguably, the generosity of Canadian governments derives from our federal system, in which different levels of government compete with one another for the political advantage which comes from supplying the security their citizens demand. Whether Canadian circumstances are peculiarly conducive to the erosion of the marketplace, or whether Canada is simply keeping pace with a phenomenon common to Western industrial countries, the pace of change is enormous. This is evident from John Howard's and William Stanbury's comprehensive review of the growth of Canadian governments and their agencies.

Instruments

Government operates through a myriad of instruments, including direct expenditures on goods and services; transfer payments to groups and individuals; public employment; tax systems riddled with exceptions for special classes of incomes and taxpayers; direct regulation of certain businesses and indirect regulation of others through social and environmental regulation; government ownership of industry; discretionary programs; subsidized lending and guaranteed loans; and assistance to private businesses. This enormous growth of government has a cumulative impact in reinforcing the political mechanisms which Lipsey and Courchene identify as inducing the government intervention in the first place.

The invisible economy

Rolf Mirus explains one reason why government growth in the economy is inexorable. He measures the growth of the invisible economy in Canada and discovers that between 10 and 15 percent of Canadian GNP is hidden from the tax collector. The avoidance of tax through shifting economic activity out of the usual transactions system into barter, exchange for cash, and "do-it-yourself" activity is a sign of resilience in a market economy, but it also encourages inefficient uses of resources, tax evasion leading to higher costs of collecting taxes, and still higher tax rates on the shrinking numbers of persons unable (or unwilling) to escape taxation. As tax burdens increase, so do the incentives to enter the invisible economy. Unless the cycle is broken, increased taxes and government regulation will push more economic activity underground which in turn leads governments to try to recapture lost revenues.

Proprietary rights and moral hazard

Herbert Grubel explains the growth of government expenditures differently. He discerns a shift in emphasis from the goal of providing a safety net for the poor and ailing, and towards the goal of establishing programs which give a broad class of persons a "proprietary right" to claim financial support. The notion that education, housing, health and income support are all "rights" rather than "privileges," and that access to them should be made largely independent of one's earnings is reflected in the figures Howard and Stanbury report on the increasing role of transfer expenditures in government budgets.

Grubel focuses only on the growth of welfare expenditures in Canada. He finds that between 1965 and 1977 expenditures rose from about $2.3 to 21 billion dollars, of which population growth and inflation account for less that $5 billion. Grubel attributes this enormous increase to the phenomenon known in the insurance industry as "moral hazard," namely that people will modify their behaviour in order to take best advantage of the programs available. Thus when funds are offered to a certain class of persons, other people will rearrange their affairs in order to become eligible for benefits.

Unfortunately, transfer payments are not costless; rather society pays twice. First, the higher taxes from which the transfer program is financed cause taxpayers to modify their behaviour, thereby leading to less productive economic activity and tax evasion. Second, in order to become eligible, potential beneficiaries must often adjust their economic status. They may, for example, choose to remain in a depressed region of the country, give up responsibility for supporting a family, squander savings on consumption, fail to provide for their retirement, or have children whom they fully expect will be supported with state assistance. The initiation of many government transfer and expenditure programs creates a class of politically influential dependents with little incentive to seek independence. The more so if they can benefit from the status as recipients of transfer payments and simultaneously participate in the active and healthy invisible economy which Mirus describes.

Future trends

How is one to respond to this unremitting gloom about the future of capitalism and economic freedom? Is the future so bleak that only morbid curiosity would motivate the observer to examine the issues raised in this volume? I think not. Despite each author's conviction that powerful forces are at work which stimulate further government intervention, all point to some indicators of the trend possibly slowing, or even reversing. Whether this is just wishful thinking or not, to leave the matter unexamined is to succumb to an unwarranted lethargy. Notwithstanding that government remains a growth industry, the economists' and intellectuals' enchantment with government seems to be waning. Since so many scholars have stressed how the intelligentsia's hostility to capitalism has helped prepare the way for government, the disenchantment of this influential group may foreshadow the redress of the balance in favour of the market. Lipsey brilliantly explains how traditional economic training has predisposed both bureaucrats and the general public to see government as a tool for remedying so-called market failures. His article is, from one point of view, a plea to officials and the public to let the market do its work. It is simultaneously an appeal to economists to teach a more full-blooded model of economic theory which confronts government policy-makers with the harsh realities of the economic options available to them, rather than the elegant but anemic pure theory that absorbs most of today's scholars.

Courchene too, despite identifying "compelling forces that will lead to an increased government involvement in all aspects of society," makes a strong plea for economists to be more realistic in their analyses in order that they might influence the choice of policy. He believes that economists can help by appreciating the role of social forces that determine public policy decisions. He advises the adoption of a "middle course" in policy analysis. Those who adopt an entirely negative attitude to all government intervention are condemned to impotence in the policy formation process. A patient and enduring program of education about the purposeful role of the market needs to be supported by an analysis that directs government away from the most egregious types of interventions to those that least damage the market economy while still satisfying the political imperatives that motivate the government to act.

Whatever one's views on issues such as the proper role of the state, the usefuness of tinkering with specific government programs, the likelihood that political and educational activities can help redress the balance of power in favour of the private sector, it is certain that reading the essays in this volume will provide a veritable feast for thought. Professor Lipsey's essay is an articulate and accessible account of the market mechanism and how government intervention frustrates its operation. His article should be compulsory reading for all politicians, bureaucrats, economics professors and their students. Courchene challenges all of us to rethink our own attitudes toward the trade-off between risk and security in our lives. He roots in Canadian political and economic reality universal concerns about the fundamental conflict between democracy and capitalism. Grubel convincingly explains why apparently reasonable and well planned government programs inevitably lead to expenditure over-runs, and he illustrates his thesis with Canada's recent experience running its welfare programs. Mirus applies the most recently developed models in order to estimate the extent of the invisible non-taxable segment of Canadian economic activity. He stresses the circularity of the process by which continued government growth will lead to ever higher tax burdens being placed in the visible sector, inducing still more tax evasion. Howard and Stanbury document the awesome scope of activities which Canadian governments already administer. For Howard and Stanbury, the future seems to have been sown but its consequences remain to be reaped. This book not only uncovers "Leviathan," as Howard and Stanbury call the government sector, but it reveals to the reader the factors in our social system which induce government growth as well as describing the harsh economic realities flowing therefrom.

George Lermer

NOTES

1 Stigler, George, J., *The Intellectual and the Market Place.* (London, Collier-Macmillan Limited, 1963, p. 85).

2 Schumpeter, Joseph Alois, *Capitalism, Socialism and Democracy* (3rd edition, New York, Harper, 1950).

3 Friedman, Milton, *Capitalism and Freedom,* (Chicago, University of Chicago Press, 1962).

PART I

RICHARD G. LIPSEY

Richard G. Lipsey was born in British Columbia in 1928. He was educated at Victoria College and the University of British Columbia, and did graduate work at the University of Toronto and the London School of Economics. He received his Ph.D. from the University of London in 1957. Dr. Lipsey is presently Senior Research Advisor for the C.D. Howe Institute in Toronto while on leave from his post as Sir Edward Peacock Professor of Economics at Queen's University, Kingston. He has held many posts in academic and public sectors, including a chair in economics at the London School of Economics, the chairmanship of the Department of Economics at the University of Essex, member of the council of Britain's National Institute of Economic and Social Research (London), and panel member for the Policy Analysis Group of the federal Department of Consumer and Corporate Affairs.

Professor Lipsey is author of several textbooks, including *Economics: An Introductory Analysis* (with P.O. Steiner) which has had seven American and five Canadian editions and has also been translated into Spanish and French. His latest book is *An Introduction to the U.K. Economy* (with Colin Harbury). His earlier book *Mathematical Economics: Methods and Applications* (with G.C. Archibald), published by Harper & Row has been translated into Spanish, Portuguese, and Japanese.

CHAPTER 1

CAN THE MARKET ECONOMY SURVIVE?*

Richard G. Lipsey

What is the market economy and does it have a future? Is it an obsolete form already heading for inevitable extermination or will its resilience and efficiency guarantee its survival in spite of all attempts to suppress it? What is the source of the rising chorus, particularly in the United States, calling for a major reduction of the role of government in the market economy, and is such a reduction likely? I address all of these questions in this paper. In the process I develop the theme that it may be much more difficult to effect a major reduction in the place of government in the economy than many seem to believe.

I. WHAT THE MARKET ECONOMY DOES

Two views of the market economy

Economists have used two ways of gaining insight into the working of the market economy. First, they have studied the economy in equi-

*This paper is a revised version of "An Economist Looks at the Future of the Market Economy," presented to the XV Annual Nobel Conference on the Future of the Market Economy at Gustavus Adolphus College, St. Peter, Minnesota, October 10, 1979. I am greatly indebted to B. Curtis Eaton, Cappy Hill, Douglas Purvis and Dan Usher for comments, criticisms and suggestions.

librium, which is a state of rest when all forces causing change have worked themselves out. The key property of free-market equilibrium is that the rewards from all lines of work open to similar individuals are equalized (allowing for both monetary and non-monetary returns) as are the rewards for all lines of investment activity (making allowance for different kinds of risk). If this were not so, people and capital would flow away from those activities that offer lower rewards and towards those that offer higher rewards. The flows would continue until rewards were equalized.

Second, economists have studied disequilibrium behaviour, which is the ways the market economy reacts to disturbances. Here the engine that drives the adaption to disturbing forces is what economists call quasi-rents, and what the general public has come to know as windfall profits. A *windfall profit* is a profit in a particular line of activity that arises out of changes in market conditions and that is not related to current production costs. (Note that windfall losses are included as negative windfall profits.)[1]

A rise in demand or a fall in production costs creates windfall profits for that commodity's producers, while a fall in demand or a rise in production costs creates windfall losses. Windfall profits signal that there are too few resources devoted to that industry. These profits induce more resources — labour, capital etc. — to enter the industry, increasing output and driving down price until windfall profits are driven to zero. Windfall losses signal the reverse — resources leave the industry until those left behind are no longer making losses.

Windfall profits and losses are thus the basic engine that drives the market economy's adaptions to changes. If the government taxed away *all* windfall profits and replaced by subsidy *all* windfall losses, it would effectively destroy the market economy by removing its driving force. Because the economy is continuously adjusting to shocks, a snapshot of the economy at any moment of time reveals substantial windfall profits in some industries and substantial windfall losses in others. A similar snapshot at another moment in time will reveal windfall profits and losses at other locations (because their existence sets up a set of decentralized decisions that have the effect of removing them).

Some basic characteristics of the market economy

If we are to study the future of the market economy, we must understand four of its most important characteristics: its operation as a social control mechanism, its determination of the distribution of income, its dynamic product cycle, and its ability to function without being understood or consciously directed.

A social control mechanism

First, consider the market economy as a social control mechanism. Every day millions of people make millions of independent decisions concerning production and consumption. Most of these decisions are not motivated by a desire to contribute to the social good or to make the whole economy work well but by fairly immediate considerations of personal or group self-interest. The price system coordinates these decentralized decisions, making the whole system fit together and respond to the wishes of the individuals who compose it.

The basic insight into how this system works is that decentralized, private decision-makers acting in their own interests respond to such public signals as prices of what they buy and sell. Economists have long emphasized price as the signaling agent. When a commodity such as oil becomes scarce, its free-market price rises. Firms and households that use it are led to economize on it and to look for alternatives.[2] Firms that produce it are led to produce more of it. This system works best when price is determined on free markets where there are many buyers and sellers. The signals about scarcities and surplus are then given to individuals through prices that are set by the impersonal aggregate forces of demand and supply.

We now come to a complication that, as we shall see later, has had important consequences for attitudes towards the price system. For many commodities, including most manufactured goods, there are relatively few producers and their prices do not change from day to day according to the conditions of demand and supply. Economists call such prices *administered prices* since firms, rather than impersonal market forces, set them. In such cases the price system still works, but it works slightly differently (and possibly less efficiently) than when prices are determined on competitive markets. Let us see what happens in such circumstances. Manufacturing firms tend to respond to price signals on the input side since many of the materials they use do have prices that are determined on competitive markets. On the output side, however, these firms respond to quantity signals. For example, having set the prices of their cars, the big automobile firms found not long ago that they could sell all the small cars they could produce, but that they were left with a glut of larger cars. The firms reacted by altering next year's plans to produce more small cars and fewer large ones at existing administered prices. What matters is that when prices are administered the market system does still coordinate decisions. It does so, however, by having firms adjust their outputs as their sales and inventories change, rather than as the prices of their products change.

Determining income distribution

The second important characteristic of a market economy is that it determines a *distribution* of the total income that it generates. People whose services are in heavy demand relative to supply—such as TV comedians and NFL quarterbacks—earn large incomes while people whose services are not in heavy demand relative to supply—possibly because they have low IQs or poor muscular coordination—earn very little and sometimes nothing.

The distribution of income produced by the market can be looked at in equilibrium or disequilibrium. In equilibrium, similar efforts by similar people will be similarly rewarded everywhere in the economy. But dissimilar people are dissimilarly rewarded. In disequilibrium, windfall profits and losses abound so that similar people making similar efforts of work or investment will be very dissimilarly rewarded. People in declining industries, areas, and occupations suffer the punishment of windfall losses for no fault of their own. Those in expanding sectors earn the reward of windfall gains with no extra effort. These rewards and punishments serve the important function of causing decentralized decision-makers to respond appropriately to changes in consumers' demands and in production costs. The "advantage" in such a system is that individuals can make their own decisions about how to alter their behaviour when market conditions change; the "disadvantage" is that temporary rewards and punishments are dealt out as a result of changes in market conditions beyond the control of the individuals affected.

While some moralists have tried to argue that the equilibrium market distribution of income is just, it does not appeal to many as satisfying general canons of justice. It does, however, have some limited appeal in that similar people making similar efforts at various places in the economy are similarly rewarded. If moralists have trouble with the equilibrium distribution, there is even more trouble with the disequilibrium distributions that actually prevail in any snap-shot of the constantly changing economy. Windfall profits and losses represent, by their very nature, rewards and penalties unrelated to the efforts of their recipients.

Thinkers who support the market economy's distribution of income from an ethical point of view usually have to rely on an argument that says something like the following: (1) No society can be made equitable from the point of view of results. Just as the good man may die of a lingering and painful disease at fifty while the evil one dies peacefully in his bed at ninety-two, so may the latter earn a higher in-come than the former. (2) Income inequalities serve a function in help-ing the market system to work effectively[3] and thus to produce as high a total income as possible. (3) It is more realistic, therefore, to look for some rough justice in opportunity rather than in results; attempts should be made to reduce the inequalities in starting points in the economic race rather than the inequalities in rewards once the race is run.

Ordinary people do, however, have strong moral feelings about economic rewards. Thus there will always be a major demand to strike at the basic engine of the free market by outlawing windfall profits in some or all markets.

When people call for more justice in market economies, there is no point in merely responding that markets are efficient. Economists can, however, introduce some rationality into the discussion by urging that measures introduced to further some concept of justice should actu-ally achieve that aim and do so at a cost that is fully understood. In many cases economists can show that measures designed to help groups such as the poor actually end up hurting them. In other cases, where the end is served by the means chosen, the costs can be calcu-lated and, once known, will sometimes be thought to be excessive. There is, however, another possibility. The public may not actually want to further some ideal of justice but only to appear to be doing so. Some measures, such as the progressive income tax with its myriad ex-emptions that are used mainly by higher income groups may not be really intended to redistribute income but only to salve consciences by appearing to do so. In these cases it does no good for economists to point out that such measures are relatively ineffective. The measures may be acceptable to the politicians, and to voters, because they do what is required of them: to appear to be redistributing income in a big way while actually only doing so in a small way.

The product cycle

A third important characteristic of the market economy is what economists call the *product cycle*. The motto of the market economy could be "nothing is permanent." New products appear continually while others disappear. At the early stage of a new product, total demand is fairly low, costs of production are high and many small firms are each trying to get ahead of their competitors by finding the twist that appeals to consumers or the technique that slashes their costs. Sometimes new products never get beyond that phase. They prove to be passing fads, or else they remain as high-priced items catering to a small demand.

Others, however, do become items of mass consumption. Successful firms in growing industries buy up, merge with, or otherwise eliminate their less successful rivals. Simultaneously their costs fall due to scale economies. Competition drives prices down along with costs. Eventually, at the mature stage, it is often although not invariably the case that a few giant firms control the industry. They become large, conspicuous, and important parts of the nation's economy.

Sooner or later further changes bring up new products that erode the position of the established giants. Demand falls off, and unemployment occurs as the few remaining firms run into financial difficulties. A large, sick, declining industry appears to many as a national failure and disgrace. At any moment of time, however, industries can be found in all phases, from small firms in new industries to giant firms in declining industries. Large declining industries are as much a natural part of a healthy changing society as are small growing ones.

Absence of conscious direction

A fourth important characteristic of the market economy is that it fulfills its function without anyone having to understand how it works. In Professor Tom Schelling's words (1978, p. 20):

> The dairy farmer doesn't need to know how many people eat butter and how far away they are, how many other people raise cows, how many babies drink milk, or whether more money is spent on beer or milk. What he needs to know is the prices of different

feeds, the characteristics of different cows, the different prices...for milk...the relative cost of hired labor and electrical machinery, and what his net earnings might be if he sold his cows and raised pigs instead....

By responding to such public signals as the costs and prices of what he buys and sells, the dairy farmer helps to make the whole economy fit together, to produce more or less what people want and to provide it more or less where and when they want it.

It is, of course, an enormous advantage that all the citizens of a country can collectively make the system operate without anyone having to understand how it works. This becomes a disadvantage, however, when they are asked, as voters or as legislators, to pass judgment on schemes for consciously intervening in the system in order to improve its operation. *Ignorance of how the system does work now becomes a drawback serious enough to invite disaster.*

II. THE CASE FOR THE MARKET ECONOMY

If we are going to understand the critics and defenders of the market economy as well as the trends of intervention, we need to understand something of the cases both for a free market economy and for some government intervention into it. The case for the free market economy has been made at an intuitive and a formal level.

The intuitive case

The general intuitive case is found in writings of such early economists as Adam Smith and in popular defenses today. I call this the *intuitive* defense. What are its major points?

Flexibility
The main defense of the market system is that it coordinates decisions on production and consumption better than any known alternative.[4] Compared with the alternatives, the decentralized market system is more flexible and leaves more scope for personal adaption and for quick adjustment to change. If, for example, a scarcity of oil raises the price, one individual can elect to leave his heating and air conditioning up high and economize on his driving while another may wish to do the reverse. In order to obtain the same overall effect by planning, the

authorities must force the same reduction in heating, air conditioning and driving on both individuals independent of their tastes, doctor's advice, or other perceived needs. Furthermore, as conditions change over time, prices change and decentralized decision-makers can react continuously, while government quotas, allocations and rationing schemes are much more cumbrous to adjust.

Responsiveness and innovation
The flexibility of the market system is very powerful in producing growth by having every avenue for cost reductions or profit-earning innovations explored by private capital and decentralized decision-makers. It also is very powerful in allowing adaptions to change. The outlook is for major changes in resource availabilities in all economies over the next decades. New products, new inputs and new techniques will have to be devised if we are to cope with those vast changes that can already be foreseen, such as the exhaustion both of fossil fuels and of the enormous water reservoirs that currently irrigate much of American agriculture. A decentralized economy will be more responsive and inventive in producing the necessary adaptions than will a bureaucratic, centrally planned economy.

Diffusion of power
Another important part of the case for a market economy is that it tends to decentralize power and thus involves less coercion than does any other type of economy. Although markets tend to diffuse power, they do not do so completely because large firms and unions clearly do have substantial power. This is a point that many existing defenses tend to ignore. Yet it must be met if conviction is to be carried.

Probably the best attempt to deal with the importance of market power was made by the great economist Joseph Schumpeter. He argued that economic power of particular firms and labour groups would not persist indefinitely. The high profits earned by monopolistic firms and unions are the spur for others to invent cheaper or better substitutes that allow their suppliers to gain some of these profits. He called this process *creative destruction,* and provided many illustrations where a seemingly well-entrenched position of economic power was eroded by the invention of new products and processes introduced to gain some of an existing monopoly's profits.

Planned or command economies tend to put larger and more permanent concentrations of power in the hands of the central authorities than market economies put into the hands of large firms and unions. If markets are not to deal with allocation of people to jobs and of outputs to consumers, then some centralized coercive power is *necessary* to do the same job. Such power creates major incentives for bribery and corruption, and for allocation according to the tastes of the central administrators. If at the going rents and wages there are not enough apartments or plum jobs to go around, the local bureaucrat will often allocate some to those who pay the largest bribe, some to those with religious beliefs, hair styles, or political views that he likes, and only the rest to those whose names come up on the waiting list.

The formal defense

Although this general intuitive defense is very strong, professional economists were not content with it. They wanted to be more precise about just what the market economy did so well and about the circumstances that tended to contribute to its success. In dealing with these very interesting questions, economists developed a defense that I shall call the *formal defense*. This was a theory showing that an idealization of the market economy called *perfect competition* would lead in equilibrium to what was in some sense the best of all possible worlds.

Perfect competition is a model of an economy in which there are so many purchasers of each commodity that no one of them can influence any price by altering his or her demand for it, and in which there are so many sellers of each commodity that no one of them can influence the price by altering his or her supply of it. This is a beautiful model in which the market responds in a purposeful way to the aggregate desires of consumers and the overall conditions of production of firms without any single buyer or seller having any power to influence the market whatever. As a model for showing that the price system could coordinate decentralized decisions in a socially useful way, the model was an intellectual triumph.

Economists then went on to show, however, that the perfectly competitive economy was not only a pretty good economy, it was an optimal economy—you could not do any better. (The only slightly technical discussion in this paper is contained in what follows. Readers not familiar with the jargon of welfare economics can skip the next three paragraphs without serious loss of continuity.)

Utility theory

Each household is assumed to care only about its own utility which in turn depends on the goods and services it consumes. In the early 20th century the theory was worked out under the utilitarian assumption of measurable, additive utility. It was shown that for given supply of resources, a perfectly competitive economy would lead to a higher money value of national income (which could be thought of as the sum of all the utilities produced by the economy and available for consumption by its citizens) than would any other economic organization. Second and third-best organizations could be evaluated by comparing the national incomes that each would produce for the same given set of resources. Then in the 1930s English-speaking economists underwent the "ordinalist revolution." Economists found that all their positive theory about consumer behaviour could be derived by replacing the dubious assumption that everyone's utility from consumption could be calculated and summed up with the much weaker assumption that each individual could order alternative consumption sets and say which was preferred to which. From the point of view of positive economics, which predicts how consumers will react to changing market situations, getting rid of measurable utility was pure gain. For welfare economics, which investigates the formal case for alternative economic systems, the ordinalist revolution had more serious consequences.

Optimality theory

The new welfare economics (founded on the ordinalist assumption that consumers could merely order alternative consumption sets) could prove that perfect competition led to an *optimum allocation* of fixed quantities of productive resources. All other forms of organizing production led to non-optimal allocations of resources (in the sense that it would be *possible* to reallocate resources so as to make at least one person better off without making anyone worse off). Perfect competition was optimal, or efficient, and everything else was non-optimal, or inefficient. The non-optimal set included "socialist" economies, market economies that contained monopolies and oligopolies, and any other form of organizing production that was not or did not exactly duplicate perfect competition. Although every organization in the non-optimal set was inferior to perfect competition, the economies in the non-optimal set could not be ranked against each other.[5]

The theory of the optimality of perfect competition became the intellectual basis of the economist's case for the market economy. While professional economists went on studying and refining the model of the optimality of perfect competition and their academically bound graduate students went on learning it, the great bulk of their students were sent out into the world with an intellectual defense of the market economy that would not stand up to five minutes rough handling by anyone who knew anything about the actual behaviour of real markets.

What was obvious to most graduate students, and to people in the outside world who were exposed to the economist's model, was among other things; that the utilitarianism on which the model is based is an unacceptable theory of social good (since most people's welfare depends in important ways on variables excluded from the theory); that the case is based on the equilibrium properties of perfect competition, but it says nothing about the allocations that will exist in any snapshot of the economy as it adjusts to continuous shocks; that the assumptions of perfect competition are not even remotely fulfilled in the world in which we live; and that the proof of perfection is too much — many who would have accepted the proposition that market economies were superior to other forms of economic organization were not willing to join Dr. Pangloss in holding that, whatever misery and injustice it produced, ours was the best of all possible economic worlds.

Logically the failure of an argument designed to prove a proposition, does nothing to prove the contrary proposition. Many people's belief in the contrary position *is* in practice, influenced by the failure of an argument to prove a proposition. Economists sent to the civil services, to law offices and to the political arena droves of students who had come to believe the contrary proposition that free markets were less efficient than available alternatives.

III. THE CASE FOR INTERVENTION

If the case for the free market economy is so strong, we must wonder why we have so much government intervention? The answer is in two parts. First there is an intellectual case, accepted at least in principle by even the most extreme intellectual free marketeers, for some government intervention. Second, there are some very strong political and social forces which are not part of the intellectual case for some intervention but which push hard for more intervention. In this section we consider the intellectual case and in the next we consider the other forces.

The intellectual case is divided between the "macro" case for stabilization policy and the "micro" case for intervention with a fully employed economy.

The macro case

We first look briefly at the macro case. As far back as records go, free market economies have been beset with alternating bouts of boom and slump. In the early 1930s the whole non-Communist world suffered from the deepest business depression in recorded history, followed by a weak recovery that left armies of unemployed and partly employed. The work of many economists, synthesized in the writings of J.M. Keynes, provided a theoretical rationale for the policy most economists thought would help: extensive public works to create income and employment until the private sector recovered sufficiently to create full employment on its own. Keynesian fiscal policy provided a strong case for intervention wherever the free market economy produced prolonged periods of unemployment.

The critical conclusions suggested by the 1930s was that the free market could subject masses of ordinary people to degrading poverty through no fault of their own and for very long periods of time. Milton Friedman and other advocates of minimal government intervention, correctly perceived this period as the critical one for discrediting their position. It is absolutely fundamental to their position that they be able to demonstrate that the Great Depression was not brought on by a failure of the free market but by a failure of government monetary policy that turned a normal, albeit severe, recession into an abnormal depression. The debate continues to rage on this point and as yet no major conclusions have been reached (see Brunner [1981] for some illustrative fireworks).

The micro case

Second, consider the very important arguments concerning the need for government intervention *even when full employment prevails.* These are arguments about (1) efficiency, (2) the distribution of income, (3) paternalism and (4) social values which are thought to transend individual values. We shall consider these in turn.

Efficiency
The efficiency arguments for intervention are of two sorts. The first refers to alleged inefficiences of monopolies and other firms that are so large as to be shielded from effective competition. The second refers to *market failures:* cases where free markets would not provide consumers with the opportunity to buy what they would be willing to pay for. Clean air and water, general reduction in pollution, and such "public goods" as defense, police protection and navigational aids are not easily provided by free markets.

Anti-interventionists have variously argued that market failures are not quantitatively important and/or that individuals affected by such failures can club together to obtain the results they desire. Public perception, however, continues (correctly in my opinion) to regard pollution of the environment as a serious problem that cannot effectively be controlled by any means other than government intervention.

Income distribution
Next comes distribution. The intellectual case for the free market recognizes that there is nothing sacrosanct about the distribution of income thrown up by the market. There is thus an intellectually defensible reason for intervention when generally accepted views of justice suggest that the distribution of income produced by the market is undesirable.

Opinions differ on how much redistribution is desirable on grounds of justice and is acceptable on grounds of not removing normal, useful incentives. But almost everyone supports taking some income from the richer members of the society and transferring it to those who would otherwise starve. Thus almost everyone supports some redistributive intervention into the economy on general grounds of social justice. The real question is "how much?"

Paternalism
The third, and very potent, source for intervention is the belief that the state understands the individual's self-interest better than does the individual himself. There is a host of such interventions including Canadian laws prohibiting the use of credit cards in liquor stores, laws for compulsory use of seat belts (on the grounds that after an accident the non-user would wish he had been a user), compulsory old-age pensions rather than voluntary provision for old age. (Such measures must be distinguished from compulsory carrying of third party insurance which protects innocent third parties.)

Philosophers and economists have long debated such paternalistic measures. I would register my personal belief that society must regard its adult members as responbible for their actions or else it will cease to function (e.g., although a disastrous childhood may help to explain, it cannot excuse in the eyes of the law, such destructive behaviour by an adult as an attempted assassination of an American President). This leads me to oppose almost all paternalistic laws as a citizen, while recognizing, as social observer, their strong appeal to many people.

Social values
The fourth source of intervention is to impose one's own tastes or values on others. Laws against gambling, prostitution, drugs, pornography, certain sexual practices, and a host of other activities thought to be immoral, probably owe their public support to these desires. Such motives are ruled out of economists' utilitarian theories of consumer behaviour but they are potent social forces revealing what economic theory denies: that consumption has a social as well as a private dimension.

Economists will get nowhere by denying this. What they can hope to do is to bring some rationality into the discussion by showing that many policies are counter-productive. For example, many of the measures designed to prevent certain forms of consumption behaviour do little to stop the activities in question. Instead, by making them illegal, they drive the activities into the hands of organized crime. This takes their income out of the reach of the tax authorities and their conditions of production out of reach of such regulatory devices as child labour and minimum wage laws. This leads to the ironic position that organized crime is one of the main supporters of laws designed to impose certain moral codes on the public. In other cases where the goals are achieved, the economist can try to ensure that the cost of doing so is estimated and publicized.

Failure of the optimality theory

Part of the apparent case for intervention has arisen out of a failure at the practical level of the theoretical defense of the free market. Social attitudes have become hostile to producers in general and windfall profits in particular. Critics of the price system have told the public that big firms do not behave in an economically useful way. The critics were left to make this charge more or less unchallenged because academic economists had, as we saw earlier, rested their case for the market economy on the optimality of the idealized model of perfect competition. This is what I earlier called the *formal defense* of the free market.

The concentration of the economists' case for the market economy on the formal defense had some disastrous consequences. First, graduate students who found the case unconvincing went off in droves to the civil service and elsewhere convinced that there was no strong case for the price system.

Second, a vulnerable flank was exposed to any critics who were prepared to admit that perfect competition bore little relation to real-world market economies. It was not long before orthodox economists suffered a crushing defeat in the battlefield for public opinion. The defeat was administered by the man who, as a result, is probably the most commonly read and best known academic economist in the world today, John Kenneth Galbraith.

In the first hundred pages of his classic *American Capitalism,* Galbraith has a wonderful time ridiculing the picture of the workings of the American economy painted by the perfectly competitive model. He has no trouble in showing that the case for the price system based on the optimality of perfect competition fails totally when applied to any modern economy. Galbraith's main point is that prices do not fluctuate with every movement of demand or supply as they do in the model of perfect competition. Instead they are administered by large firms and unions having market power. In this he is undoubtedly correct, and his point is sufficient to destroy the possibility that actual market economies could be optimal. Academic economists who rested their case for market economies on perfect competition had no effective reply, and Galbraith was left in possession of the field. The academics returned to the classroom to continue to show that the optimality of perfect competition survived a host of purely formal obstacles that were suggested by the new, set-theoretic approach to mathematics.

Having destroyed the academics' case for market economies in *American Capitalism,* Galbraith proceeded to build his own case against such economies in his subsequent books, of which *The New Industrial State* is typical. The basic story is that (1) firms do not produce to satisfy consumers' wants but create, through advertising, wants for those goods they choose to produce; (2) firms squander resources rather than economize on them; and, (3) the market puts very little discipline on the pricing policies of firms who can and do price more or less as they wish.

This leads Galbraith to the conclusion that there is no case for the free market since it does not work to satisfy consumers with even relative, let alone absolute, efficiency. Also the arbitrary behaviour of firms, free from any discipline of the market, creates such undesirable aggregate consequences as continual cost-push inflation. Galbraith advocates government intervention in the form of wage-price controls to cure inflation. To the obvious objection that in the long term such controls destroy the workings of free markets (e.g., Lipsey 1977), Galbraith replies that this does not matter since these markets do not work to any useful purpose in any case.

Need for an intuitive defense

Had academic economists rested some of their case on what I earlier called the intuitive justification, they would not have had to suffer any major defeat at the hands of Galbraith. The general case for the price system as being *relatively* effective in coordinating decentralized decisions in a socially useful way is still valid with administered prices even if full optimality is not. This is because economies with administered prices still allocate resources in response to consumer demand and relative scarcities of basic materials. Also arbitrary power of firms and unions is severely limited in the long term by Schumpeter's process of creative destruction.

As it is, however, Galbraith's attack has been very widely read and no really popular statement of the modern intuitive case for the free market has received one-tenth as wide a distribution. Galbraith's views continue to be very influential, and if the market system is further eroded in the United States over the next decades, Galbraith will be able to take much of the credit.

Main-line economists have only themselves to blame for this. (1) Almost no effort has been, or is, devoted to developing the theoretical cases for more or less government intervention in the kinds of market economy actually found in the real world. (2) Even today, graduate students are, as a matter of course, put through a rigorous training in proving all the theorems about the optimality of perfect competition, and left with the view that this is the intellectual basis of the case for the market economy; they are seldom given help in core courses in thinking about the real questions of more or less intervention into existing market economies. (3) No really good intellectual case for actual market economies has been publicized by those capable of doing so at the popular level; the intellectual case for our mixed market societies has yet to be made with a popular force equal to that of *The New Industrial State.*[6]

IV. THE EROSION OF THE FREE MARKET

The intellectual defense for intervention has been referred to in the previous section. To a pragmatist such as myself, who accepts that the market is full of imperfections, its defense is much more difficult than it is to a dogmatist who believes that the free market is perfect and there is no case for any intervention. At the political level intervention is usually based on some perceived need to protect the general public from being harmed by some particular group within the society. Even when the motives are genuine, such interventions are easily corrupted to fulfilling a second motive—to enhance the welfare of a particular group at the expense of the general public.

Practical forces for intervention

In this section I look at a few forces for intervention that have been important in practice. These are sometimes related to the intellectual case and sometimes depend on very strong motives of self-interest that are independent of any broad philosophical justification. The discussion in this section, which is illustrative rather than exhaustive, prepares the way for the case to be argued in the final section, that it will be harder than is often thought to reverse the last century's trend towards increasing government intervention.

Regulation of natural monopolies
One major reason for intervention has been to regulate "natural monopolies." The intellectual case for this intervention relies on consideration both of efficiency and distribution. It is argued that natural monopolies prevent the market system from working efficiently, and that, left to themselves, they earn very high profits at the expense of their customers. Transportation, communications and public utility industries come under this heading. The *failure* of many of the regu-

latory schemes for national monopolies has been extensively discussed elsewhere, so I need only make a few summary points here.

1. Very often the regulatory agencies are co-opted by the firms in the industry and end up supervising monopoly practices that would be illegal if instituted by the firms themselves.

2. Very often government intervention in terms of regulation or nationalization protects firms from the consequences of their own errors. A government enforced monopoly has, for example, shielded post offices in many countries from the consequences of bad investment decisions over the last two decades. The legal distinction of whether the post office is privately or publicly owned is irrelevant; what matters is that its economic position as a monopoly is protected by the full force of the law. Without this, most branches of postal services would be fiercely competitive, providing more and better service at lower prices than are charged by existing postal monopolies. In the few places, such as mail delivery to the Canadian North, where private services would not be profitable but are thought desirable in the social interest, services could be provided by taking competitive bids for the minimum subsidy needed to persuade a private firm to do the job.

3. Government regulation of natural monopolies has a danger of maintaining the industry's monopoly position by legal means long after technological change destroys the "naturalness" of the monopoly. One of the major characteristics of modern economies is that nothing remains static. Railroads were once natural monopolies in rural areas but this position has long been challenged by trucks, airlines and buses. Telephones were until recently a natural communication monopoly, but technological changes in communications are currently eliminating the "naturalness." This once again illustrates Schumpeter's creative destruction: any monopoly position that has high profit potential sets up strong incentives for technological breakthroughs that will attack the monopoly, allow the new innovators to gain some of the profits, and benefit consumers by reducing costs and prices of existing products and/or by producing new products. Government regulation may, however, perpetuate the legal monopoly.

4. When a regulated industry is deregulated, a period of confusion often ensues. In the process, many formerly protected giants may go broke. For example, opponents of airline deregulation pointed

to the bankruptcy of Braniff Airlines as evidence of the hazards of deregulation. Instead it may have been a triumph of deregulation that such inefficient firms were eliminated, and a condemnation of regulation that they were for so long shielded.

Belief in benefits of government control
A second potent reason for intervention into the productive process is the belief that the government can do it better. This has been the motive behind much of the nationalization of existing industries, the subjugation of private industries to the government will, and the growth of new public enterprises. A typical case of the last-mentioned type occurred in the 1950s when Premier W.A.C. Bennett set up B.C. Ferries after an unsuccessful attempt to persuade a cautious CPR executive to take on what proved to be a wildly successful business risk. B.C. Ferries prospered since, as a good entrepreneur, Bennett perceived a good chance when he saw one. But the ferries were nonetheless a nationalized industry subject to all of the political forces that affect such industries. By the 1970s they were unprofitable. Their politically determined high wages and low fares were influenced by the pressure groups who gained from them at the expense of the general B.C. taxpayer who footed the bill.

As an example of the subjugation of a private firm, Dome Petroleum in Canada became the government's chosen instrument for Canadian oil development. This favouritism encouraged extreme borrowing and bad risk-taking until, under the force of enormous debt, a government bailout became necessary.

In the face of what happens when economic decisions about prices and costs become politicized, it is hard to imagine an efficiency case for government control of those industries, such as B.C. Ferries, that could be left in the private sector. Yet the belief that the public sector can do better — particularly when, as in the CPR-B.C. Ferries case, private industry is obviously performing below par — will continue to encourage governments to get into ownership and control of production when in the long run they will, on all past evidence, do substantially worse than the private sector could.

Shoring up declining industries
Another reason why government gets into production is to shore up declining industries. The large mature industries in the product cycle are the most visible parts of the nation's industrial strength and also

the largest employers of labour. When these industries enter a declining phase both employers and employees suffer windfall losses. It is very easy to think that the nation's continuing economic prosperity depends on preventing this decline. The industry calls for help and the political economy of the state makes it popular to offer such help. Country after country has been seduced into a policy of supporting its declining industries. In the past the British have tended to nationalize these industries; more recently they poured funds into privately held ones in an effort to prevent unemployment from rising above its already currently high level. Chrysler and U. S. Steel are recent American firms to look to the government for such help and to get it.

Yet protection of industries in late stages of the product cycle is usually the wrong policy. Sooner or later the industry must decline, and protecting it now only puts off the evil day. It also makes the eventual decline sharper than it would otherwise have been. A case can be made for easing the transition by helping displaced workers to move and retrain, but there is no economic case for pouring scarce funds into industries that cannot cover their costs with the present level of demands for their products. Among other things, such protection may deny funds to new industries that will eventually grow to fill the gap left by the declining giants.

A new form of government support for declining industries (and other sectors) has been the government guarantee of loans made by the private sector to private industries. This intervention has the seductive appeal that it initially costs nothing. Yet if the guarantees are needed, many of the loans must be expected eventually to be defaulted. Thus the cost for the public is merely postponed and, as the lender of last resort, the government may find itself forced to nationalize or otherwise take control of a growing number of the country's most unsuccessful enterprises (which only exist in their present form because of earlier government guarantee of their borrowings). These guarantees are a series of time bombs currently being constructed and ready to force increased government intervention over the next decades.

Protecting individual and special interests
As well as owning or controlling particular industries, governments have from time to time regulated almost every aspect of economic activity: security transactions, loans, bank interest, professional associations, building regulations, safety standards, hours of work, mini-

mum working age, minimum wages, prices charged by taxicabs, standards for admission into countless occupations, qualities of countless products, advertising claims, and so on almost ad infinitum. The ostensible motive for intervention varies greatly. There seems little doubt that the motive is often protection of the individual, and that a majority feels that this is successful in some cases, such as child labour laws, safety standards for canned goods and truth-in-lending laws.

In other cases, such as laws that make it illegal to try to recruit a fellow air traveller to share a cab with you, the objective is clearly to provide more income for producers at the expense of their customers. It is evident that any group would like to gain a monopoly over what it sells and to raise prices. As Adam Smith long ago observed about businessmen:

> People of the same trade seldom meet together, even for merriment and diversion, but the conversation ends in a conspiracy against the public, or in some contrivance to raise prices.

The same is clearly true of labour unions and professional organizations.

Marxists have often viewed particular classes as having distinctive motives: capitalists are grasping, self-seeking, and ever ready to grind the faces of the poor while workers are noble, altruistic and concerned with the general good. Adam Smith viewed peoples' motives as independent of their class: no group has a monopoly on either virtue or vice; indeed, give any group — a firm, a union or a professional association — a monopoly, and their members will exploit it for their own self-interest. I have no doubt myself that the Marxist view is sentimental nonsense that prevents many from seeing the enormous importance of Smith's message: any monopoly, of labour or capital, public or private, is a serious threat to the public interest.

Potential new entrants provide severe checks on private monopoly practise. Raise the profits or wages in any line of activity above what can be earned in comparable lines elsewhere in the economy and a flood of new entrants will drive profits and earnings back down again. Throughout history potential monopolists have realized that success requires an agreement about price among existing firms *plus* the ability to restrict entry.

In the absence of government support of entry restrictions, most monopolies of firms or labour would sooner or later be attacked by new entrants. If the industry or labour group cannot be entered by a frontal assault, it will be outflanked by the invention of new products or new techniques using a substitute labour group. For example, when carpenters' wages became very high, building contractors turned to standardized doors, window frames, and other wooden parts made in factories. This substituted cheap assembly line workers for carpenters whose wages were three to four times as high.

Potential substitutes provide a powerful check on the long-run ability of a restrictive union to raise the wages of its members. But if the union can line up the government on its side, the full force of the state can be used to prevent this substitution from occurring. In this case closed-shop legislation is needed, saying that anyone who in any way builds the wooden parts of a house must belong to a carpenters' union, which is then allowed to control its own entry. Such legislation has gone much further in the United Kingdom and Canada than in the United States, but wherever it occurs its purpose is the same: to allow a monopoly group to restrict its supply and protect it from the consequences of substitutions. In the United States, building codes have accomplished somewhat the same purpose.

Very often government regulation of quality of product or of training standards and licensing of craftsmen serves to restrict entry where this could not be done privately. The American Medical Association is one of the most effective professional organizations that enforces such a supply restriction, with the full support of the government, as has been cogently argued by Milton Friedman.

Governments will continue to support monopolies in these ways until the general public gains a greater awareness of the extent to which this support works to their disadvantage. Here we have one of the many illustrations of how the advantage of the market system, in working without being understood or consciously run, becomes a disadvantage when the public supports intervention and conscious direction.

Protection from free market consequences
We may now pass to another class of reasons for intervention: to protect the people from the full consequences of the operation of free markets even where these markets have no hint of monopoly. Such policies fall into two types: those that allow markets to work and then seek to compensate for some adverse effects, and those that seek to prevent the adverse effects by interfering with operations of the markets.

Compensating for adverse effects

The goals of such policies are to alter the distribution of income. In the first type of policy, funds are directly transferred. Benefits for long-term unemployment and disability, manpower policies that retrain or relocate labour, welfare payments to those without marketable skills, Medicare, Medicaid, and a vast variety of other "welfare" expenditures come under this rubric. I shall not go into the debate over such measures now except to observe that they are no doubt here to stay, that the current climate of opinion suggests their high water mark has probably already been passed, and that, to me, although they are sometimes abused, they represent some of the great triumphs of the liberal program born early in the century and intended to make the world a little less unjust a place in which to live.

Interfering with market workings

I want now to focus attention on the second type of program, that seeks to help by changing the workings of individual markets. When assessing such policies economists and politicians often misunderstand each other because without realizing it they approach the same issue with very different objectives in mind, the economist being concerned about efficiency and the politician about income distribution.

An illustration: response to the energy crisis. When, for example, OPEC imposed its startling increase in the price of oil in the early 1970s, many economists argued that domestic oil prices should be allowed to rise fairly quickly to the world level. In doing this they were concerned about the efficiency of the price system. The real price of oil — measured in the quantities of goods that had to be exported to pay for oil imports — had risen substantially. If the domestic price of oil rose to reflect this, a series of reactions would occur to this "price signal." On the demand side, users would have to economize in countless ways. On the supply side the first effect would be large windfall profits for the oil companies. A scramble to share in these profits would then lead to numerous supply reactions, from the discovery of more oil to the development of technologies of alternative energy sources.

Policymakers argued, however, that a rapid increase in domestic oil prices would cause unacceptable hardship. The poor would find their heating and transportation costs rising dramatically and the sudden severe fall in their living standards would be unjust. Also, the enormous windfall profits for the giant international oil companies would entail a transfer of income from the community at large to these companies, that was as unnecessary as it was socially harmful. The President's Economic Report (1978, p.8) stated the view as follows: ". . . The (energy) program must be fair: No segment of the population should bear a disproportionate share of the cost or burden of adjustment, and no industry should reap unnecessary and undeserved [!] windfall gains." Here we see two of the driving forces behind much modern government intervention: a hostility toward windfall profits and a concern about the effects on the poor of increases in the prices of key products. Let us consider these forces in turn.

Windfall profits are, as we have seen, part of the very mechanism of market economy adjustment and by their very nature they are *always* "undeserved." If windfall profits were eliminated either by price controls or taxes, then decrees, regulations and controls would be needed to reallocate resources by central authority. Since energy shortages and exhaustion of many key raw materials will put great strain on the economy and require much adaption in the coming decades, we can be sure that large windfall profits will occur over time at various places in the economy. In the current climate of opinion, governments will be led to intervene to eliminate these profits and will then have to resort to countless further interventions to accomplish what the price system would have accomplished had it not been frustrated by government policy.

There is something faintly ludicrous in the view that the citizens of what is still one of the wealthiest countries of the world cannot afford to pay the full world price of oil when citizens in countries with tiny fractions of the U.S. per capita income do so at present. The best case for hardship is that, although when the dust is settled Americans could no doubt adjust to paying the full price of oil, the transition would be very hard for the poor, the old, and those whose incomes are already fully committed to installment payments, etc. But this was a case for transitional payments to select groups, not for subsidizing everyone to the extent that domestic prices were held below world prices, nor for giving the subsidies through price controls that frustrate the myriad adjustments the free market would otherwise produce. Coupons giving select groups the right to buy fuel cheaply would have protected the poor at a minute fraction of the economic cost of the control program.

In the event, U.S. and Canadian prices of oil were held down. The Carter administration tried to enact a set of laws that would produce through the cumbersome apparatus of the command economy some of the reactions that the free market would have produced as decentralized decisions if oil prices had been permitted to rise. But the Congress refused to act, and even if it had, the cumbersome apparatus of the command economy is a poor substitute for the myriad subtle adaptions of the free market. Finally Americans decided to leave the job to the free market. Even at the time of writing, however, Canadians still live with the consequences of the attempt to rely on a centrally planned, command solution to the energy crisis.

Rent control: another illustration. Other examples of intervention in particular markets for distributive reasons abound. Rent controls are an example of rapidly growing importance. Rent controls have been used in many European countries for decades and their consequences are well documented. They are intended to protect the poor, the old and others by preventing landlords from making windfall profits. They cause housing shortages by removing the windfall-profits signal that more rental accommodation is needed and by driving the return on investment in apartments below the return on other investment. They cause a transfer of accommodation from the rental to the owner-occupied market. To stop this, security-of-tenure laws are passed making eviction difficult or impossible and also further reducing the attractiveness of new investment in rental accommodation. They end up helping those who are already in rental accommodation and hurting those seeking rental housing as well as hurting landlords, many of whom are of modest means. Over time, the control-induced shortage becomes massive. The controls then end up hurting the very groups they were designed to protect. The final solution becomes socialized housing with the state providing from tax revenue subsidized rental housing that private investors will not provide at the controlled prices.

Yet the controls are spreading, and it is not hard to see why. The old and the poor are very hard pressed by inflation and the rapidly rising demands for housing. Rent controls do help those now in apartments, and if they hurt those that follow, that is someone else's problem. Those who are desperately pressed now can hardly be blamed for trying to help themselves. But when the state gives in to this pressure it creates a major housing problem further down the line and heavy suffering for the aged and the poor of that not-too-far distant future.

A direct income transfer is a much surer way to secure "adequate" living standards for the poor, while rent control helps a haphazard selection of sitting tenants while hurting landlords and all unsuccessful would-be tenants with a bias towards hurting, in the long run, the poor, the meek and mild, and the excessively honest. But direct income payments to the poor cost tax money while controls do not, since they transfer income directly from landlords to tenants.

Political realists sometimes reply that it is all very well to argue for direct income supplements but politicians are reluctant to grant these. If we want to help the poor—or any other underprivileged group—income supplements would be a "first best." Intervention in such markets as rental housing and oil is a "second best"—that is, better than nothing.

I used to support this argument myself, but experience has led me to reject it because I feel that the important caveat "second best is better than nothing" is often not correct empirically. When special privileges for particular groups are put up for grabs in the political "market-place," the evidence suggests that the groups with most power and votes will get the most. Although a few measures may well help the special groups they are aimed at, the sum of all such special measures hurts them. For this reason economists are not inclined to say "What about the poor?" every time a policy for a particular market is being considered. This is not because they are insensitive to poverty, but because evidence suggests that intervention in particular markets is a dubious and, in the long run, a very costly way of helping the poor—or any other group of consumers for that matter.

Owner-occupied housing: a final example. A third market where great pressure is building up for further intervention is owner-occupied housing. Not long ago young people could look forward to moving out of their parents' homes to get married and move directly into homes of their own. Rising population, scarcity of land in urban areas where most people want to live and rising incomes means that a growing demand for housing is driving prices up. The price system is signalling that housing is becoming scarce and that people will have to economize by buying smaller houses, buying them later in life and making a host of other adaptions. This is an unpleasant development for those affected by it and there is growing pressure to try to eliminate this real scarcity by passing laws that will only end up aggravating the problem.

V. THE FUTURE OF THE MARKET ECONOMY

Of course, we cannot foretell the future with any accuracy. We can, however, show what will happen if existing trends are not reversed, and we can establish the existence of various forces affecting these trends. First let us look at some forces leading to decreased government intervention.

Forces for decreased intervention

There has been a trend since the 1930s for increased government intervention to produce full employment and other macro goals. The intellectual and the public opinion tides are beginning to flow the other way. There is a strong feeling, stemming partly from the belief that government is itself responsible for the stagflation of the 1970s, away from so much government macro-intervention in the economy. One form that this takes is a call to balance budgets while also cutting taxes.

An important attitude favouring government intervention earlier in the century was the decline of the belief in individualism and an increasing willingness to accept a more coercive society. People were not upset by the idea of the state forcing people to act in a socially desirable way. Today the pendulum is swinging the other way, partly as a result of more perception of what has happened in dictatorships of the left and the right.

Another strong force in the last century and earlier parts of this one was a sense of outrage at the conditions of the ordinary working household. Zola and Dickens at the imaginative level and the Hammonds and the Webbs at the factual level voiced this feeling. Observations of working class living standards in socialist societies currently in the same stage of development as capitalist countries in the late nineteenth century have served to temper the perception of causes as seen by earlier generations. We are no longer so sure that the deplorable state of the average worker in late nineteenth century Britain or America was due to capitalism, or that it would have been any better under socialism.[7]

A major force pulling towards less intervention in individual markets is a growing recognition of the failure of many regulatory policies. Repeal of regulation is strengthened by a growing hostility to big business shown in many attitude surveys. Thus once the public is convinced that regulation helps big business, support grows for deregulation.

Forces for increased intervention

The forces working towards less government intervention are well publicized today. But there are strong forces working in the other direction as well. Indeed, the deregulation movement may be a special case fuelled by hostility to big business. On this view it is no accident that airline deregulation was accomplished easily while trucking deregulation was not. Shedding the myriad of monopoly-creating regulations in areas of the economy other than those served by big business may prove very difficult and it is not coming quickly. Furthermore, the growing public hostility to big business is ominous. It may encourage a host of regulations, price controls and profit taxes that seriously inhibit the workings of the market economy.

Many other forces are also at work to make a general pull-back from the existing scale of government intervention difficult. Major changes in the supplies of raw materials and energy over the next decades will mean that the market economy will produce large changes in relative prices. Large and rapid changes will impinge on everyone, but the most noticeable effects will be on the windfall profits of large companies and the living standards of lower income groups. The media will continue to call for measures to protect the poor and eliminate windfall profits of large companies. Politicians will find it popular to be seen to be protecting consumers from the consequences of large price rises, although price rises that reflect rises in costs cannot be voted out of existence, but merely shifted from one group to another.

The pressure for intervention in markets will be very strong indeed. Industries that should decline as a result of changes in resource availabilities will be shored up. Price controls and windfall profit taxes may frustrate the normal adjustments of the market economy and make a host of centrally administered, coercive adjustments necessary. The predictable success of the controls in frustrating the free-market adjustments will be taken as evidence that the free market doesn't work (just as Galbraith said it wouldn't) and this will justify further centrally administered price controls, quotas, rationing schemes and compulsory orders to alter consumption and production habits.

Similar developments are likely to occur in the housing markets where rent controls and security-of-tenure laws are spreading rapidly. We have already discussed the growing pressure for rent controls and there is no reason to expect this pressure to subside. I have also referred to the pressure to intervene in the market for owner-occupied housing to keep its cost "within reach of ordinary people." This illustrates a general phenomenon — the market is often the bearer of un-welcome news. Growing pressure of population, and shortages of some resources, often mean that some consumption patterns that were taken for granted in the past are no longer physically possible. Such a development causes a large rise in price of the commodity affected. The market is signalling that a cherished consumption habit must be abandoned — by many citizens even if not by all. Past rulers executed the messengers who brought news of defeat; today's rulers pass laws seeking to suspend the actions of the market economy and end up executing it. We can look forward to much pressure in this direction as the public — unaware of how the economy works — seeks to avoid the harsh economic facts of growing scarcity of some products.

Another force pulling for more intervention is the political process itself. Although the dynamics of political decisions are often difficult to understand, politicians naturally are more responsive to the forces of votes and campaign money than to what economists tell them is efficient for the economy. The immediate distributional effects of any policy are much more obvious and immediate than the efficiency effects, and they therefore tend to have more influence on policy-makers — both because distributional effects may carry more weight with the electorate and because policy-makers are often not trained to look beyond distribution to the efficiency effects. Also the distributional effects of many policies are asymmetric in the sense that resulting gains are concentrated on specific groups while losses are diffused over the general public. Thus more votes may be attracted from the small number of large gainers than are lost from the large number of small losers. Although the losses suffered by any one person as a result of each measure that aids special-interest groups may be small, the cumulative loss caused by a large number of measures, may be substantial. The economist who totals the losses over all these measures may take a dim view of them while the politician who totals the votes gained by each may be favourably disposed.

What all this amounts to is that the general interest is very diffuse while self-interest is focused and very immediate. Thus there will always be very strong pressure put on politicians to redistribute income in favour of powerful pressure groups wielding votes and campaign money. Unless something drastic and unexpected changes in the political process, we must expect that many of these pressures will be yielded to.

No matter how often economists may try to persuade politicians that it is better to use the tax and expenditure system to redistribute income than to fiddle with particular markets, their arguments will have no effect on politicians responsive to the demands of pressure groups. If politicians are redistributing income according to generally accepted ideas of social justice, it is a virtue of a tax and expenditure system that its redistributions are open, obvious, and relatively clear, at least in their impact effects. If, however, politicians are yielding to pressure groups with no overall ideas of social justice in mind, these same characteristics of a tax and expenditure system are a disadvantage. Those who are helped will know they are helped, but it is better that the rest do not realize what is happening to them. For these purposes fiddling with particular markets is the superior alternative.[8]

Another reason why we may see more pressure for government intervention in the future is the demand for "justice" in income distribution. Inflation hurts people on fixed incomes very severely. They find food and rents "going out of sight." The appropriate solution (until inflation is contained) is to insulate their incomes with cost-of-living adjustments or coupons that allow them to get such specified commodities as housing and fuel below the market price. The obvious solution to those who do not understand the workings of the economy is to control the prices of commodities that are important in these people's budgets (but thereby creating even bigger shortages).

The call for justice in distribution and the growing hostility towards big business will lead to a call to tax away windfall profits at least of large companies. The resulting destruction of the mechanism that drives the market system will lead to a host of interventions that will further inhibit the workings of the market and, in the classic sequence by which controls breed controls, lead to yet further interventions.

For all of these reasons it seems very likely to me that we will continue to see major, even growing, government interventions into the workings of markets in the foreseeable future. This then sets up conditions for some very difficult political times ahead. For years politicians have gotten elected by calling for a balanced budget and then found themselves voting piecemeal for measures that increased the deficit. I foresee a generation of politicians who will analogously get elected by calling for a reduction in the place of government in society and then find themselves voting piecemeal for increasing the degree of government intervention. The call to help special groups while also cutting taxes will give a real bias towards the most harmful and self-defeating types of intervention and of controls over particular markets. In short I find myself in the same camp as the great advocate of the market economy, Joseph Schumpeter. I believe that the market economy carries the best promise for a system that adapts reasonably effectively to the stresses to which society will be put over the next one hundred years, but I have no optimism that public opinion or the political process will allow the market to do that job. Instead I suspect we will see an increasing barrage of measures that will hamper its ability to do so. I hope I am wrong, but awareness of what I foresee as a possibility may encourage some to work to prevent it.

If the price system becomes less important in our day-to-day life, and if we move toward a command economy, we will not be able to say that the *market economy* failed because of its own internal economic contradictions. It will be closer to the truth to say that the *democratic market society* failed because of its own internal political contradictions. It will have been voted out of existence piecemeal by successive administrations and legislators who, while accepting the rhetoric of the value of the market, were unwilling to put up with some of its harsher consequences. If told what they were doing, they would register shocked disbelief. Since there can be little doubt that their reactions would be genuine, we must conclude that our legislators, and the public who back them by their voting pressures, are unconsciously the potential executioners of a system they genuinely think they are protecting. Once again we see the unfortunate implications of a system which works without having to be understood.

Moderating forces

Finally I want to give one major balancing argument to the gloomy view I have just painted. A common mistake of social scientists is to identify forces leading to particular changes and then to overlook the natural corrective forces that these changes themselves generate.

Those who do not see these balancing forces often think only of what mathematicians call "corner solutions"—the economy goes *all the way* in one direction or else *all the way* in the other. Hayek, in his famous book *The Road to Serfdom,* argued for a corner solution: once we started on the road of government intervention we would be pushed all the way to a complete, dictatorial, command economy. Looking at the United Kingdom and Sweden, which have gone further on that road than any other developed economy, I find myself unable to accept Hayek's conclusion. The reason is that most social processes set up natural checking forces that lead to what mathematicians call an "interior solution"—an equilibrium where opposing forces are balanced somewhere away from either extreme.

A whole paper would be required to lay out these checking forces, so I will merely mention two. First, there is a limit to what the state can raise in taxes. When tax rates get too high, people just refuse to pay. They spend money learning how to avoid taxes, they emigrate or they resort to downright cheating. Second, markets are so efficient that they always grow up beside state, non-market production and distribution unless suppressed by the full vigour of a strong dictatorship. (Markets for prostitution and drugs in the United States and black markets for all kinds of scarce consumer goods in the Eastern Bloc countries show just how hard it is to suppress markets which sell things people want to buy.) It took only a short time living in modern Britain—as I did for five months in 1979—to learn that you do not go to the Gas Board to have your gas central heating repaired or to the local council to have your building rubble removed, even though you paid taxes to support these services. If you do, you wait for months before a shoddy job is done. But if you phone a private contractor, the job will be done in hours. This sort of knowledge has done more to create popular resistance to further nationalization than countless speeches predicting collapse and dictatorship.

Hayek argued that interventionism leads to dictatorship.[9] I think he had the causal sequence wrong. I think that only a society with well-established dictatorial traditions, such as pre-revolutionary Russia, is likely to go the whole way towards complete interventionism, because dictatorship is needed to suppress the natural forces that check the interventionist trends. A society with strong democratic roots such as Britain or Scandinavia is unlikely to go too much further than its citizens want to go, because when it does, the natural corrective forces will be activated and the democratic state will be unable or unwilling to take the measures needed to suppress them.

Thus, I do not offer you total gloom. We will never, as long as our democratic traditions hold, get to abject serfdom. But do not be too encouraged, for there is a lot of momentum in our present course and a lot of fuel in terms of self-interest and ignorance to drive us further along Hayek's road. Unless we are very careful, we Canadians and Americans may easily get to the London or the Stockholm stations, even if we stop short of the Siberia station on the road to serfdom.

NOTES

1. The economists' concept of quasi-rent extends the idea of windfall profits to cover all productive resources. If, for example, market conditions drive the wage in one occupation above that earned by similar workers elsewhere in the economy, these workers earn a quasi-rent — a return above returns to similar efforts by similar people elsewhere in the economy. I shall use the more familiar term windfall profits but understand it to refer to all resources.

2. Throughout history, observers have often thought in terms of fixed proportions in consumption and production: believing, for example, that: "if only one key material can be denied the enemy, his war effort will come to a halt; consumers will buy this 'essential' product at any price." The overwhelming weight of evidence is that in consumption and in production things are highly substitutable. Firms and households can and do cut down on their use of things whose prices rise, turning to cheaper existing substitutes and inventing new ones.

3. It is possible to imagine a situation in which the state taxed away all windfall losses. This would yield the limited ethical appeal of having similar effort similarly rewarded everywhere in the economy. But nothing is without a cost, and the cost of doing this would be that some method would have to be found of coercing individual decision-makers to respond to changes in demands and costs, because their own self-interest incentive to do so would have been removed.

4. This view is often called into question when queues develop in a market economy. But in mixed economies such as our own, shortages and queues that persist for any appreciable period of time are almost always caused by government intervention rather than the working of the market. For example, gasoline shortages and queues in the 1970s were caused by government price controls plus a moderately inefficient system of allocating scarce supplies by government decree. In other words they were a fairly typical experience of a command economy.

5. Economists did go on a long search for a social welfare function, or a set of compensation criteria, that would allow the results of various sub-optimal market organizations to be compared with each other. The outcome of this long search was, however, that as long as only ordinal assumptions are made about consumer behaviour, the outcomes of non-optimal states cannot in general be ranked against each other. The only exceptions are certain obvious cases where one economy produces less of *all* goods than another or where some very restrictive and unrealistic assumptions are made about people's tastes.

6. This passage was written before the Friedmans published *Free to Choose* which is certainly a counter blast at Galbraith's level. I still await a balanced defense for a middle-of-the-roader who recognizes the imperfections of the market but defends it, as Bernard Shaw did democracy, on the basis that all the alternatives are even worse.

7. What socialist societies have done, by such measures as free hospitalization, medicine, retirement pensions, and housing, is to remove the bottom tail of low living standards that existed, and still exists, in free market societies. But they have not raised the average living standards of all workers. Indeed, with their concentration on growth and hence on heavy investment, they may have reduced average living standards (at comparable stages of development) by diverting a larger fraction of national income to investment than would have gone to "capitalist profits."

8. The relatively few milk producers will realize, for example, that the milk-quota system makes them better off. The large number of milk consumers may not realize, however, that the government's attempts to bring "order" into the milk market have the effect (and are for the purpose) of redistributing income from them to farmers. Probably the moralists, who would be revolted by a scheme that was consciously designed to redistribute income from the poor to the relatively rich, will also not realize that this is the purpose of the policy. Such redistribution from lower to middle and higher income groups are the function of many market intervention schemes since those at the lower end of the income scale are seldom owners or members of the firms and labour and professional organizations who are "assisted" at their consumer's expense.

9. Dan Usher (1981) also argues that government intervention means the end of democracy. He does this using a novel theoretical model whereby he argues that democracy is incompatible with serious government intervention into the distribution of income.

REFERENCES

Brunner, K. (ed). *The Great Depression Revisited*. Boston/Hague/London: Kluwer-Nijhoff, 1981.

Friedman, Milton and Rose. *Free to Choose*. New York/London: Harcourt, Brace Jovanovich, 1980.

Galbraith, John K. *American Capitalism*. Boston: Houghton and Mifflin, 1956.

————. *The New Industrial State*. Boston: Houghton and Mifflin, 1971.

Hayek, F.A. *The Road to Serfdom*. Chicago: University of Chicago Press, 1944.

Lipsey, R.G. "Wage Price Controls: How to Do a Lot of Harm by Trying to Do a Little Good." *Canadian Public Policy,* Winter 1977, pp. 10-17.

Schelling, T.C. *Micromotives and Macrobehaviour*. New York: Norton, 1978.

U.S. Government. *Economic Report of the President*. Washington, D.C.: U.S. Government Printing Office, 1979.

Usher, Dan. *The Economic Prerequisite to Democracy*. New York: Columbia University Press, 1981.

THOMAS J. COURCHENE

Thomas J. Courchene is Professor of Economics at the University of Western Ontario. Born in Saskatchewan in 1940, he was educated at the University of Saskatchewan and received his Ph.D. from Princeton University in 1967. He has also been Professor in Residence at the Graduate Institute of International Studies in Geneva, and has done postgraduate study at the University of Chicago. Professor Courchene has been a member of the editorial boards of the *Journal of Money, Credit and Banking* and the *Canadian Journal of Economics.* He has served on the advisory boards of the Fraser Institute and the C.D. Howe Research Institute. He is currently the Chairman of the Ontario Economics Council.

Professor Courchene is the author of many books, articles, and reviews, including: "Energy and Equalization," in *Energy Policies for the 1980s and Economic Analyses,* Ontario Economic Council, 1979; "Towards a Protected Society: Politicization of Economic Life," (The Innis Memorial Lecture), *Canadian Journal of Economics,* 1980; "Post-Controls and the Public Sector" in *Which Way Ahead?* published by the Fraser Institute; and "Avenues of Adjustment: The Transfer System and Regional Disparities," *Canadian Confederation at the Crossroads,* published by the Fraser Institute.

He has also written several studies for the C.D. Howe Research Institute, including: *Money, Inflation and the Bank of Canada: An Analysis of Canadian Monetary Policy from 1970 to early 1975* (1976), *Monetarism and Controls: The Inflation Fighters* (1976), *The Strategy of Gradualism: An Analysis of Bank of Canada Policy from Mid-1975 to Mid-1977* (1977), and *Refinancing the Canadian Federation: The 1977 Fiscal Arrangement* (October 1979).

His most recent book, *Equalization Payments: Past, Present and Future,* is forthcoming from the Ontario Economic Council.

CHAPTER 2

THE CITIZEN AND THE STATE: A MARKET PERSPECTIVE*

Thomas J. Courchene

I. INTRODUCTION

Has the role of government in the economic system reached its apex and is it now being rolled back? An affirmative answer to this fundamental question might seem to follow from recent events. The passage of Proposition 13 in California, and the electoral victories of Margaret Thatcher in Britain, Ronald Reagan in the U.S. and, to a lesser extent, Joe Clark in Canada, can contribute to this perspective. And this perception lingers still, particularly in the U.S. where significant measures have been taken to curtail government intervention. One can point to the various deregulation measures in airlines, oil, etc.; one can point to the U.S. tax cuts and the on-going expenditure restraints; and more recently one can point to the proposal for the devolution of power from Washington to the states. The latter measure by moving these activities closer to the people reduces the heavy

*This article draws very substantially on my Innis Memorial Lecture, "Towards A Protected Society: The Politicization of Economic Life," *Canadian Journal of Economics* XII, no. 4 (November 1980), pp. 556–77. I gratefully acknowledge the Journal's permission to reproduce substantial portions of this article.

hand of uniform governmental measures and introduces at the state level some healthy competition in delivering these public services to the citizen.

These developments notwithstanding, at this juncture of Canada's economic and political history there are, in my view, other and more compelling forces which will lead to an *increased* government involvement in all aspects of society. More importantly, this new wave of government intervention is likely to be particularly inimical to the viability and flexibility of the market economy. Therefore, my task in this paper is first to identify some of the factors which point to an increasing role for government and, second, to address the related issue of how this encroachment by government is likely to affect the future of the market economy.

There are three strands to my analysis. The first focuses on the perception of the state by citizens, from their vantage point both as consumers and as producers. This analysis builds on the valuable framework developed by Scott Gordon in *Welfare, Justice and Freedom*, (1981). There Gordon analyzes the manner in which the three primary social goals — welfare, justice and liberty, — have contributed singly and together to the growth and perception of the modern state. To these primary social goals, I would add an important fourth, the quest for economic security or protection, even though Gordon probably embedded this somewhere in the concepts of economic welfare and social justice. It is in this drive for increased security and protection including, for example, claims for proprietary rights to the status quo, that I foresee generating an enhanced role for the state.

The second part of the analysis essentially pits this security-oriented conception of social motivations against the uncertainty and adjustment characterizing Canada's current economic challenges. This confrontation portends a substantial further intrusion of government into all facets of the economy — an intrusion that has the potential for dealing a severe blow to the market system. There is a certain irony in all this. The Keynesian revolution gave birth to macroeconomics and, in turn, to the mushrooming of the role of the government sector. Indeed, since the government first took upon itself responsibility for stabilizing economic activity at a high level of employment, a large area of economic activity has become dependent upon *political* rather than market processes. Today, because of the apparent failure of macro policies together with the evolution of rising expectations of citizens, in large measure facilitated by the Keynesian revolution, government intervention is likely again to increase. The difference between the last and the next states of government expansion is — and it is a critical difference — that the new intervention will occur not in the stabilization function, but in the allocation and distribution activities of government to use Musgrave's phraseology (1959).

In the final section, the analysis leaves the private sector-public sector perspective of the earlier sections and directs attention to the process of government itself, or more specifically to the current intergovernmental confrontation in Canada and the impact of this on the well-being of the market economy. Inherent in the manner in which Canadian federalism is developing is a tendency to balkanize our already small national market and to transfer economic decision-making from the domain of the marketplace to that of the political arena.

To be sure, the rise of neo-conservative political and social philosophy may effectively slow the rate of further government encroachment into the private sector. In my opinion, however, the neo-conservatism movement is borne out of the general malaise caused by recent economic history and it is directed principally against the growth of expenditures and taxes that characterized the Keynesian revolution. It has not demonstrated a similar ability to act at the leading edge of the increased demands for government intervention in the economy. It is not directed against the expansion of government's role arising from society's growing preoccupation with economic security.

II. THE PROTECTED SOCIETY

Should economic security emerge as the winner over the requirements of economic efficiency and growth, Canada could in a few years find itself well advanced toward what I call the "protected society." I outline briefly the principle elements in the protected society scenario, not so much to persuade but rather to construct a backdrop which provides the motivation for much of the analysis which follows. A protected society is one in which many or most groups (from small special-interest associations to entire provinces) have turned towards government both to help them attain income which they perceive might be unattainable without such regulation, but also to render them immune to the vicissitudes and discipline of the market economy. Naturally, some groups in the economy are already partially or fully under the protective umbrella of the state either as a result of conscious policy decisions (e.g., equalization payments for the have-not provinces and indexation of income maintenance programs) or as a possibly unintended by-product of regulation. But what happens if and when more and more groups succeed in being so regulated? At some point society clearly becomes engaged in a negative-sum economic game. Relative price signals become muted, economic adjustment is impeded, under-employment and unemployment abound. The system becomes internally driven toward still greater government intervention as the increasing cost and inefficiency arising from the increasing rigidity of the economic structure leads inexorably to further government intervention. Within such a framework, resource allocation increasingly becomes a political, rather than a market phenomenon. Moreover, with the decline of the market system as a co-ordinating institution, the regulation of social and economic activity becomes progressively more personalized and paternalistic. The logical culmination of the protected society scenario is aptly captured by Edward Gibbon's comment, albeit in a different context, on the fall of Athenian democracy: "in the end they valued security more than they valued freedom, and they lost both" (Owen and Braeutigam, 1978, 36).

The drive for economic security and the interaction between citizen and the state

A. The domestic and public households
The citizen's perception of the role of the state (or the public household) in relation to his/her well-being has altered dramatically over this century. It was not all that long ago that individuals turned to family, the church, or to private charity in times of economic insecurity or crises. This has now changed. Today, charity is institutionalized. More importantly, it has been transferred from the realm of benevolence into the realm of justice. Put somewhat differently, the state has conferred upon its citizens the right to assistance from other citizens with a minimum of reference to the sentiments of compassion and benevolence which activated the older forms of charity. Scott Gordon (1977), (1981), links this development to Sir William Beveridge's famous report on the British social security system in 1942 which in effect committed the government to providing full employment. Referring to this report as the "Beveridge transform," he asserts

that "it may turn out to be the most significant change in the socio-economic relationship of Western society since labour became a commodity that was bought and sold in the marketplace" (1977, p. 44).

Over the years, with the refinements in the conception of economic welfare and social justice, the demands on the state have transcended the domain of human *needs* and have entered the realm of human *wants*. Indeed, they have broadened until now they are a very encompassing set of claims — social, political, environmental, etc. As Daniel Bell has remarked, "the revolution of rising expectations which has been one of the chief features of Western society in the past 25 years, is being transformed into a *revolution of rising entitlements* in the next 25" (1974, p. 39). Moreover, it is increasingly the case that the "satisfaction of private wants and the redress of perceived inequalities are not pursued, individually, through the market, but politically by the group, through the public household" (*ibid.*, p. 51). Below, when focusing on the uncertainties associated with the current economic situation, I shall argue that one of the entitlements claimed by the citizenry is a property right to status quo and that this will almost of necessity have to be pursued through the public sector. Since the market is signalling the need for abandoning the status quo, it cannot be the vehicle for resisting adjustments.

Traditional economic theory does not handle this issue well because it is essentially a *distribution* issue. To take an extreme view, assume that what individuals desire is to rise in society's *relative* income ladder. Immediately, one runs up against the distributional equivalent of the "paradox of thrift" — what is possible for one individual (i.e., to rise in society's relative income ladder) is not possible for all. The economic theorists' typical answer is that these are inappropriate expectations for people to harbour. Why attempt to wrestle $1 away from your fellow man when for the same effort you can wrestle $10 from Nature. But this argument is entirely beside the point if people do have strong moral feelings about the distribution of income. For example, a widely held expectation is that the key to success in the relative income scramble is to invest in human capital. But what happens when all your peers also get a university education? The time-honoured path of the acquisitive society runs you smack into the reality of the macro fallacy. Expectations are dashed, you feel that the market system has let you down, so where do you turn? One obvious answer is to turn to the state, in short to "politicize" the issue of distribution. Thus the rationale for individual maximization weakens as the importance in utility functions of these relative income goods increases.

At this juncture, it seems appropriate to ask if the current thrust to reduce government expenditure and curtail deficits will successfully dampen these demands on the state for accommodation from the rising flood of special interests. One might expect them to since rather than competing for a share of an increasing government pie, these interest groups will be pitted *against each other* in order to gain priority for a share of a constant (or at least slower growing) pie. However, expenditures are only one method of placating special-interest groups. To control expenditure growth only to find that claims on government are being satisfied via the tax-expenditure route is hardly a victory for those espousing a reduced role for government. Obviously curtailing government expenditure in combination with a cessation of borrowing from future generations would effectively limit the ability of governments to buy off these groups with direct payments. But this is clearly not the end of the matter. There still exists what Douglas Hartle (1979, p. 1) has identified as the essential, and far and away the most pervasive function of government, namely government regulation. I believe that the real battle over the future role of government and, therefore, the future role of markets, will be fought on the regulation front. And it seems to me that the neo-conservative movement is concerned more with up-front operations of government that can be readily tabulated in terms of expenditures and taxes than with the hidden costs of regulation of economic activity, let alone the rising claims for regulation in the environmental, moral, and social spheres. Moreover, as far as government regulation is concerned, the political spectrum does not really dichotomize into two groups — one favouring more and one favouring less regulation. Rather there exists a fascinating schizophrenia — those espousing economic liberty typically are in favour of moral and social regulation (with some degree and misrepresentation we can call these persons "Republicans"), and those persons espousing moral and social liberty are typically in favour of economic regulation (the "Democrats").

B. The enterprise sector and the public household

If government regulation is coming to the fore as an avenue for bestowing property rights on groups of citizens, its role as a device for granting protection to the enterprise sector is greater still. It has become recognized recently that much of the so-called "public interest" regulation of enterprise embodies significant aspects of income distribution. This has come to be known as *Stigler's Law* — regulation normally tends to be in the interest of those being regulated. Put another way, Adam Smith's view of the invisible hand in economics was that individuals pursuing their own interests are led as if by an invisible hand to further the *public interest*. Milton Friedman (1977, p. 35) writes of the invisible hand in the political sphere — individuals who attempt to further the public interest are led as if by an invisible hand to further private interests which it was not necessarily their intention to promote.

One could give a good deal of attention to the demand and supply of regulation, but I will not dwell on this important area because it is the focus of other papers in this volume. I focus on only one aspect. The regulatory process protects expensive investments from sudden, unexpected reductions in value that might occur if these economic agents were subject to the discipline of an unfettered market. Two implications derive from this approach to regulation. First, unlike the domestic household which often aspires to proprietary claims on the status quo, regulation can provide the enterprise sector with legal rights to the status quo. Second, allocative decisions are transferred from the market sphere to the realm of the administrative process or the courts — in other words, politicized.

I recognize that this argument for private protection is difficult to distingush empirically from the more traditional argument that regulation is designed to achieve an increased return on investment through acquiring property rights. Yet in the current enthusiasm for deregulation, this distinction is frequently absent. I agree fully that regulation does typically embody one or more of the evils ascribed to it, for example, inhibiting innovation, suppressing technical change, depressing economic growth, overinvesting in plant and equipment, tilting the income distribution in favour of the regulated, bestowing property rights. But if one of the principle goals of those seeking regulation is to acquire legal rights to the status quo, it seems to me that one does not make many converts by arguing for the elimination of regulation and a return to the discipline of the market, which threatens to deliver the very antithesis of the status quo. Unless and until these perceptions alter and the public recognizes the vital role played by decentralized markets in coordinating production and consumption decisions, in adjusting to altered underlying conditions and in allowing more scope for the exercise of personal freedom, it is my opinion that the deregulation movement will be frustrated and will achieve little success.

One final point deserves mention. Economists are prone to describe the cost and efficiency losses associated with such institutions as marketing boards, provincial preferential purchasing policies, etc. Yet we tend to forget that there is a great deal of economic activity that is currently under the umbrella of protection or shelters, e.g., civil servants, academics with tenure, etc. For how long, in good conscience, can we turn the powerful tools of economic analysis towards the unregulated sectors and proclaim that in the name of economic efficiency their livelihood should be governed by the discipline of the market? As long as some economic agents are able to fall under the protective umbrella of government regulation in the sense of having valuable property rights bestowed on them, what canon of justice or equity can we fall back upon which would suggest that others be excluded?

It seems to me, therefore, that increasingly we have to turn our attention towards facilitating the degree to which the market governs those sectors that currently benefit from protective regulation before we can with any force argue that regulation should not increase in the "market sector."

This leads to another aspect of the protected society scenario, namely the tendency for regulation or protection to beget further regulation and protection. Consider Canada's generous unemployment insurance program, for example. There are no doubt many ways to rationalize its existence. One of them, I would suggest, ought to include the fact that by offering compensation to those who are victims of protected markets elsewhere in the system, government facilitates the preservation of these sinecures. The pressure for wage flexibility in protected spheres would be enhanced substantially if there were no unemployment insurance. It is clearly in the interests of the current beneficiaries of these shelters to ensure that government steps into accommodate the victims of their actions. Therefore, if governments are unwilling to introduce more flexibility into currently regulated markets, they are inevitably going to be faced with the necessity of introducing more protection elsewhere in the system.

Protectionism and the realities of the 1980s

I now want to turn to the real world and address the issue of whether or not one is likely to find the seeds of further government intervention in the economic malaise and insecurity that is currently gripping the country. My answer is a resounding yes, even though on the surface one could plausibly argue that governments have done a fairly good job of resisting the clamors from the flood of special interest groups seeking special privileges. What underlies my pessimism? Let us look at some of the current problems in turn.

(a) Inflation
Many, perhaps most, economists overestimate substantially the abilities of various institutions, let alone individuals, to adapt to instability in the monetary system. In inflationary periods the socio-economic outcomes are less influenced by careful allocative calculations and more by being able correctly to forecast future inflation.[1] This leads to a situation where people tend to rely less on private contracts and more on political compacts to ensure for themselves a more reliable frame into which to fit their economic lives. In short, there exists a tendency for numerous firms to turn away from the market and towards the political sphere in order to create a more predictable environment for themselves. I think that this is a major part of the reason why the corporate sector was not openly hostile to the AIB and also why they now appear to be in the process of agreeing with Ottawa to a similar compact.

There is a second consequence of inflation, best expressed by Governor Gerald K. Bouey in his 1976 *Annual Report* (p. 8), "Experience with inflation undermines the confidence of people in the fairness of economic processes." Examples are easy to come by. Assume that interest rates are 20 percent and that the inflation rate is 12 percent for a real (after inflation) cost of borrowing of 8 percent. On the surface, it appears as if everybody is treated equally. But we are forgetting about the *tax system*. For the large corporation, with a 50 percent tax rate, the after-tax borrowing cost is 10 percent for an after-tax real cost of credit of -2 percent. For the small corporation, with a 25 percent tax rate, the cost of credit is 15 percent, for an after-tax real cost of borrowing of +3 percent. For the homeowner, and the small businessman with no profits, and hence no ability to write off borrowing costs, the after-tax real cost of credit remains at 8 percent. It was precisely this inequity in shouldering the burden of inflation that every provincial premier raised at the February, 1982 First Ministers' Conference. This is the reform — an intelligent approach to inflation accounting coupled with an equitable approach to taxing non-labour income — that should have been in the Finance Minister's last budget.[2] It is this inequity across sectors of the costs of high interest rates that is calling into question the role of the market as an allocative mechanism.

More generally, societal consensus in favour of a market economy depends upon, among other things, free markets having proven able to generate high average incomes and that the resulting income dispar- ities reflect, to a large degree, relative social rewards for different con- tributions. Inflation, however, renders the latter aspect of the market system highly suspect, because it becomes progressively more difficult to explain the distribution of income by variations in social produc- tivities. Once this situation occurs, the perception of the price system becomes for many incompatible with socially approved goals. In- evitably, there is aroused the temptation to resort to greater and greater political intervention (Krueger, 1974, 302). There is no ques- tion in my mind that experience with inflation has convinced a goodly number of Canadians that political rather than market allocative mechanisms are preferable across an increasingly broad range of goods and services.

(b) Slowth (slow growth)
Another characteristic of the present economic environment is that it is a period of slow growth, or slowth. Growth is the solvent which dissolves much of the potential conflict in a society that is increasingly conscious of redistributive norms — the poor can become richer with- out the rich becoming poorer. Unfortunately, with slowth it becomes progressively more difficult to escape from the rigours of scarcity — we are bound up at best in a zero-sum game and, after tax, often a negative-sum game. Earlier, I noted that it might be irrational to try to pry $1 out of your fellow man when you can get, for the same effort, $10 from Nature. But in a period of slowth, Nature becomes more nig- gardly and the returns from exploitation of one's neighbour through the political system become more attractive. This behaviour has been called the "new enterpreneurship" or "rent-seeking" behaviour and it has spawned a fascinating literature. I do not want to dwell on this in detail here, except to mention that the problem of building political and constitutional defences against this type of exploitation, while at the same time maintaining the advantages of market-type societies, is emerging as a major challenge to society. This will continue as long as our economy remains in the shadow of the stationary state. (See Boulding (1973, p. 95.)

(c) Government policy

It is easily argued that the net result of recent government policy has been to force Canadians to look even more to the government to solve their problems. If one were the least bit paranoid, one could view government policy as a well-executed Machiavellian scheme to undermine confidence in the market economy. I prefer to attribute it to mistaken government policy. Regardless, the problem is a serious one for the future of the market system. Two examples will suffice to make my point, one related to energy and the other to investment. Canadian energy policy, as a result of a combination of federal-provincial rivalry and inappropriate policy has managed to emasculate Canada's one area of sure growth in an otherwise depressed economy. As Richard Lipsey points out in his excellent paper (1982), the predictable success of these government interventions in frustrating the workings of the market will be taken as evidence that the market will not work and will justify still *further* government intervention.

The current situation with investment is just as serious. The latest Balance of Payments data reveal that net direct long-term capital *outflows* for 1981 reached $10 billion, thereby dwarfing figures from previous years. Moreover, at least half as much again is probably buried in the unclassified outflows. Some of this can be attributed directly to the Canadianization features of the National Energy Program. Some capital is also leaving because of the retroactive and banana-republic approach that the NEP took with respect to the "back-in" or expropriation measures for energy finds in the Canada Lands. Capital is also being frightened away by the November, 1981 budget, because many Canadians suddenly find themselves saddled with enormous costs or losses associated with the retroactive measures. The entrepreneurial environment has turned sour in this country and capital, which is by its very nature a nervous commodity, is taking shelter in more favoured climates.

The point at stake here is not so much that these policies are undesirable. Rather it is that with no place to turn because of this substantial outflow of capital and investment, Canadians will be forced to petition the government for help — in spite of the fact that the government perpetrated the problem — and this will lead to even greater control and regulation over the market economy.

Federalism and the market system

In a recent paper, University of Toronto economist John Dales (1975,

p. 502) put forth the proposition that "government is our most precious scarce resource, and probably one of those special, common pool resources." Therefore, Dales argued, "access to government should be made difficult and the cost of political participation kept high in order to prevent government from transforming itself into a common property and succumbing to overuse." (p. 502). For present purposes, and from an economist's vantage point as well I should think this is a useful analogy. Government does preside over a vast pool of *potential* property rights, dispensing them in pursuit of its own ends as well as in response both to society's prevailing attitudes towards basic goals such as justice, equality, and liberty and to the myriad demands from special-interest groups. In an important sense, the efficiency gains arising from a well-functioning market system are embodied in the "rent" shared by society which arises from government maintaining restricted access to these potential property rights. Privatizing these rights directs benefits toward particular sectors of society, and the resulting efficiency loss can be characterized as rent diminution arising from the overuse of a common property resource.

One problem with this analogy, and indeed with the entire analysis to this point, is that government is viewed as a single entity. The viability of the market system has been cast in terms of the interaction between the public sector and the private sector. But what about the interaction *within* the public sector itself? The reality of the Canadian version of federalism is that there are precious few ground rules which allocate, or more importantly which prevent the allocation of, this pool of potential property rights *among* governments. In the final analysis the outcome of this intergovernmental struggle will surely play a major role in determining the degree to which Canada moves along the route towards the protected society.

On the surface, the economic theory of federalism would appear to be particularly appealing to market-oriented economists. Provinces are viewed as providing alternative bundles of public services, and citizens can choose their province according to preferences for these various bundles. This "voting by foot" aspect introduces into the government sphere some of the flexibility and competition that characterizes the operations of decentralized markets.

Yet the practical reality of federalism is that provinces, too, can and should be viewed as special-interest groups. And it may not be too farfetched to view federalism itself as a regulatory process, the beneficiaries of which on many occasions, as Stigler's Law would suggest, are the provinces — as *provinces*, not as the collection of individuals who comprise them. For example, it has struck me as intriguing that we now have a guaranteed annual income scheme for provinces embodied in the Constitution (the Equalization Program) but we lack a correspondingly comprehensive scheme for individuals.

One of the problem areas is that the BNA Act did not provide the necessary constitutional guarantees for a common market in goods, labour and capital across provinces. Thus Ottawa and the provinces can collaborate to fragment the internal common market. And they do. The best example relates to marketing boards. In the 1950s there was a court case in which the Supreme Court ruled that a provincial marketing board was illegal because it was influencing the interprovincial flow of agricultural products. This might have been a victory for consumers. But Ottawa came along and amended the Agricultural Products Marketing Act in 1957 which authorized provincial boards to engage in extra-provincial activities.

Another example is the recent provision enacted by Quebec whereby residents who purchase new share issues of Quebec-based companies can treat a large portion of this as the equivalent of a Registered Retirement Savings Plan for tax purposes. This tends to fragment the internal capital market. Other provinces attempted to follow Quebec's lead but Ottawa stepped in and disallowed their programs because they were inconsistent with the spirit of the tax collection agreements. These provinces are now faced with the choice of abiding by Ottawa's decision on this or, like Quebec, withdrawing from the tax collection agreements and setting up their own personal tax systems, which would probably further contribute to the fragmentation of the internal common market. It is easy to extend this list *ad infinitum*, including federal barriers to internal trade as well.

As part of the recent constitutional review, Ottawa brought this issue of an internal economic union to the fore. It proposed an economic bill of rights as part of the overall Charter which would provide some safeguards for individuals and enterprises. This was an admirable proposal for it would have set some limits to government action in the marketplace that would have been binding on all levels of government. However, what actually found its way into our new Constitution is quite the opposite. To be sure, there is a freedom of mobility clause. However, also in the Constitution is the right of any province with an above-average unemployment rate (which excludes only Ontario, Saskatchewan, Alberta and, on occasion, Manitoba) to discriminate in favour of its residents. This is hardly an acceptable outcome given that the initial thrust was to enhance the rights of citizens and enterprises against governments.

There is one other area of federal-provincial interplay which will continue to have a deleterious impact on the performance of the market sector. This is Section 125 of the Constitution which states, in effect, that the Crown cannot tax the Crown. In practice, what this means is that the interest earnings of the Alberta Heritage Savings Trust Fund cannot be taxed by Ottawa. It means that if any province nationalizes a profit-making enterprise, it will henceforth not pay any federal tax. This is going to become a much more serious problem in the future. How long is it before the Heritage Fund is going to undercut a chartered bank in a major loan placement? When this occurs the tax privilege of the provinces (and of federally operated enterprises as well) will come to the policy centre stage. As it stands now, a very substantial incentive exists for nationalizing or provincializing enterprises and the incentive is such that it places private sector agents at a severe disadvantage.

Finally, it seems to me that the exercise of "executive federalism" (decision-making conferences of senior executives from federal and provincial governments) is not entirely conducive to serving the interest of the enterprise sector. Just as the regulatory process is usurping the role of the market in the private sector, executive federalism is usurping the role of the courts in the public sector. Take the recent energy agreements for example. As part of the compromise, both governments agreed to refrain from referring contentious constitutional issues to the Supreme Court. The Alberta-Ottawa Agreement included an arrangement not to test the legality of Ottawa's export tax on oil. In the Ottawa-Saskatchewan Agreement, both parties recognized that some of Ottawa's revenue was deriving from Crown corporations but that the legality of this would not be brought before the Supreme Court. An early version of a proposed Ottawa-Newfoundland Agreement included a clause suggesting that control over offshore oil would not be brought before the Supreme Court.

The substantial uncertainty caused by intergovernmental rivalry over who has ultimate control is but another example of the manner in which the pool of potential property rights associated with government is being dissipated within the government itself.

III. CONCLUSION

I began this paper by focusing on the drive for economic security or protection on the part of individuals, groups or even provinces and the implications of this for the future of the market economy in Canada. My analysis has focused on those aspects which are likely to generate problems for the viability of the enterprise system. In this sense it may be overly pessimistic, because there co-exist with these forces some positive signs. We *are* toughing it out on the monetary front. Adjustment *is* taking place. Canadians are now beginning to adopt a more realistic set of expectations. So there is hope. But we cannot, and should not, take for granted the maintenance of a viable market sector. Neither in the private nor the public sector, is there much respect for, and perhaps more importantly, much understanding of, the market mechanism. For this reason, those of us who believe in the importance of decentralized markets for generating real growth and for maintaining a large degree of personal freedom must take this message beyond the classroom. Similarly, we must bring more of the real world into the classroom. It is at our own peril that we pontificate on the policy implications of various theories without a much better appreciation and analysis of the institutional fabric of modern economies. In the Canadian context this framework would include such institutions as the regulatory process, the Supreme Court, the governmental decision process and federalism itself.

It is important to return to one of the key points in the analysis, namely the desire on the part of all agents in society for an increased degree of economic security. It is not an evil motive. Far from it. It is a natural and societal instinct. I am sure that we all desire more economic security in our own lives and in those of our fellow citizens. Yet, by our very history and perhaps even our culture, Canadians have a tendency to look towards government as the vehicle for attaining security. By contrast, Americans tend to look toward government more as a last than as a first resort. I prefer their attitude because an economy that places a higher value on individual initiative and the enterprise system will dominate one that looks instead to government to provide economic well-being.

To put this somewhat differently, longer-term economic security requires short-term adaptability and flexibility in light of the rapidly changing pattern of world demands. To pursue security in the here and now at the expense of this required flexibility will serve only to rigidify our economic structure and endow future generations with a lower standard of living. This said, it is important to remember that we cannot turn a blind eye to those less fortunate among us who are burdened most by economic adjustment. The crucial task before us is to design social safety nets that, while providing for those who, for whatever reason, are casualties of the march of economic events, facilitate the necessary allocative adjustments that are dictated by the market.

In conclusion, society's perception of the role of the market, like the market itself, is anything but static. Thus, it would appear essential to gain an overview of the march of political, social, and economic events in order to maintain a proper perspective both as to how the market system is likely to evolve and as to the sorts of policy measures likely to be appropriate at any given time. For example, it accomplishes little to argue against any and all intervention when it is clear to everybody that the government is going to act. It is far better, in situations like this, to support the type of government intervention that will least damage the market and allow it a maximum of freedom from political influence. On this need for perspective, the philosopher of summer, Yogi Berra, stated rather aptly, "If you don't know where you're going, you may end up somewhere else."

NOTES

1. The idea in this sentence and the following two are adapted from Leijonhufvud (1977).
2. Interestingly enough, a proposal along these lines was included in the June 1982 budget package. See MacEachen (1982). While I am obviously in favour of the philosophy underlying these proposals, the particular manner in which they are currently designed is far from satisfactory. For an analysis of these proposals, see Ontario Economic Council (1982).

REFERENCES

Bell, Daniel (1974), "The Public Household 'Fiscal Sociology' and Liberal Society," *The Public Interest*, vol. 37, pp. 29–68.

Bouey, Gerald K. (1977), *Annual Report of the Governor to the Minister of Finance: 1976*, (Ottawa, Bank of Canada).

Boulding, Kenneth (1973), "In the Shadow of the Stationary State," in M. Olson and H.H. Landsberg, ed., *The No-Growth Society*, (Toronto: George J. McLeod Ltd.).

Dales, John H. (1975), "Beyond the Marketplace," *Canadian Journal of Economics*, vol. 8, pp. 483–503.

Friedman, Milton (1977), *Friedman on Galbraith*, (Vancouver: The Fraser Institute).

Gordon, H. Scott (1977), "The Demand and Supply of Government: What We Want and What We Get," Economic Council of Canada, Discussion Paper (Ottawa: ECC).

Gordon, H. Scott (1977), *Welfare, Justice and Liberty*, (New York: Columbia University Press).

Hartle, Douglas C. (1979), *Public Policy Decision Making and Regulation*, (Montreal: Institute for Research on Public Policy).

Krueger, Ann O. (1974), "The Political Economy of Rent Seeking," *The American Economic Review* LXIV, pp. 210–303.

Leijonhufvud, Axel (1977), "Costs and Consequences of Inflation," in C.G. Harcourt, ed. *The Microeconomic Foundations of Macroeconomics*, (London: The MacMillan Press).

Lipsey, Richard (1984), "Can the Market Economy Survive" in this volume.

MacEachen, Honourable Allen J. (1982), *Inflation and the Taxation of Personal Investment Income*, (Ottawa: Department of Finance).

Musgrave, Richard A. (1959), *The Theory of Public Finance*, (Toronto: McGraw-Hill).

Ontario Economic Council (1982), *Inflation and the Taxation of Personal Investment Income: A Council Position Paper on the Canadian 1982 Reform Proposals*, (Toronto: O.E.C.).

Owen, Bruce and R. Braeutigam (1978), *The Regulation Game*, (Cambridge: Ballinger Publishing Company).

PART II

HERBERT GRUBEL

Since 1972, Herbert Grubel has been a Professor at Simon Fraser University in the Department of Economics specializing in international trade and finance. In addition, he is presently Director of the Centre for Economic Research. He has held academic posts at Stanford University, the University of Chicago and the University of Pennsylvania. In 1984 he was Visiting Professor at the University of Cape Town, South Africa and in 1978–79 was CIDA Visiting Professor at the University of Nairobi, Kenya. In 1974–75 Professor Grubel was a visiting Research Fellow at Nuffield College, Oxford and during 1970–71 he was a Senior Policy Analyst for the U.S. Treasury Department in Washington, D.C.

Born in Germany in 1934, Professor Grubel was educated at Rutgers University and Yale where he received his Ph.D. in Economics in 1962. His latest books are *The International Monetary System* (Penguin, 1984); *Free Market Zones* (The Fraser Institute, 1983); *International Economics* (Irwin-Dorsey, 1981); *Intra-Industry Trade* (Macmillan, 1976). Professor Grubel has been the recipient of research grants from both the National Science Foundation and the Canada Council and is listed in "Who's Who in Canada" and "Who's Who in Economics."

CHAPTER 3

THE COSTS OF CANADA'S
SOCIAL INSURANCE PROGRAMS

Herbert Grubel

I. INTRODUCTION

It is unusual to start a paper with graphs, but this is the best way to set
the stage for the following analysis. As can be seen from Figure 3.1,
during the last twenty years Canada's inflation and unemployment
rates have steadily increased. In addition, and economically disturbing, except for a temporary improvement during the world-wide raw
materials boom of the early 1970s, there has been a pronounced downward trend in real income growth per person.

Figure 3.2 shows the growth in total government expenditures during the same period. As can be seen, accompanying the deterioration
in the economy's performance indicators is a steep increase in government expenditures as a percentage of GNP. In data presented below it
will be shown that over 40 percent of the increase in these expenditures
can be explained by the growth in spending on social welfare. The
main theme of this paper is that *growth in welfare spending has contributed substantially to the deteriorating performance of Canada's
economy by depressing the output of actual and potential beneficiaries of welfare and by creating a disincentive to produce on the part
of those taxed to pay for the benefits.*

Figure 3.1

Canada's Economic Performance
Five-Year Averages, 1961-81

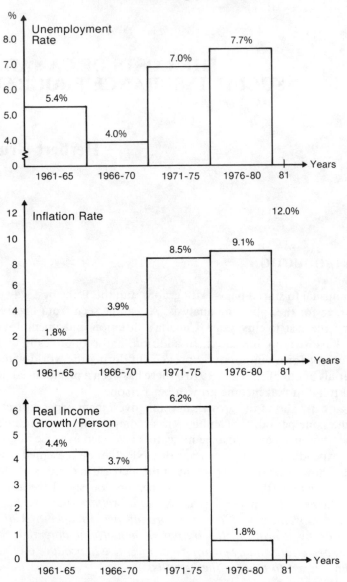

Source: *International Financial Statistics, 1981 Yearbook.*

Figure 3.2

**Total Government Spending as Per Cent of GNP
Five-Year Averages, 1961-81**

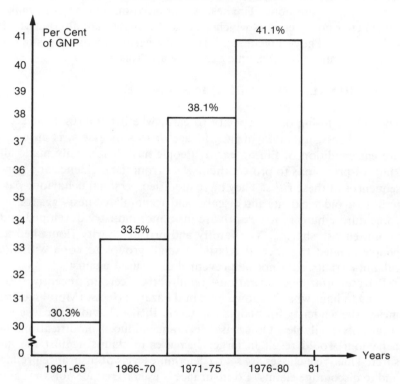

Source: *Economic Review, 1981.*

My emphasis in this paper should not be read as meaning that I believe Canada's problems are due solely to the growth in welfare expenditures. Blame, of course, also falls on monetary policies, excessive regulation, national energy and other policies. But the program of welfare expenditures represents an excellent case study of how liberal policy enthusiasm for fixing free markets has gone awry because of a blatant disregard of prices, incentives and the nature of man.

After presenting a brief rationale for social welfare programs, I review the recent growth in welfare expenditures and then discuss the unexpected side-effects of these programs that contribute to the deterioration of Canada's economic performance. In the concluding section I would have liked to offer solutions to these problems. Unfortunately, there are none. The best we, as a nation, can do is to make some better policy choices which include the unpleasant alternative of reducing direct government support for the needy as a prerequisite for a healthier and more dynamic economy and society.

II. RATIONALE FOR PUBLIC INSURANCE

The risk of losing one's capacity to earn, whether the result of accident, sickness, unemployment, old age or loss of assets, is an ever-present condition of life on earth. People have historically made all kinds of provisions to protect themselves from the incidence and consequences of these risks. They have modified personal behaviour patterns to avoid accidents and disease, and accumulated nest-eggs for income during hard times. A private insurance industry developed and permitted risk-sharing. The family and private charity flourished as people banded together in relatively small groups to cope with the calamities that could not be prevented or insured against.

Private insurance operations require that certain incentives be created to limit what is known as moral hazard effects. (Moral hazard means the tendency for people to modify their behaviour because insurance is available.) Otherwise, insurance-induced modifications in behaviour would result in larger increases in claims against the insurer. Thus, risk classes are set to determine levels of insurance premia and to discourage claims. Co-insurance is used to reduce nuisance and non-economic claims. Other institutions have also adapted to the reality of moral hazard behaviour. Private charity, by operating at a decentralized level, is able to limit moral hazard by the use of effective means tests and surveillance of claimants by methods that meet the group's standards of morality. It can be shown in a logically rigorous fashion that this private system of risk-reducing institutions tends to yield efficient results in the sense that individuals actually obtain the level of reduced risk they prefer and are willing to pay for it (Grubel, 1971).

Nonetheless, liberal critics of the free market process have found the private system of insurance deficient on several grounds. First, it is considered to be inefficient in that it requires private insurance companies to employ sales forces, portfolio managers and officers to police against moral hazard behaviour. It is argued that most of these expenditures could be saved by the use of universal, compulsory public insurance which also could reduce costs by exploiting economies of scale in administration. Second, private insurance fails to provide for such risks as unemployment and poverty after retirement. Third, private insurance is inequitable. It charges the highest rates to, and insists on the greatest degree of co-insurance from, the very people who frequently suffer from the insured risks and who, because of poor health and poverty, can least afford the costs of insurance. Healthy, well-to-do persons who can afford high premia and co-insurance rates typically enjoy low premia. Fourth, private charity forces dehumanizing means tests and procedures on the poor. Dickens' stories about crippled children being abused by their guardians and forced to beg and about the squalor of nineteenth century English work houses are symbolic of the shortcomings of private charity. The tendency for people to care for each other through several generations of a family living together, leads to dependence, exploitation and all kinds of horrors for which sociologists have found vivid terms.

On the above shortcomings, the inequity of private insurance looms largest as a motive for the public and uniform provision of many forms of insurance, but the dehumanizing effect of submitting oneself to means tests and facing continuous pressure to get off private charity's relief roles also explains public demand for the collective provision of insurance without such conditions.

The question of rights

Private methods for dealing with the risks of living have come under attack on grounds other than their inefficiency and inequity. In our time we have witnessed the rise of a philosophical movement promoting the view that the enjoyment of economic security is a right and that the state has an obligation to provide it.

The moral and natural rights philosophy which in eighteenth century England led Thomas Hobbes and others to argue that man has a moral right to a freely chosen government, provided the intellectual foundations for the French and American revolutions. It is now popular to apply much the same reasoning by which certain philosophers have defended the self-government right, to argue that the road from barbarism to higher levels of humanity and civilization can be travelled only through enshrining the right to economic security. A good society will not allow some unfortunate members to remain in need. This view has been expressed eloquently in Article 25 of the U.N. Declaration of Human Rights, which Canada signed in 1956:

Everyone has the right to a standard of living adequate for the health and well-being of himself and of his family, including food, clothing, housing, and medical care and necessary social services, and the right to security in the event of unemployment, sickness, disability, widowhood, old age or other lack of livelihood in circumstances beyond his control.

I believe that today this philosophy is deeply rooted in the minds of a majority of Canadians.[1] It is important to appreciate this fact for the study of the growth and effects of Canada's social insurance programs as well as for designing potential changes in policies.

In conclusion, by concentrating on alleged inefficiencies and inequities, critics of private and free market means for dealing with life's risks have successfully attacked these institutions. In this attack they have been joined by those who see economic security to be a moral right of all citizens. In the kind of civilized society we want Canada to be, the state has an obligation to provide this security. Canada's politicians have responded affirmatively to these criticisms. As will be seen, they have fashioned a magnificent tapestry of programs for the provision of economic security. These programs eliminate inequitable risk classes, co-insurance provisions and means tests. Public insurance programs redistribute income and encourage the belief that the benefits are a right, not a privilege.

Need for utilitarian cost-benefit analysis

Before turning to the empirical part of my paper, I consider two important points raised by the preceding sketch. First, Canada's social insurance programs do not fare well in my critique, not because I believe they do no good, but because I find they do far more harm than good. The moral philosophers are certainly right – the fewer needy in a society, the better the society. Indeed, as we contemplate the size of welfare expenditures today, one cannot doubt that they do a lot of good for some and relieve the misery of many. Moreover, it is true that the operating cost of public insurance schemes per dollar of benefits provided is lower than that of private insurance. It is also true that savings in selling costs, management and economies of scale do exist.

Nevertheless, this paper shows that welfare programs have led to far higher costs than liberal critics of free markets have estimated and that philosophers tend to neglect entirely. The existence of the extra costs alone does not imply that welfare programs should be abandoned. After all, private insurance which would replace them also would incur large costs. The recognition of the existence and magnitude of the costs of social insurance merely suggests that it may be rational to modify terms at which public insurance is offered. Now that more evidence on the cost of welfare programs is available than when they were initiated, realistic and rational approaches to the design of the system should replace the original design that was largely motivated by emotion and forged in innocence of true costs.

Second, the cost-benefit analysis of Canada's social insurance system proposed below is, no less than the liberal welfare model, hallowed by a powerful philosophical tradition—the utilitarianism of Jeremy Bentham. Utilitarianism proposes that laws should not be based on absolute moral rights, but should all be subjected to a calculation of resulting gains and losses in the well-being of the members of society. Economists, with a well-known propensity for subjecting everything to cost-benefit analysis, are in this sense true Benthamites. Perhaps, if my findings and analysis are convincing, more utilitarians and economists will be hired in place of moral philosophers, lawyers and sociologists, by those institutions that formulate and administer Canada's social insurance programs.

III. SOME FACTS ABOUT WELFARE SPENDING

The complexity and scope of Canada's social insurance programs are often underestimated. Table 3.1, in which I list the programs under which Canada's federal, provincial and municipal governments are disbursing funds to the needy, should dispel any notion that Canada's social insurance arrangements are simple and lacking broad coverage. The table lists 47 programs, indicating for each the year when the program was inaugurated and expenditure levels for 1959, 1969 and 1979. For the major programs, the table shows the percentage growth rates between 1959 and 1979.

The data in Table 3.1 provide eloquent testimony to the rapid expansion of the Canadian welfare system. The number of programs has risen from 20 in 1959 to 43 in 1979. While this is not a precise measure, it is at least symbolic of the broadening of the social welfare effort during the period. The dollar value of expenditures rose from $2.7 billion in 1959 to $35.6 billion in 1979, or 12.9 times.

TABLE 3.1

Social Security Expenditures by Program ($ million)

	Year first in table	1959 $	1959 %	1969 $	1969 %	1979 $	1979 %	$ Growth 1959-79
1 Family Allowances	(1957)	475	17.2	560	7.4	2093	5.9	441
2 Youth Allowances and Quebec Schooling Allowances	(1965)			73	1.0			
3 Child Tax Credits	(1979)					874	2.5	
4 Old Age Security	(1957)	559	20.2	1297	17.1	4131	11.6	739
5 Guaranteed Income Supplement	(1967)			244	3.2	1234	3.5	
6 Spouses Allowance	(1976)					126	.4	
7 Canada Manpower Institutional Training Allowances	(1973)			108	1.4	117	.3	
8 Canada Manpower Industrial Training	(1967)					84	.2	
9 Registered Indians, Social Assistance	(1968)			22	.3	104	.3	
10 War Veterans Allowances	(1957)	55	2.0	96	1.3	236	.7	429
11 Veteran Disability and Dependent Pensioners	(1957)	151	5.5	223	2.9	437	1.2	289
12 CPP and QPP Retirement Beneficiaries	(1967)			7	.1	1055	3.0	
13 CPP and QPP, Surviving Spouse Pensioners	(1969)			20	.3	408	1.1	
14 CPP and QPP, Disability Pensioners	(1970)					229	.6	

#	Program	Year							
15	CPP and QPP, Orphans and Dependent Children of Disabled Pensioners	(1968)			3		109	.3	
16	UIC, Unemployment Beneficiaries	(1957)	406	14.7	499	6.6	3917	11.0	965
17	UIC, Sickness Benefits	(1972)					156	.4	
18	UIC, Maternity Benefits	(1972)					200	.6	
19	UIC, Retirement Benefits	(1972)					15		
20	UIC, Fishing Benefits	(1972)					69	.2	
21	UIC, Persons in Manpower Training	(1976)					118	.3	
22	Workers Compensation, Temporary Disability	(1961)			69	.9	274	.8	
23	Workers Compensation, Pensions for Permanent Disability and Survivors	(1957)			104	1.4	494	1.4	581
24	Old Age Assistance	(1957)	85	3.1	13	.2			
25	Blind Person Allowance	(1957)	60	2.2	5	.1	1		
26	Disabled Persons Allowances	(1957)	8	0.3	29	.4	1		
27	Unemployment Assistance	(1957)	31	1.1	34	.4			
28	CAP, Direct Financial Assistance	(1967)	62	2.2	522	6.9	2179	6.1	
29	CAP, Homes for Special Care	(1968)			91	1.2	495	1.4	
30	CAP, Child Welfare	(1968)			78	1.0	165	.5	
31	CAP, Other Welfare Services and Work Activity	(1968)			60	.8	462	1.3	
32	Vocational Rehabilitation of Disabled Persons	(1963)			8	.1	63	.2	
33	Registered Indians, Social Services	(1968)			8	.1	41	.1	
34	Mothers Allowances, Provincial-Municipal Cost-Shared	(1957)	41	1.5					
35	Provincial Tax Credits and Rebates	(1974)					965	2.7	
36	Other Provincial Welfare Programs	(1957)	142	5.1	457	6.0	1582	4.4	1114

TABLE 3.1 (continued)

Social Security Expenditures by Program ($ million)

	Year first in table	1959 $	1959 %	1969 $	1969 %	1979 $	1979 %	$ Growth 1959–79
37 Hospital Insurance and Diagnostic Services	(1958)	64	2.3	812	10.7	3858	10.8	6222
38 Hospital Insurance and Diagnostic Services, Provincial Costs	(1958)	64	2.3	814	10.7	2631	7.4	4110
39 Medical Care Insurance	(1970)					1325	3.7	
40 Medical Care Insurance, Provincial Costs	(1970)					925	2.6	
41 Extended Health Care, EPF	(1978)					521	1.5	
42 Other Health Programs	(1957)	112	4.1	228	3.0	632	1.8	564
43 Worker Compensation, Hospital and Medical Care	(1957)	32	1.2	65	.9	198	.6	818
44 Other Hospital Care, Provincial	(1957)	234	8.5	451	5.9	835	2.3	357
45 Other Provincial Health	(1957)	70	2.5	426	5.6	1710	4.8	2442
46 Net Municipal Welfare	(1957)	35	1.3	84	1.1	339	1.0	969
47 Net Municipal Health	(1957)	75	2.7	95	1.2	210	.6	280
Total Expenditures		2762	100.0	7604	100.0	35619	100.0	1290
Total Number of Programs		20		33		43		220

Source: *Canada Yearbook* 1981–82, Table 8.16.

TABLE 3.2

Welfare Expenditures in Canada 1957-79

	Per capita expenditure in constant 1971 dollars	Annual increases in per capita constant dollars	Ratio of expenditures per $100 of personal income
1957	145	8.3	6.9
1962	174	0.5	7.9
1972	342	21.0	10.1
1977	502	4.4	11.3
1979	539	5.2	12.0
Average		6.1	

Source: *Canada Yearbook* 1980-81, Table 8.19.

Although the table records the growth of the system, the raw data it provides requires considerable further analysis. To convey a fuller appreciation of the growth in social insurance programs, Table 3.2 eliminates social insurance expenditures, on health, items 37–45 and item 47 of Table 3.1, leaving only welfare expenditures. Eliminating health expenditures makes the analysis of causes and effects of welfare spending simpler to follow.

As can be seen from Table 3.2, per capita expenditures in constant 1971 dollars rose from $145 in 1957 to $739 in 1979, an annual compounded rate of growth of 6.1 percent. Since per capita income during this period grew at only about half that rate, welfare expenditures rose from 6.9 to 12.0 percent of personal income.

Figure 3.3 shows major categories of government expenditures as a percentage of GNP for the years 1965-77, for which consistent data are available. This graph shows dramatically that social welfare expenditures rose more rapidly than any other category, both absolutely (by 5.7 percentage points) and in terms of rates from the base in 1965 (233 percent). Of the total increase in government expenditure noted in Figure 3.2, about 40 percent is accounted for by growth in welfare expenditures.

Figure 3.3 also shows that during this period defense expenditures

Figure 3.3

Government Expenditures as Per Cent of GNP
(Consolidated Federal, Provincial and Local)

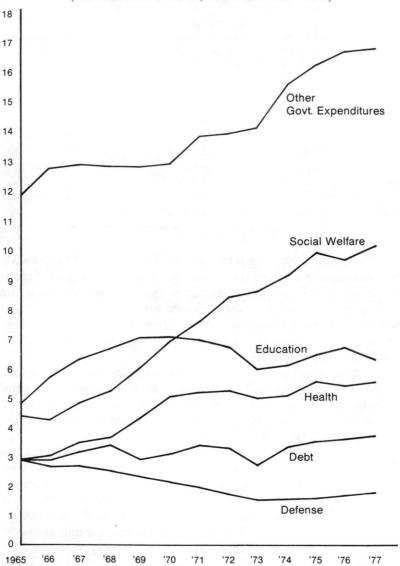

Source: Calculated from *Canada Statistical Yearbook*, various issues, Tables 22.1
and 23.1.

fell by one half while education spending rose a miserly average annual rate of 1.5 percentage points or 25 percent on the 1965 base. Health expenditures rose at an average of 2.5 percentage points annually or 196 percent on the 1965 base. The largest category of government expenditures is a catch-all "other." It also rose sharply, but started from a much higher base. It contains many government services which might be categorized by some under the title social welfare. These include expenditures under programs for housing, agriculture and Indian affairs.

The adjustment of published welfare expenditure figures to reflect the welfare component of other spending programs is a difficult and contentious task and will not be undertaken here. The government presentation of statistics is subject to some manipulation, as may be seen from the treatment of defense expenditures. Until the early 1970s they were shown as such and exhibited a steady downward trend. They were then combined with domestic security expenditures to create a category entitled "Defense of Persons," which has shown a steady increase. To construct Figure 3.3 with consistent defense data, I had to consult different tables in government publications before and after the switch in nomenclature. I believe that by analogy, other government expenditures may contain substantial elements of social welfare spending that it is politic to hide.

G. Gilder (1981 estimated that in 1979 in the United States a welfare family of four received an *average* of close to $18,000 in government benefits and subsidies. This figure is meaningfully compared with the $9,000 annual earnings accruing to someone working full time at the minimum wage. I could not find similar calculations for Canada since there appear to be no data on the number of benefit recipients. A simple calculation may, nevertheless, usefully convey an idea of the per capita and per family level of Canada's welfare expenditures.

In 1979, Canadian social security expenditures totalled $36 billion. After subtracting the costs of health ($13 billion), family allowances ($2 billion) and UIC unemployment benefits ($4 billion), we are left with expenditures of $17 billion for retirement and welfare. By assuming that all two million Canadians over 65 were beneficiaries of the retirement programs, and that 10 percent of the remaining 20 million Canadians, received benefits, we calculate that $17 billion was spent on four million individuals. This would mean that in 1979 each welfare recipient received about $4,200 and a family of four received about $17,000. This figure is close enough to the one quoted by Gilder for the United States to give us some confidence, but it should be treated with great caution given the casual nature of the preceding calculations. Whatever the level of accuracy of this figure, there can be little doubt that per capita and family transfer payments have reached lofty heights in both Canada and the United States.

The above data document what most Canadians have believed for some time and have noted painfully at the end of April every year when income taxes are due. The Canadian system of welfare benefits has grown rapidly, is very generous to its beneficiaries, and costs taxpayers a great deal of money.

What are the causes of growth in welfare expenditures? Is there simply an increasing willingness of the middle and wealthy classes to share wealth with the needy, as some social workers, politicians and intellectuals argue? Or is there something to the widespread belief that the welfare system involves a great deal of cheating and generates its own need? The purpose in writing this paper is to provide answers to these questions.

IV. MORAL HAZARD

Most Canadians would agree that in 1965 the level of welfare in Canada was, by general standards, reasonable. True, the needy, poor and wretched of the earth were with us, but the combination of government welfare expenditures together with family and private charities provided these groups with the essentials. Twelve years later, in 1977, real per capita government welfare expenditures had risen threefold from 1965 levels. Despite this enormous expansion in per capita support levels, the needy, poor and wretched appear still to be with us. Few Canadians have strong personal experiences with welfare recipients and our knowledge comes largely from the CBC and the testimony of social workers. I tend to distrust the objectivity of both sources of information, but their testimony is the most persuasive available. Statistics on income and wealth inequalities are notoriously difficult to construct and interpret, but they basically support the CBC's and social workers' views that the vast growth in welfare expenditures has not created a correspondingly more equal society. What, if anything, has gone wrong?

Relation to welfare cost growth

The answer to this question is obviously complex and a full answer that would meet the most rigorous standards for evaluating evidence may never be possible. I do defend, however, the hypothesis that a very significant proportion of the growth in welfare expenditures has been due to what popularly is known as welfare "cheating," known in the insurance industry as "moral hazard," and interpreted by economists as rational behaviour towards changes in relative costs and opportunities introduced by the welfare system itself. In other words, the growth in expenditures is due largely to the broadening and deepening of demand for welfare services that would not have occurred in the absence of their availability. This is a case of supply engendering much of its own demand.

At the outset of the analysis I find it useful to allocate the observed growth in expenditures to different, easily assignable causes. To do this I show in Figure 3.4 the level of welfare expenditures in 1965 at $2.4 billion. The upward sloping lines from the 1965 origin indicate the levels of expenditure that would have been necessary to maintain real services per recipient at their 1965 levels. I have assumed that total need varies proportionally with the general population, the share of the aged in the population and the general rate of inflation. Accordingly, we see that expenditures of $7.7 billion in 1977 would have provided for delivery of the same level of real services per needy person in 1977 as was provided in 1965.

Because during the 1965-77 period real income per person in Canada rose substantially, it can be convincingly argued that the need to increase benefits declined proportionately, since public charity is supposed only to provide a minimal safety net for the needy. By the same token, others would argue that higher incomes permit a more generous treatment of the needy and that benefits should increase more rapidly than income. In Figure 3.4 I reflect the view which may well appeal to most Canadians' sense of fairness, that the needy should receive a *constant proportion of average incomes*. As can be seen, on this basis and after adjusting for inflation and changes in the age distribution of the population, in 1977 welfare expenditures should have totalled $14 billion. The true amount Canada spent in that year was $21 billion, or 50 percent more than my standard. I submit that this extraordinary growth was caused by the operation of moral hazard.

The dynamics of moral hazard

Moral hazard is a term used in the insurance industry to describe the

Figure 3.4

Social Welfare Expenditures
in Canada

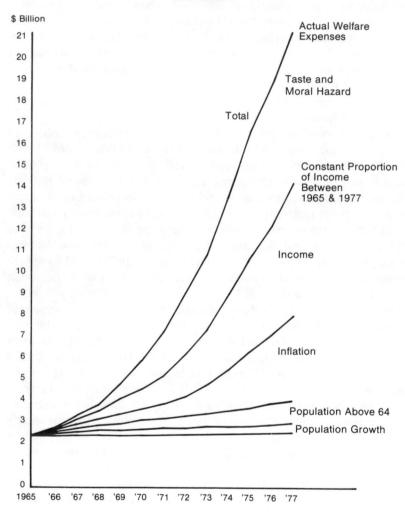

Note: $WE_{p,i} = (WE_{65} \cdot P_i)/(P_{65})$, where WE is welfare expenditure, P indicates adjusted
for population growth, 65 refers to value in 1965, i is the year = 66, 67, ...,77.
Further adjustments are made by multiplying $WE_{p,i}$ by $A_{65,i}/A_{65}$ where A is
population aged 65; and so on for each variable. The final value adjusted for
population, age, inflation (I) and income per capita levels (Y) is:

$$WE^* = (WE_{65} \cdot P_i \cdot A_i \cdot I_i)/(P_{65} \cdot A_{65} \cdot I_{65})$$

phenomenon that whenever a class of risks is insured, the incidence of the hazard increases. For example, restaurants insured against fire damage burn down more often that those that are not. Persons with dental insurance make more frequent visits to the dentist than those who do not have the same coverage.

Unfortunately, though moral hazard is a catchy term to describe the phenomenon, it is misleading. Only a few insured risks lead the insured to engage in outright cheating, which violates universal standards of morality, as for instance when someone torches a restaurant. Most increases in damage to insured property are due to more subtle changes in behaviour that economists identify as rational responses to changes in relative prices. For example, restaurant owners tend to become less careful about the removal of hazardous rubbish and kitchen grease simply because the return to expenditures for such services is lowered by the insurance. People with dental insurance have fewer cavities for shorter periods, replace lost teeth sooner, and have fancier replacement work done than those without such insurance coverage, for the good reason that their dental work costs them less.

Moral hazard behaviour is induced also by government insurance designed to pay benefits to those who suffer from unemployment, single parent status, blindness, other physical and mental handicaps, old age and many other conditions. The potential beneficiaries under these programs have one of the strongest of incentives to refrain from employment, because the schedule of benefits dramatically lowers their effective returns from work.

For example, a single mother who could earn $5 an hour or $200 a week working full time might, given the welfare system, be left with as little as $1.25 per hour. The welfare system taxes her $2.75 on each hour worked. (To arrive at this figure I assume that after work-related expenses, paying a babysitter and taxes, the disposable income from work is $150 a week. If the government pays the single mother $100 a week in support, the net gain from work is only $50 a week, or $1.25 an hour.) Many people who would find it worthwhile to work for $5 an hour would not do so for $1.25 an hour. Furthermore, by not working the single parent can earn additional income through the increased availability of discretionary time, to do informal and casual work for pay, learn skills and do work around the house that would otherwise have to be bought. Similar incentives, of course, affect all recipients of benefits when the benefits are conditional on not working.

The impact of moral hazard behaviour on welfare expenditures in recent years has grown because of changing public attitudes and beliefs, as well as changes in relative prices. As was noted above, increasingly large sections of the community have accepted the idea that social welfare benefits are a right. This view is sometimes supported by the argument that most beneficiaries have in the past, as taxpayers, paid in advance for the funds they now claim.

Measurements of effects

Few people, not even socialists, moral philosophers or lawyers would deny today that moral hazard incentives of welfare programs exist and operate in the manner described above. What is in dispute is the magnitude of the effects. To decide the dispute over magnitudes, measurement is necessarily of the utmost importance. Unfortunately, little direct and reliable evidence is available.

One of the first direct measures of moral hazard effects was published by Grubel and Maki (1975) in connection with Canada's unemployment insurance program. We found that the 1972 increase in unemployment insurance benefits relative to wages, together with other liberalizations in the program concerning eligibility for benefits, led in 1975 to unemployment rates 1.5 percentage points above the 5.0 percent would have prevailed in the absence of the 1977 changes in the UIP.[2] This study of the unemployment insurance program, was possible because of the availability of data collected by the UIC. Such data, unfortunately, are rarely available for other social insurance programs. Therefore, all that can be done instead is to outline the typical changes in behaviour called forth by the availability of insurance to support the thesis that much of the recent growth in welfare expenditures is due to moral hazard.

Behaviour modifications

Some of the behaviour modifications stimulated by increasingly generous unemployment insurance follow:

1. Employers are quicker to lay off workers during slowdowns in business because they know benefits prevent extreme hardship, and allow workers to seek temporary employment without penalty and take holidays while awaiting recall.

2. Workers are more prone to leave when they are dissatisfied with the package of work conditions, pay, etc. because benefits cushion their income while they search for new jobs. Employers and workers often collude to disguise quits as lay-offs since to do so costs the employers nothing, and creates good-will among workers, and this collusive behaviour is not closely controlled by the authorities.
3. Once on unemployment insurance benefits, the worker is induced to extend job search time. Workers can set higher quality standards for the job they will accept and reduce the intensity of their search. They resort to many well-known techniques for resisting government pressures on them to accept job offers or for preventing offers from being made.[3]
4. Benefits are equivalent to government subsidies for seasonal workers and industries. In the absence of such subsidies, seasonal industries would be less prevalent in Canada and average unemployment would therefore be lower.
5. Benefits are equivalent to subsidies for people who prefer to live away from rapidly growing labour markets. In recent years, though there were labour shortages in the West, unemployment benefits permitted people to remain in remote areas and economically declining regions.
6. Benefits raise the effective wage rate earned while working. As a result, people with secondary interest in labour force participation, such as mothers, the young and elderly, are induced to enter the job market for short periods, quit after eligibility for benefits has been established, and contribute to the measured unemployment rate.

Because so much is known about the effects of unemployment insurance, the above list stands alone with little additional comment. On the other hand, it may be tempting to argue that moral hazard behaviour in the case of unemployment is a unique situation and tends to be high because co-insurance is very low while most other genuine welfare programs, such as aid for such groups as the blind, single mothers, etc., are associated with high levels of co-insurance and leave little room for what the English call fiddling. After all, it is hard to imagine someone going blind or becoming a single parent in order to become eligible for relatively miserly benefits. This line of argument misses the subtle effects of moral hazard behaviour.

Many people think of welfare aid for single parents as funds supporting a widow with five children who lost her husband in an industrial accident. However, reality tells a different story. The majority of beneficiaries of aid to single parents are young mothers with a single child. The ranks of the latter group have been swelled greatly in recent years by such benefit-induced changes in behaviour as the following:

1. More children are born out of wedlock because of the widespread awareness among young parents that the single mother will be supported by the state.
2. people move geographically for many reasons, but in the past, mobility was reduced by the desire to keep several generations of a family together for mutual assistance, including help with the raising of children if, for any reason, a parent became single. The availability of benefits for single parents has eased restraints on geographic mobility and left many single mothers unable to work since there are no babysitting grandparents nearby.
3. Sociologists have found that in families with low-income fathers, disputes that would otherwise be simple quarrels may lead to separation and divorce. This occurs because a mother experiences little and often no reduction in net income when she shows her husband the door, while a departing father leaves knowing the state will look after his family. This explains why the number of single parents reaches such high proportions in New York's Harlem, where wages are low, and at the other extreme in Sweden, where welfare benefits are high.
4. Since eligibility ceases upon marriage or remarriage, many relationships between single mothers and potential husbands remain informal, and in many jurisdictions, surreptitious.

The preceding short review of benefit-induced changes in behaviour in the case of the unemployed and single parents is designed merely to provide some rough indications of the types of adjustments that social insurance programs call forth and that have increased the cost of operating them. This kind of behaviour is as diverse as are people and it is ubiquitous, affecting every welfare program. Unfortunately, direct evidence is scant on the quantitative effect of moral hazard behaviour, except in the case of unemployment insurance, and even in the case of unemployment insurance the measured effects document only the reaction to recent liberalization of the program, not the program itself. Therefore, regarding the increase in welfare expenditures from 1965 to 1977, which I find excessive, attribution of this excess to moral hazard rather than another reason must remain indirect and circumstantial. Readers must, in the end, trust their own intuition and draw on personal experiences in reaching a final judgement on the validity of my hypothesis and the resultant need for policy changes.

V. COSTS THROUGH CHANGES IN THE NATURE OF SOCIETY AND HIGH TAXES

The availability of the social welfare system has other important influences on economic and social behaviour that most people identify as inducing extra costs on society. These can only be sketched here, but they may be more important than the expansion of demand for benefits and the subsequent financial outlays created by the types of moral hazard behaviour noted above. These changes are sometimes obvious and in other cases rather subtle.

For instance, attitudes towards work, education and savings are changed because the traditional penalties of failure are much reduced. One obvious influence is revealed by employers' complaints about the poorer work habits of the young, which are likely correct on average. Also, budget studies show that people include public pensions and medical benefits in their planning for retirement and emergencies, reducing correspondingly their private savings. On the other hand, more subtle effects occur when people make decisions for a lifetime. In Sweden, Lindbeck (1980) notes that universities have trouble filling engineering classes because this type of training demands serious effort whereas they face overcrowding in easier fields of study.

Another less apparent change is the growing social and political tension between those holding traditional values and paying high income taxes and those of the younger generation holding the new values, for whom welfare benefits and personal behaviour patterns are a matter of right. There are grave social and political consequences of this split in the community. Aid to people with marginal ability and willingness to work, such as single parents and the blind, engenders a sense of frustration and dependence. It is difficult to find the extra energy and resourcefulness to learn new skills, develop work habits and face the discomfort of working when the effective pay rate, the premium earned over and above the level of available benefits, is lowered so much by the availability of welfare benefits. Single parent support programs increase the number of children who are raised with only one parent in the home. Many of the crime problems of Harlem are attributed to the effects which this welfare program has had on generations of black families living there. The traditional multi-generation family relationship is broken up as welfare programs reduce intergenerational dependence. This may be welcomed for the extra mobility and personal freedom it sometimes brings but on the other side of the coin is the harm done by reducing the influence of grandparents and increasing the influence of television on the formation of character and values of young people.

Welfare programs have led to a vast proliferation of laws and regulations that invite fiddling to allow citizens to maintain their relative standard of living. This erosion of general standards of honesty has serious and as yet unconsidered consequences both for individual mental health and for the preservation of those standards of human interaction without which civil society can hardly survive. "Everyone is doing it" and "I've paid my taxes" are the easy rationalizations used.

In sum, social insurance programs erode the traditional values, constraints, penalties and institutions of society, the loss of which threatens the viability of that society. Even if many such changes taken individually are welcomed by some Canadians, especially those among us who often, for romantic reasons, dislike free market solutions to economic and social problems, these same Canadians would shrink from the prospect of the sum of these social changes bringing about a new type of society with unpredictable and potentially highly undesirable characteristics. There remain serious doubts about the productivity of a Canada in which the work ethic is replaced by the social attitudes induced by the welfare state.

Impact of taxation

The effect of benefits on recipients is possibly less serious for the economy than the impact of the taxes raised to pay for the benefits. The continued growth of unemployment and the rise in numbers of dependent single parents, retired and the disabled persons induced by social insurance shrinks the tax base. As a result, given the progressivity of Canada's tax structure, increasingly high marginal tax rates are needed to raise revenues. The hardest hit are the productive middle classes, with effects that only now are entering into society's consciousness.

Traditional economic theory teaches that taxation may or may not decrease work effort, depending on the relative size of the income and substitution effects. This may well be true for taxes used to pay for defense and roads, but it is not similarly true for taxes used to supply otherwise privately supplied services. Under these conditions the substitution effect is clearly cut and these taxes reduce work effort. Let me explain. When the government initiates a pension program and at the same time taxes me to pay for it, my wealth position is unchanged because the reduction in my flow of income is matched by the reduced obligation to provide support for my parents or save for my own retirement. All that is left is a tax-reduced return to effort and a guaranteed benefit that is independent of my own effort.

The traditional view of the incentive effect of taxation has tended to downplay the potential magnitude of all substitution effects because it was believed that most people had only limited opportunities to vary their working hours. This neglects three important long-run adjustments.

The first adjustment is made possible by the social insurance programs noted above. Sick leaves, absenteeism, temporary unemployment, early retirement, and work-related injuries all present opportunities for the enjoyment of leisure without significant loss of income. Germany and Sweden every year are setting new records in the number of work days lost through sickness and absenteeism even though the people of both countries are enjoying increasing levels of health by everyone's medical standards.

Second, young people rationally and in increasing numbers choose occupations which allow more opportunity to earn income in kind. Executives refuse promotions requiring geographic mobility because after tax income increases fail to compensate for the untaxed costs of settling in a new community. It is well known, for instance, that executives are increasingly unwilling to move from Vancouver to eastern locations even for significant promotions.

Third, there has developed in Canada a large underground economy, which has been estimated to be about one quarter of the size of the officially recorded economy (Mirus and Smith, 1981). It provides ready opportunities for strictly illegal activities, but for the purpose of the present analysis it is important to note that it consists in large part of work done in the home, for barter or for money which is not reported to the income tax authorities. Opportunities for such work are especially great for temporarily unemployed people who are recorded as sick or absent for unexplained reasons.

The preceding analysis suggests that there exists a synergistic link between the size of moral hazard, tax rates and the underground economy. Encouraged by a growing indifference to traditional values and the law, these developments feed upon and reinforce one another, thereby lowering incentives to work, decreasing productivity and changing the nature of Canadian society.

Implications for the future

Descriptions of life in the socialist paradise of Eastern Europe make depressing reading for most Canadians. Not only are living standards lower than in Canada, but still more depressing are the pictures of the drabness of everyday life, the omnipresence of the state and the hopelessness of ordinary citizens. I believe that through the expansion of the welfare state in Canada, our society is encouraging such conditions here. The blunting of incentives to work, savings and risk-taking has proceeded at a steady rate from both ends of the social scale — it removes penalties for failure as well as imposing high tax penalties on success. This decay has entered our perceptions only slowly, it takes more than one generation to accept the realities of a new economic and social environment and to learn that economic security is a citizen's moral right. In Canada, the second generation is now coming to the fore.

As in Eastern Europe, the protection of the achievements of the rights ideology justifies state paternalism and ever increasing regulation. Fortunately, our police institutions are still strongly steeped in democratic traditions, but troubles loom as the underground economy draws away increasing resources and reduces the tax base. It will not be a nice country to live in when there are three sharply distinct classes of people in the country — one class living off social insurance benefits, another working in the legitimate sector, paying high taxes and being only marginally better off in terms of consumer goods than the welfare section, and finally, a third class given over wholly to the underground economy and enjoying non-taxable incomes and high living standards.

VI. POLICY CONCLUSIONS

The sketch of historic trends in the growth of Canada's social insurance scheme just presented is unpleasant, but who would doubt its validity? Projections from the described trend into the future probably would be excessively alarmist. There must be a slowdown in the growth of the welfare state, if just because 100 percent of GNP is an absolute ceiling for the claims of the state. However, this is no basis for being sanguine.

Nothing in the above analysis of moral hazard as a main cause of the rapid growth in the demand for social insurance has not been known in principle and predicted by the opponents of the welfare state from its inception, and yet growth of the programs has been irresistible. Nevertheless, I believe that the beginning of the 1980s is an opportune time to re-examine these arguments in light of the experience of twenty years of welfare state expansion and of the economic crisis in unemployment, inflation and slow growth that has appeared in tandem with the welfare state.

None of this is to say that I have *proved* in this paper that the economic crisis is *caused* by the welfare state. Undoubtedly many other forces have contributed to the development of the crisis, from government policies of monetary inflation and social regulation to exogenous technical change and the global population explosion. If, like the lemming, we hide from reality and do not act until someone succeeds in proving absolutely that the welfare state is the *cause* of economic malaise, we may well be doomed to the fate of Eastern Europe. My analysis is a plea to move the Canadian system of social insurance from its pedestal as the political sacred cow that no one dares criticize, let alone touch. We need to have our intellectuals, business leaders and politicians openly discuss the trends and issues presented here. We must end the idea that anyone wanting to question the wisdom of the welfare state model is necessarily a fascist and a successor of Genghis Khan, bent on destroying the achievements of Western civilization and its system of moral rights.

VII. RECOMMENDATIONS

Unfortunately, there are no "solutions" to the problems posed by the existence of economic risks in the world which do not bring problems of their own. Private and market methods for dealing with risk leave many Canadians unhappy about resulting inequities, indignities and the suffering of some. The government approach to dealing with risks has the costs noted above. The mistake made by many critics of the market's means of distributing and allocating risk is to compare its shortcomings with the idealized perfect working of a mythical government-run system. We need to compare the results of both approaches in the real world, not someone's conception of their ideal norms.

When there are no "solutions" to problems, it is necessary to choose rationally between the available alternative ways of dealing with them. In the case of economic risks, there are no methods for eliminating them. We can only choose ways that minimize the costs of insuring against them.

In my view, the state provision of economic security is a distinctly inferior method for dealing with economic risk. The entire preceding analysis of the costs of the welfare system serves to support my judgement. In comparison, free market solutions are superior through their preservation of private incentives for self-protection, the reliance upon a dynamic and efficient private insurance industry with a strong self-interest in the control of moral hazard, and the reliance on private charity for dealing compassionately with unfortunately situated people and for limiting moral hazard. Thus, I believe that the true welfare of Canadians would be served by turning away from the collective provision of insurance and returning to the decentralized choices of individuals.

NOTES

1. I recently attended a colloquium sponsored by the Liberty Fund at which academic lawyers, sociologists, political scientists, moral philosophers and economists discussed the history and issues surrounding constitutional guarantees of human rights. After lengthy discussions and after the economists had pointed to the growing evidence of the very serious costs of welfare spending and taxing, 60 percent of the intellectuals at the colloquium remained convinced that Canadians had the "right" to the economic benefits mentioned in the U.N. Charter and that the state had an obligation to deliver them. None of the economists present voted with the majority.

2. Studies of unemployment compensation programs in other countries modelled after the Grubel-Maki study came up with analogous results. See the proceedings of a conference on this subject sponsored by the Fraser Institute, Grubel and Walker (1978).
3. One such technique involves going to mandated job interviews with a two-day-old beard and in old clothing over which some alcohol has been poured.
4. For a technical analysis of these issues in a world with complementary and substitute government services, see Lindbeck (forthcoming).

REFERENCES

Economic Council of Canada. *Reforming Regulation 1981.* Ottawa: Government Publishing Centre, 1981.

Gilder, G. *Wealth and Poverty.* New York: Basic Books, 1981.

Grubel, H.G. "Risk, Uncertainty and Moral Hazard." *Journal of Risk and Insurance,* March 1971.

———and Maki, D. "Real and Insurance Induced Unemployment in Canada," *Canadian Journal of Economics,* May 1975.

———and Walker, M., ed. *Unemployment Insurance: Global Evidence of Its Effects on Unemployment.* Vancouver: The Fraser Institute, 1978.

Lindbeck, A. "Tax Effects vs. Budget Effects on Labour Supply." *Economic Inquiry* (forthcoming).

———. "Work Disincentives in the Welfare State." Summer Paper 164, Institute for International Economic Studies, University of Stockholm, 1980.

Locke, J. *Second Treatise of Civil Government.* Laslett, ed., Cambridge: Cambridge University Press, 1960.

Mirus, R. and R.S. Smith. "Canada's Irregular Economy." *Canadian Public Policy.* VII, 3, Summer 1981.

JOHN L. HOWARD, Q.C.

John L. Howard is Senior Vice President, Law and Corporate Affairs of MacMillan Bloedel Limited. He obtained degrees in business administration and law from the University of British Columbia and Harvard, was appointed a federal Q.C. in 1977, and is a member of the Bars of Quebec and British Columbia.

In addition to his business and law practice experience, he spent twelve years working for the federal government, eight of those years as an Assistant Deputy Minister in Consumer and Corporate Affairs Canada. He was involved in programs related to consumer protection, competition law and patent and trademark law standards in Canada as a member and chairman of an advisory board of the Canadian Institute of Chartered Accountants.

He has participated as author or consultant in the publication of several major policy studies and has co-authored *Proposals for a New Business Corporate Law for Canada,* Consumer and Corporate Affairs Canada, 1971 and *Proposals for a Securities Market Law for Canada,* Consumer and Corporate Affairs Canada, 1979.

W. T. STANBURY

W. T. Stanbury is UPS Foundation Professor of Regulation and Competition Policy in the Faculty of Commerce and Business Administration at the University of British Columbia, having joined U.B.C. in 1970. Between June 1978 and November 1979 he was Director of Regulation Reference for the Economic Council of Canada and then became Director of Research for Regulation and Reference until August 1980. Between November 1977 and August 1982 he was Director, Regulation and Government Intervention Program of the Institute for Research on Public Policy.

Dr. Stanbury received his B.Comm. from U.B.C. (1966) and his M.A. (1969) and Ph.D. (1972) degrees in economics from the University of California at Berkeley. His research has ranged quite widely — from the problems of native peoples, to competition policy, government regulation and the growth of government in Canada. He has been a consultant to the Bureau of Competition Policy of the federal Department of Consumer and Corporate Affairs, the Law Reform Commission, the CRTC, the Treasury Board, MacMillan Bloedel Ltd., and Cominco Ltd.

He is the author or co-author of more than 95 publications. His latest book, written with P. K. Gorecki, is *The Objectives of Canadian Competition Policy, 1888–1983* published by The Institute for Research on Public Policy.

Chapter 4

MEASURING LEVIATHAN: THE SIZE, SCOPE, AND GROWTH OF GOVERNMENTS IN CANADA*

John L. Howard and W.T. Stanbury

Dictionaries define Leviathan as "a sea monster embodying evil." In 1651 Thomas Hobbes applied this term to the sovereign state. Three and one-quarter centuries later, we use the term only when we discuss government and political processes pejoratively, and then only when our purpose is to call attention to the dangers inherent in an expanding public sector of society.

—James Buchanan, 1975

Government, it seems safe to say, is one thing that has been growing rapidly in the West. Wherever governments were once small they have become big, and wherever they were big they became bigger. Nothing is so rare as shrinking government.

—Warren Nutter, 1978

In Canada you are reminded of the government every day. It parades itself before you. It is not content to be the servant but will be the master...

—Henry Thoreau, 1886

---

*We are indebted to the Word Processing Staff of the Faculty of Commerce, University of British Columbia for superb quality work and to George Lermer and Michael Walker for their helpful comments.

I. INCREASING CONCERN ABOUT THE ROLE OF GOVERNMENT

About seven years ago Judith Maxwell (1977, p.1) observed that "the debate about the growing size and impact of government in industrial economies has been gaining intensity for the past few years as analysts from all sides of the political spectrum have begun to worry that governments are out of control and are doing serious economic and social damage to the communities they are trying to serve." A survey of Canadians' attitudes toward government (Hurley, 1981) conducted in 1980 and 1981, indicates we have become more critical of our governments. The summary included the following statements:

1. Increasingly, people are taking a more hostile and cynical view of governments.
2. In many ways government is being seen as the cause, rather than the cure of many of society's problems today, particularly inflation and poor economic performance.
3. Government [is seen as] setting up a double standard between itself and the public it is supposed to be serving.
4. [People] see governments indulging in what they regard as extravagant wasteful spending with no attempt being made to control or correct such abuses.
5. We are on the verge of a middle class revolt in this country. In the next five years we are likely to see a much more politically active and vocal middle class as they attempt to defend and protect their position in society. We are likely to see increased resistance to tax increases. . . .
6. There will be pressure on government to curb its perceived extravagant and wasteful spending, but not at the expense of public services...; the public will be very reluctant to accept cuts in government services. Canadians will look increasingly to government to protect them and shield them from worsening economic conditions.
7. In the face of continuing economic problems, support for government intervention in the economy will increase. There is strong support for various forms of government economic controls — such as rent controls, or wage and price controls.
8. There is widespread support [88 percent] for the [federal] government's Canadianization policy in the oil industry.

In mid-1982 a Gallup poll indicated that "distrust of government has grown markedly in the past 2½ years while concern about labour and business has declined...." [1] Table 4.1 shows the national trend since 1975.

TABLE 4.1

"Speaking of the future, which do you think will be the biggest threat to Canada in years to come—big business, big labour or big government?"

National Sample	Big Business	Big Labour	Big Government	Don't Know
July 1982	13%	29%	46%	12%
Oct. 1981	16	28	44	12
Jan. 1980	20	36	29	16
1979	18	34	37	14
1978	21	38	35	12
1976	18	43	33	13
1975	20	36	29	16

Source: Gallup poll reported in the Toronto *Star*, August 18, 1982, p. A3.

While the question posed by Gallup was very general, it seems evident that Canadians' trust in their governments has decreased in recent years. At the same time, it appears that the calls for more government intervention outweigh those for less. It is somewhat surprising that complaints about "big government" are being heard in Canada, where citizens have historically had a generally positive attitude toward the various manifestations of the state. Anthony Westell (1982 p.11) has summed up the difference between the political cultures of Canada and the United States as follows: "In Canada the state has been viewed, by and large, as a beneficent agency, protecting the citizen and promoting the general welfare; in the United States, the state has been regarded with suspicion, as a potential threat to the liberty of the individual." Despite the differences in attitude (and rhetoric) toward government, however, the relative size, scope and growth of governments in the two countries have been quite similar.

Although the debate may be heating up, it is not supported by accurate information concerning even the size and scope of government activities in Canada. Perhaps one reason is that governments[2] effect their many purposes through a considerable number of governing instruments, as we shall document.

The problem of describing government in quantitative terms is an old one. For example, Sir William Petty wrote in *Political Arithmetic* in 1676 that he was seeking to "express himself in terms of number, weight and measure instead of using only comparative and superlative words and intellectual arguments" and one of Petty's students defined political arithmetic as "the art of reasoning by figures upon things relating to government" (as cited in Schumpeter, 1954, p.210, 211). Despite the vast volume of work on the problem over the past 300 years, we are still struggling with our political arithmetic. For example, Larkey, et al. (1982), after reviewing a dozen measures of the scope of government and while ignoring such aspects as public enterprises and tax expenditures, state that such measures "individually and collectively" are "poor surrogates for the scope of public sector activity in any complete sense."

We concur with Bird, et al. (1979, p.6), who emphasize that "many important dimensions of what the state does do *not* lend themselves to systematic quantitative treatment. This does not mean that these aspects of activity are less significant, either in total or in their effects in the lives of individual Canadians. . . . " However, we also agree with Jonathan Hughes (1977, p.xi), who wrote as follows about the problem of appreciating the scope of governments in the United States:

> What seems not to be known, and needs to be, is the fact that there is a totality of social control beyond the decisions of the market in this country, and that totality has a certain shape. It can be comprehended in aggregate.

In the Appendix to this paper we bring together data and analyses from a wide variety of sources in an attempt to provide a more comprehensive picture of the size, scope, and growth of governments in Canada. It is not possible to provide a single datum which measures even the size of a single level of government, let alone all three levels. It is possible, however, to provide a dozen quantitative measures that make it clear that the ratio of government expenditures to GNP — the statistic most commonly used to describe the size of government — grossly understates the significance of the state in our economic life.

As there are many dimensions to government activity, a number of measures must be used. But these measures cannot be "added up" as they are incommensurable. However, our various measures of government expenditures, public employment, tax expenditures, regulation, Crown corporations, loans and guarantees, equity interests, chosen instruments and suasion, when taken together, do provide a more comprehensive view of the size and scope of government activity in Canada than has previously been available. We believe we can make some progress toward our objective of measuring the *impact* of government upon the behaviour of firms and individuals in the private sector by examining the size, scope, and growth of the use of the major governing instruments.[3]

II. SUMMARY OF THE MAIN FINDINGS[4]

Expenditures
Total government expenditures in Canada in constant 1971 dollars (including hospitals and the Canada and Quebec pension plans) amounted to 45 percent of GNP in 1982 (Table A-2 in the Appendix). Exhaustive expenditures (both current and capital) now absorb one-fifth of aggregate output. Transfer payments to persons (including CPP/QPP payments) amount to over one-eighth of Personal Income while total government transfer payments amount to one-quarter of Personal Income. In contrast, at the time of Confederation, government's share was about 5 percent of GNP (Table A-3 in the Appendix). Even 20 years ago the ratio of total government expenditures to GNP was slightly less than 30 percent of GNP.

Public employment
The public sector, including hospitals, educational institutions and public enterprises, employs almost one-quarter of all persons employed in Canada. This ratio was virtually constant between 1961 and 1975. Government departments, however, employ less than one-half those classified as being in the public sector (Bird, et al., 1979, and Appendix Table A-5).

Tax expenditures
Federal tax expenditures in 1979 amounted to 46 percent of federal direct expenditures. These revenues forgone amounted to 56 percent of all federal revenues actually collected. While precise comparisons

are not possible, it appears that federal tax expenditures, as a ratio of actual expenditures, have more than *tripled* in the past decade.

Regulation

Government regulation is ubiquitous (Economic Council, 1979, p.11). Yet federal regulatory expenditures and employment are not large, amounting to about 2 percent of the budget and 6 percent of federal employment (Stanbury and Thompson, 1980). However, based on U.S. estimates, the cost of regulatory programs to the private sector in Canada probably amount to ten to fifteen times the outlays of the federal government. It is estimated that (prior to the National Energy Program) 29 percent of Gross Domestic Product at factor cost is subject to some form of federal or provincial regulation with respect to prices, entry and/or output. The intensity of regulation, it should be noted, varies greatly, e.g., from supply management marketing boards to the far less stringent control over railroad freight rates.

There was a substantial growth in regulation in the 1960s and 1970s. For example, the federal government passed more new regulatory statutes between 1970 and 1978 than it did in the previous three decades. Thirty percent of provincial regulatory statutes in place in 1978 were enacted since 1960.

Crown corporations

There are at least 233 provincial Crown corporations (excluding subsidiaries) and 464 federal Crown corporations (including subsidiaries) and corporations in which the government has a minority interest (Vining and Botterell, 1983; Langford and Huffman, 1983). Federal and provincial Crown corporations may produce about one-tenth of the GNP. The two largest non-financial enterprises in Canada in terms of assets in 1983 were Ontario Hydro and Hydro Quebec. Thirty-nine of the largest federal and provincial Crown corporations ranked in the top 500 non-financial corporations in Canada in terms of revenues in 1983.

Loans and guarantees

The value of federal and provincial loans and investments, loan guarantees and credit insurance provided to the private sector amounted to 18.5 percent of GNP in 1980 (Economic Council, 1982). In 1950 the ratio was 4.3 percent. In some sectors, government financial assistance is of particular importance. For example, in agriculture governments account for 30 percent of all credit outstanding and 58 percent of all long-term loans. In 1978/79 the size of the indirect subsidy in government loans to the private sector was estimated to be $906 million, measured on a social opportunity cost basis.

Equity interests (Mixed enterprises)
Certain provincial and federal agencies have begun to acquire an equity interest in privately owned corporations. Elford and Stanbury (1984) estimate there were over 300 mixed enterprises in Canada in 1983. The Caisse de Dépôt in Quebec, has an equity portfolio of over $3 billion, said to be the largest in Canada (Olive, 1982). For example, the Caisse (in conjunction with another Quebec government agency) owns 45 percent of Domtar Inc., one of Canada's largest forest products enterprises. The Caisse also owns slightly less than 10 percent of Canadian Pacific Ltd. This interest prompted the federal government to introduce a bill limiting provincial agencies to 10 percent of the equity of federally regulated transportation firms. (It was subsequently withdrawn.) The Alberta Heritage Fund has begun to acquire common shares. Given the size and growth of the fund, its potential as an instrument of intervention is enormous. The implications of this new governing instrument have not yet been fully appreciated.

Chosen instruments
Through a variety of instruments such as preferred procurement, special tax provisions, subsidies, and loan guarantees, the federal government appears to have introduced the concept of the private sector firm as a "chosen instrument" of public policy (Shepherd, 1981). The identification of companies as chosen instruments is difficult, yet it is evident that certain firms are able to form a symbiotic relationship with government that advances the interests of both. As a governing instrument, the use of private sector firms as chosen instruments is an example of the substitution of "less obvious" instruments for the traditional, more overt instruments of taxation, expenditures and Crown corporations.

Suasion
While it is difficult to document, there is some evidence suggesting that federal and provincial governments (particularly the former) are making greater use of *suasion* (Stanbury and Fulton, 1984). This most subtle of governing instruments produces apparently voluntary

changes in the behavior of firms and individuals without resort to legislative action of any kind. Rather, the government relies on hints and nudges which remind the object of persuasion that the business-government relationship is a reciprocal one on many levels. Anticipation of the potential loss of benefits or the imposition of additional costs or constraints is often enough, for example, to persuade firms to comply with wage and price "guidelines" or, persuade the major banks to sharply reduce their loans to finance the takeover by Canadians of U.S.-owned companies in Canada in mid-1981 (see the discussion in the Appendix). The potential for abuse in the use of such a "subtle" method of government intervention should be cause for concern to many Canadians.

III. UNDERSTANDING LEVIATHAN: CONCLUSIONS AND IMPLICATIONS

Government has become Leviathan

Canadians have shown a remarkably strong and consistent taste for more action by government designed to influence the economic behavior of firms and individuals in the private sector. They have freely elected governments which, at the end of their term, have left a larger public sector than when they came to office. The cumulative effect of millions of small decisions has changed government from a small but important actor in the economy to the dominant entity in the nation's economic life. Indeed, *Canada has become a government-centered society*.

By a number of measures it is evident that the government sector in Canada has become Leviathan. The scope of government activity is simply awesome. For example, it is virtually impossible to think of any economic activity in the private sector that is not directly or indirectly regulated by one or more levels of government.

It is clear that all previous estimates of government activity in Canada have substantially *understated* its size and scope. This is because most researchers have been content to examine only one or two facets of government activity in isolation from the others. In trying to measure the scope of the public sector in relation to nine governing instruments (described in detail in the Appendix), we have demonstrated that government activity in Canada is far more pervasive than even its severe critics had believed. Yet one is struck by the virtual absence of publicly-expressed concern about the consequent loss of individual freedom and the "politicization" of economic decisions formerly made on a decentralized basis by impersonal market forces (Courchene, 1980). In Canada, unlike the United States for example, there has been only a modest amount of serious public debate about the growth of governments. A massive transformation has been wrought without fanfare and with only a few political skirmishes over its nature and its consequences.

Growing redistributive transfers "on the books" and off

Perhaps the most significant change in the composition of public *spending* has been the rise of transfer expenditures of all kinds. For all governments combined, transfer expenditures (excluding the enormous intergovernmental transfers) now exceed the total of exhaustive expenditures. While a large component consists of interest payments on the public debt,[5] "pure" transfers form a substantial fraction of personal income. But these transfers are only a small part of a much larger phenomenon—that of massive flows of income that are moved back and forth by government action in an effort to redistribute income and wealth in Canada. This is not limited to unemployment insurance, old-age pensions, family allowances and social welfare payments on which many are dependent.[6] For example, much direct regulation is used to redistribute income from consumers to producers and between groups of consumers, to prevent market-induced shifts in income or wealth, and occasionally to redistribute income from producers to consumers (see Stanbury and Lermer, 1983).

Government loans to the private sector often contain large implicit subsidies conveniently hidden from public view. Federal tax expenditures embedded in the personal income tax system, which more than tripled in the 1970s, have the apparent effect of benefiting upper income tax payers (Government of Canada, 1981), partially offsetting the "progressive" income tax. Crown corporations are used to provide transfers in kind when their prices are substantially less than the social opportunity cost of production.

We must recognize that many actions by governments to redistribute income are not the result of a broadly based consensus as to who should be taxed to improve the economic position of others. Rather, governments are the vehicle by which the members of some interest groups are able to make themselves better off at the expense of their fellow citizens. As more people appreciate the nature of the "game," rent-seeking activities convert transfers into social waste (see Tullock, 1983).

The irony is that despite the large and growing private efforts to seek economic rents and despite the redistributional programs of governments, the *net* effect on the distribution of income (and wealth) appears to be rather modest — see Osberg (1981).

Increased use of "less obvious" governing instruments

In general, we have seen the substitution of "less obvious" instruments for the traditional fiscal tools of taxes and direct expenditures. We emphasize that less obvious does not mean less obtrusive to those in the private sector. It is not surprising that the increased scope of public sector activities has created a need for new governing instruments. In some cases the traditional tools (taxes, direct expenditures, regulation and Crown corporations) simply were not as effective or efficient as others that were developed.

Taxes, direct expenditures, Crown corporations, loans and guarantees to the private sector, and regulation were well known at the time of Confederation, although the last three instruments were used only sparingly. However, tax expenditures, the use of private sector firms as "chosen instruments" of policy, and equity ownership in private sector firms (e.g., the Caisse de Dépôt in Quebec now owns $3 billion in equities)[7] did not emerge as significant governing instruments until at least the 1960s.[8] Suasion, the most subtle form of intervention, was hardly a feasible instrument when spending by all governments accounted for only 5 to 7 percent of GNP, as it did until the turn of the century.

Considerations of technical substitutability do not appear to have been the main reason for the shift to less obvious instruments. Rather, there was a need to intervene in ways *less visible* to the public. There was also a desire by politicians, some bureaucrats and the beneficiaries of the government's largesse to escape the restraints of formal scrutiny by the legislature that the tax and expenditure system required. In politics, perception is reality. The less obvious instruments permit governments to apply more easily the canons of marginal voter politics together with the use of targetted, selective, subsidized information to increase the probability of re-election (see Trebilcock et al., 1982). With continued fiscal constraints we can expect to see greater use of the less obvious governing instruments.

Less obvious instruments are essential to governments desiring to redistribute income and wealth. It is not too strong to say that deception is necessary to effect transfers financed by a broad cross-section of voters to small, politically influential groups.[9] Cash subsidies or "welfare payments" (whether for individuals or corporations) leave official tracks. Money must be voted annually. But a supply management marketing board, for example, can operate "off the government's books" and yet tax the consumers of eggs, milk, tobacco, broiler chickens and turkeys, and transfer the proceeds to farmers. Moreover, the enormous social costs of effecting such transfers are also well hidden (see Lermer and Stanbury, in press).

Ambivalence about government

Governments are deeply embedded in the Canadian economy and in the psyche of individuals. For that reason it will be all but impossible to reduce their size relative to the economy. This difficulty stems from the fact that we are all ambivalent about government. Governments confer benefits, but they also impose burdens. Taxes may be "the price of civilization" but they are always too high.[10] On the other hand, contemplation of economic insecurity prompts positive thoughts about the elaborate set of "safety net" programs ranging from unemployment insurance to social assistance, retraining grants, old-age pensions and crop insurance for farmers, to name but a few. Marie-Josée Drouin (1983, p.21) acutely observes:

> A paradox of our modern age: we have achieved such a high standard of living and quality of life that anything which appears to threaten this comfort is no longer accepted. Hence, the door is open for more and more government intervention in our day to day lives.

Businessmen damn governments for introducing more cost-increasing environmental protection or various types of health and safety regulation. Yet a few paragraphs later in their speeches they will demand that the federal government act to resrict the flow of low-priced imports that are "destroying the Canadian market" or that their provincial government provide capital subsidies to permit them to install the latest high-technology equipment.[11]

While endorsing general calls for getting "government off the backs of business," the executives of Bell Canada, CP Air, most large trucking companies, and marketing boards have fought tenaciously to *re-*

tain the "burdens" of the existing regulatory framework under which they operate.[12] The public expects Crown corporations to be efficient and profitable, yet they are *also* supposed to perform a wide variety of "social chores" while competing with privately owned firms. They are to be market-oriented and at the same time politically accountable to a minister, the Cabinet or the legislature (Tupper and Doern, 1981). The contradictions abound. The public sector as an employer is expected to exemplify the most enlightened terms and conditions of employment but, at the same time, is not to be a wage leader or the first to introduce expensive employee benefits such as maternity leave or four-weeks vacation.

The larger governments become, the larger the constituencies they create. The fact is that any move by government creates winners and losers. The potential losers are not anxious to sacrifice themselves, no matter how large the net increment in the nation's welfare.

Can the growth of government be controlled?

Substantial efforts to reduce the size and scope of governments in Canada have been very rare. Reagan-type rhetoric is all but absent, reflecting the different political and economic culture of this nation.[13] Moreover, the few serious attempts to reduce the role of governments have been conspicuously unsuccessful. These efforts, however, may have had the result of slowing the rate of increase in the size of the public sector.[14]

To support this conclusion we point to four initiatives in the past five years. First, there has clearly been no political support to either reduce the stringency of federal and provincial regulation or truly deregulate parts of the economy.[15] The contrast to the American experience in this regard is stark. Second, we refer to the abortive effort of the short-lived Clark government in 1979 to "privatize" some federal Crown corportations. The Conservatives found that Petro-Canada, for instance, had very substantial popular support—even in Alberta. Third, in a desire to obtain greater visibility and to "cap runaway shared-cost programs," the federal government has sought to renegotiate the massive transfers to the provinces that are at the heart of Canada's fiscal federalism. Despite the bellowing of the provinces (some of which have reaped very large amounts of resource revenues in recent years), there has been only a modest reduction in federal transfers (including tax abatements) to the provinces in real terms.

Their rate of growth has slowed, however. Fourth, we point to the highly vocal adverse response to the federal government's timorous attempts to "de-index" (or cap the increases in) certain transfer payments and the basic personal exemptions under the income tax. Also there was an outcry against ruminations by federal ministers suggesting that certain transfer programs be "de-universalized." Opponents raised the spectre of means testing which they said would "stigmatize" millions of Canadians.[16]

Apparently a national unemployment rate of over 12 percent, a projected federal deficit of about $30 billion in 1983/84 ($23.3 billion in 1982/83), and the most severe recession since the 1930s is not a sufficient crisis to force serious action to restrain the growth of the federal public sector. For example, in 1983/84 federal spending alone is expected to exceed 23 percent of the GNP. For 1984/85 federal spending is estimated at $98 billion. In nominal dollars, federal outlays grew by 13.0, 17.6 and 17.8 percent annually between 1980/81 and 1982/83 (Government of Canada, 1983, p.7). During the same period *real* output per capita declined slightly.

In simple terms, the public sector, particularly federal and provincial governments, is widely believed to be beyond the effective control of politicians and even of the bureaucracy's central agencies. With respect to the federal government, this point was made indelible by the Royal Commission on Financial Management and Accountability (1979). A more recent investigation by the Auditor General of Canada (1982) reinforces the point, noting in particular, that Crown corporations have taken on a life of their own. Their managers in many cases are not responsible to a minister, central agency officials or Parliament. The tether of accountability has been cut and we are forced to rely on the goodwill and political sensitivity of the corporations' senior managers to ensure that they fulfill their usually ill-specified mandate.

Government is likely to grow in the near future

Despite both the enormous bulk and rapid growth of government activity over the past three decades or so, it seems destined to continue growing relative to the total economy, in the near future at least. Several reasons may be suggested. First, the poor performance of the economy, for which the federal government must accept a large part of the responsibility, has produced and will continue to produce more demands for government action. Existing "safety nets" are seen as inadequate to cope with a prolonged, severe recession. The "discomfort index" — the sum of the inflation rate and the unemployment rate — has grown consistently since 1965, when it was less than 7, to a level of almost 21 in the first six months of 1982.[17] (It has since dropped as inflation declined from an annual rate of about 13 percent in January 1981 to about 5 percent in early 1984.)

Second, there is no strong political movement in Canada advocating a serious retrenchment of government activity. While all governments appear to be "economizing" and making some efforts to reduce their deficits,[18] the results of such marginal adjustments will be, at best, to slow the rate of growth of public spending somewhat. There is, however, no serious effort to bring about a net reduction in the public sector (all governing instruments considered) at any level.

Third, according to a 1982 survey summarized in Table 4.2, opinion leaders assign moderate to high probabilities to the expansion of government activity on a variety of fronts. For example, 75 percent of the sample thought it "likely" that federal and provincial governments will "develop a focused industrial strategy" which would use grants or tax expenditures to assist certain industries. A slightly greater fraction expected that in the next decade governments would require all employers to match the pension plan contributions of employees and that "much stricter occupational health and safety regulations would be enacted."

It is notable, however, that the fraction of respondents believing the nine types of intervention to be "most probable within 5 years" was much smaller than the fraction believing them "likely during the next 10 years." For example, 86 percent thought legislation requiring greater public disclosure of corporate information "likely" in the next decade, but only 10 percent saw it as "most probable within five years." The implication would appear to be that the rate of expansion of governments will slow during the next five years but increase in the following five. (As we are frequently reminded, prediction, particularly where it concerns the future, is a hazardous activity!)

It should be noted that the same survey one year later indicated there has been a shift in expectations about future government intervention — see Hay Associates (1984).

Constraining forces

Are there any forces presently operating or likely to become stronger

TABLE 4.2

Predictions of Future Government Intervention in Canada
By 185 Opinion Leaders, Mid-1982

Type of Intervention	Likely during next 10 years	Most probable within 5 years
• The federal and some provincial governments will develop a focused industrial strategy which funnels grants or preferred tax status to certain industries to improve their international competitiveness.	75%	16%
• The federal government will reduce its involvement in and regulation of business activities.	31	4
• Major efforts to increase Canadian ownership similar to the National Energy Program will be made in other areas.	56	9
• Wages will be controlled or frozen by the federal government.	68	28
• All employers will be required to provide a pension plan in which they match employee contributions.	78	11
• Much stricter occupational health and safety regulations will be enacted.	79	10
• Genetic engineering will be stopped or strictly regulated.	35	1
• Legislation will be enacted to require greater public disclosure of corporate information.	86	10
• Fears of resource depletion will lead to regulation of the amount of exports in the forestry and/or mining industries.	20	1

Source: Hay Associates Canada Ltd. (1983).

in the future that would restrain the growth of government activity? Yes, there are, but their strength is difficult to ascertain. A major constraint on the growth of government is the openness of the Canadian economy. About 30 percent of our GNP is exported (imports make up a similar fraction). A large fraction of our exports are sold in competitive markets—hence Canadian firms are price-takers. Such firms (e.g., in forest products, mining and agricultural products) are the natural enemies of government activity, which increases their costs or constrains their freedom of action to meet international competition. Their particular concern is that government-induced cost increases should be greater than those imposed on their trading competitors. In the short run, particularly when product prices are high, governments can impose substantial cost increases on natural resource exporters (e.g., through environmental and health and safety regulations, higher taxes — including payroll taxes, and protective labor legislation which increases the bargaining power of unions). The short-term "safety-valve" is the government's ability to reduce the amount of economic rent it collects as owner of the primary resources. When commodity prices fall, however, such rents fall more than proportionately. In such cases, unless governments recognize "negative rents" (i.e., pay subsidies to the companies), the firms are stuck with higher costs induced by government policy. Since price is exogenous, the shareholders will be squeezed and the managers will exercise one or more of Hirschman's (1970) three options: (1) "exit" (i.e., move to other jurisdictions where the economics are more favorable); (2) "voice" (i.e., lobby against government-induced cost increases or to obtain offsetting subsidies — usually hidden); or (3) "loyalty" (i.e., accept the situation and hope commodity prices will rise, but as a corollary, probably accept subnormal returns to capital in the longer run).

Provincial governments are generally more vulnerable to external financial constraints than the federal government. Only the latter can literally print money or use the central bank to swallow its IOUs, which has the same effect. To the extent that they finance their public debts abroad, the provinces are vulnerable to international financial markets. For example, one of the reasons that Premier Levesque has tried to rein in the expenditures of the Province of Quebec is the judgment of the international financial community, reflected in their reduced willingness to lend Quebec huge sums at reasonable rates. The international bond-rating services have vastly more power than the opposition parties and the media combined.

There are other potentially constraining forces. The larger government becomes the greater the probability that it will be beset by scandals, massive policy failures and periodic paralysis. Michael Walker has remarked:

> We have now had the opportunity to experience the governmental alternative to the market in a wide range of activities. The sup-

posed superiority of governmental action has not materialized and in many cases the intrusion of government has caused a noticeable deterioration. In effect, we have discovered that government reflects all of the human frailties which led to the excoriation of the market. And, because of the size and scope of present day government, the frailties are magnified and their consequences widespread.[19]

Scandals serve to focus public attention on the most egregious forms of government activity. They can be turned into symbols of a vastly greater problem. As a result politicians and/or bureaucrats lose credibility as, for example, the enormous losses of Canadair and de Havilland have indicated.[20]

Wedged firmly between a fiscal rock and a monetary hard place, the federal government — long the champion of Keynesian macro-economic interventionism — offed a form of suasion with the "6 and 5" program and states that it is up to the private sector to pull us out of the worst recession since the 1930s. The federal government has suffered a paralysis of will and a severe loss of credibility.[21] Even if it does act, its policy initiative may have the effect of pushing on a string.

Tragic as the consequences would be, it may be that only a massive crisis would have the necessary effect of sharply altering expectations and, more importantly, would usher in efforts to change the constitutive rules and structure of incentives that bias all the actors to support more government activity instead of less.

The structure of incentives favors more government intervention

The set of incentives facing all the major actors in the political system — politicians, senior public servants and voters — bias rational, self-interested behavior toward actions that generally increase the relative size of the public sector. The existing state of the world is not the product of a handful of clever villains, nor is it attributable to some vital but limited flaw in the rules of the game. The problem is more pervasive, more subtle and far deeper than that. If it was not, we might have moved toward its amelioration by now.

Consider the structure of incentives facing the major actors in the political system. Voters as individuals and as members of reasonably homogeneous interest groups seek to have the benefits of government action concentrated on them and the costs of such action diffused widely on others. In this desire they are helped by politicians or would-be politicians who seek to do the same thing — or at least give the impression of doing so. At one level, the voters know the pieces of the game "don't add up," yet each operates on the reasonable assumption that he or she can be a net winner.

How many politicians can make a career out of promising less (except taxes) and offering to eliminate major governmental programs?[22] All government programs have a constituency. Psychologically, both voters and politicians are disposed to believe in growth, new programs, and more positive action that will benefit people. In short, they are captives of the idea of "progress" and the idea that it is possible to use government both extensively and wisely to improve the human condition.[23] If it is possible to land a man on the moon and bring him back safely, surely we can spur economic growth in lagging regions. Surely we can virtually eliminate the spectre of poverty. Surely we can eliminate the economic and physical hazards that threaten the path to a better life. These are the assumptions upon which the welfare state has been built.

Public servants, particularly those in the senior ranks, offer specialized expertise in the design and management of various governing instruments. How many can make a successful career from advising their political masters that: (1) the real problem is not as great as it seems to voters or politicians; (2) the total costs of proposed forms of intervention, although largely hidden, are likely to outweigh the potential benefits; and (3) government, no matter how well-intentioned, cannot perform certain activities as well as admittedly imperfectly functioning markets? The fact is that, with few exceptions, the rank, status and income of senior public servants is roughly proportionate to either the size of their departmental budgets or other measures of their activity, *or* it is a function of the bureaucrat's ability to help formulate *new* programs and policies that will bring their political masters electoral success.

But bureaucrats, in general, operate within a system of incentives that is within the power of politicians to change. Senior public servants are often specialists who study problems or potential problems in some detail. They become convinced that their problems have particular importance *and* can be at least ameliorated by government action. At the same time, politicians, in general, are hungry for policy ideas or potential programs to either "sell" to the electorate to meet some latent need or to respond to the competitive "offerings" of other parties. Voters want politicians to propose *solutions* to the myriad problems they face. They don't want to be told that some problems cannot be "solved" by government action. No practical politician can afford to be unconcerned, no matter how individual the problem or how far it is beyond the domain where government action may be effective.

Moreover, politicians operate on a fairly short electoral cycle. This is most obvious in civic politics where elections are held on a fixed schedule every two or three years. Even where the legal maximum is five years, political action must take into account the much shorter "attention span" of voters. A few months before an election a few issues (out of the scores a government must deal with) must be defined and impressed upon the consciousness of voters. There is an enormous incentive to promise or even implement policies/programs that have (or appear to have) large positive pay-offs in the very short term — regardless of their long-term net consequences, which may be bad indeed. In most cases, when the "chickens come home to roost" no one may connect the costs with the original decision and besides someone else may be in power.

Ultimately the size of government is a value judgment

Ultimately the appropriate type and amount of government activity is a value judgment that must be made by each individual. Government activity can both enlarge and severely constrain individual liberty. It can improve the efficiency with which our scarce resources are allocated, but it can also impose a substantial dead-weight burden on the economy. Governments can redistribute income. Indeed, the evidence suggests that in Canada they have become obsessed with "who gets what" at the expense of prudent actions that encourage the growth in the *total* amount of income.

But value judgments about the appropriate type and amount of government activity need to be well informed. In this chapter (with its Appendix) we have tried to lay the foundation for a thoughtful reassessment of the role of governments in our daily lives by providing some facts and analytical insights concerning the size, scope, and growth of governments in Canada.

NOTES

1. Toronto *Star*, August 18, 1982, p.A3. The poll was based on interviews with 1,050 adults early in July 1982. For more recent information, see Gregg (1984).

2. We use the terms "government" and "state" interchangeably. Unless otherwise indicated, the terms refer to all three levels of government — federal, provincial, local/municipal — together with hospitals, pension plans and educational institutions which are largely funded by a government.

3. This concept is discussed at length in Trebilcock et al. (1982) and Doern and Phidd (1983).

4. This summary is based on the much more detailed analysis in the lengthy Appendix to this paper — see pp.127–223.

5. The federal government's debt has grown from 11.7 percent of GNP in 1974/75 to 37 percent in 1983/84. The net debt per capita has increased from $1,000 in 1975/76 to over $6,000 in 1983/84. The cost of servicing the federal debt has risen from $50 per capita in 1973/74 to about $200 in 1979/80 to over $500 in 1983/84 (*Financial Times of Canada*, February 28, 1983, p.1.) The federal deficit in 1982/83 was $23.34 billion (*Globe and Mail*, August 30, 1983, p.B4). The total net liabilities of the federal government amounted to just over 30 percent of GNP in the early 1960s. This ratio decreased to 7 percent in 1974 and then began to increase steadily to about 24 percent in 1983 ("Fiscally sensible or tragic?" Vancouver *Sun*, April 20, 1983, p.H6).

6. It has been estimated that early in 1983 one-third of the population of British Columbia were dependent in whole or in part on government transfer payments in the form of old-age pensions (294,720 persons), unemployment insurance (257,000 persons supporting another 147,000), and social welfare payments (104,000 at the end of December 1982 supporting another 95,800). See Rick Ouston, "1 in 3 depend on government aid," Vancouver *Sun*, March 2, 1983, p.A13.

7. Wendie Kerr, "Business group urges caisse to stay within fiduciary limits," *Globe and Mail*, March 15, 1983, p.B17.

8. We recognize, of course, that the CPR was originally a chosen instrument of federal transportation policy. We also note that depletion allowances which originated in the 1920s were an early form of tax expenditure.

9. This point is emphasized by Tullock (1983). A useful review of this book can be found in *Fortune*, March 21, 1983, pp.173–175.

10. We don't even like to *think* about paying taxes, hence the demonstrated preference for hidden rather than overt taxes. Even property taxes have been converted into part of the monthly "mortgage" payment.

11. A sophisticated plea by the president of Ford of Canada for government help to fend off Japanese imports can be found in Kenneth W. Harrigan, "A Critical Force in Competition in World Markets," *Chimo*, February/March 1983, pp.26–30.

12. See Stanbury and Thompson (1982, Ch.4) for details.

13. An excellent example of the differences can be found in *Chimo* (February/March 1983, pp.15–51), which contains the opinions of more than a dozen senior Canadian executives on "the growing trend of government intervention in the private sector and its effect, for better or worse, on the future of our country."

14. It is too early to say if the July 1983 budget of the Bennett government in British Columbia will go further and actually reduce the absolute size of provincial government activities. The newspapers and a variety of commentators have referred to the "severe cuts in public programs," the plans to reduce the number of public servants by 25 percent, the "privatization" of certain government programs, and the imposition of higher taxes. The Leader of the Opposition is quoted as saying, "When do the brown shirts come out? It's an ultra-right wing Government. They are union busting, job busting. It's fear administration.... They're nuts." However, total expenditures were budgeted to rise by 12.3 percent at a time when the inflation rate was about 6 percent implying a net growth in the size of government. In the longer run, the government may succeed in actually reducing the scope of its activities, although it seems most unlikely that it can eliminate 25 percent of public sector employees as it says it wants to do. (See the many stories in the Vancouver *Sun*, July 8, 1983, pp. A1, A2, A4, A5, B1-B4 and E5 and on July 9, 1983, pp.A1, A2, A4, A10. See also the *Globe and Mail*, July 9, 1983, pp.1-2.) The government's budget and relaxed legislation has provoked a strong response from labor unions (which created Operation Solidarity) and other concerned groups and individuals.

15. See Stanbury and Thompson (1982a), (1982b) and Reschenthaler et al. (1982).

16. Michael Walker (*Financial Post,* April 21, 1984, p.8) estimates that if federal transfers to individuals were *not* paid to those with a family income of $29,000 some $3.9 billion would be saved—and this figure excludes Unemployment Insurance payments. If they are included *and* the cut-off is lowered to $23,200, the savings amount to $6.1 billion.

17. National Bank of Canada, *Economic Review*, 4th Quarter 1982, p.5. Between January 1981 and July 1983 the monthly rate of inflation, converted to an annual basis, declined from almost 13 percent to 5.5 percent.

18. See, for example, Terence Corcoran, "The great deficit debate," *Financial Times*, February 28, 1983, pp.1, 12, 13, 15; Clayton Sinclair, "Governments strive for fiscal restraint," Financial Times, January 17, 1983, pp.2,

15; and Wendie Kerr, "Quebec public service unions are Government's target," *Globe and Mail*, April 7, 1982, p.B3. See also Thomas Walkom, "Credit rates come to PEI," *Globe and Mail*, August 18, 1983, p.8.

19. *Financial Post*, October 2, 1982, p.6.

20. Canadair Ltd. reported a loss of $1.4 billion in 1982, the largest loss for any corporation in Canadian history. De Havilland lost $265 million in the last seven months of 1982. See Vancouver *Sun*, June 27, 1983, p.A13. More generally, see *Globe and Mail*, June 20, 1983, pp.1-2; editorial June 18, 1983, p.6; Michael Valphy's column June 28, 1983, p.6. See also *Financial Post*, June 18, 1983, p.4; *Globe and Mail*, June 16, 1983, pp.1-2, June 8, 1983, pp.1-2, B-15, June 9, 1983, pp.1-2. In the first six months of 1983 Canadair Ltd. lost $107.3 million and de Havilland lost $76.6 million. See Edward Clifford, "Aircraft units of CDIC lost $184 million," *Globe and Mail*, September 1, 1983, p.B1. The losses continued in 1984.

21. See Peter Cook, "Study finds strong public dissatisfaction with economy," *Globe and Mail*, March 10, 1983, p.B3.

22. It should be emphasized that the recent actions by the B.C. government (see note 14) do not promise less for everyone. Certain groups, notably business and those with above-average incomes, stand to benefit. See William Boli, "Socred ideology victimizes poor, economist says," Vancouver *Sun*, July 9, 1983, p.A10. More generally, see Vaughn Palmer, "Bennett's New Deal," Vancouver *Sun*, August 30, 1983, p.A6.

23. See Ronald Anderson, "Tendency seen in economy to greater government role," *Globe and Mail*, September 2, 1983, p.B2.

REFERENCES

Auditor General of Canada. *Report to the House of Commons: Fiscal year ended 31 March 1982*. Ottawa: Minister of Supply and Services, 1982.

Bird, Richard M. et al. *The Growth of Public Employment in Canada*. Montreal: The Institute for Research on Public Policy, 1979.

Courchene, T.J. "Towards a Protected Society: The Politicization of Economic Life." *Canadian Journal of Economics*, Vol. 18(4), 1980, pp.556-77.

Doern, G. Bruce and Richard Phidd. *Canadian Public Policy.* Toronto: Methuen, 1983.

Drouin, M.J. "Redefining the Role of Government." *Chimo*, February/March 1983.

Economic Council of Canada. *Responsible Regulation.* Ottawa: Minister of Supply and Services, 1979.

————. *Intervention and Efficiency: A Study of Government Credit and Credit Guarantees to the Private Sector.* Ottawa: Minister of Supply and Services, 1982.

Government of Canada. *Estimates, 1983-84. Part I.* Ottawa: Department of Supply and Services, 1983.

Government of Canada, Department of Finance. *Analysis of Federal Tax Expenditures for Individuals.* Ottawa: November 1981.

Gregg, Allan R. "The Corporation and the Public" in J. D. Fleck and I. A. Litvak (eds.) *Business Can Succeed.* Toronto: Gage Publishing, 1984, Ch. 7.

Hay Associates Canada Ltd. *Report to Opinion Leaders.* Toronto, January 1983.

————. *Navigating Uncharted Waters: Canada's Next Ten Years, Report to Opinion Leaders.* Toronto, February 1984.

Hirschman, Albert O. *Exit, Voice and Loyalty.* Cambridge, Mass.: Harvard University Press, 1970.

Hughes, Jonathan R.T. *The Government Habit.* New York: Random House, 1977.

Hurley, Douglas. "The Social Environment, Social Trends and Consumer Attitudes and Behaviour," in *Through a Glass Darkly: A Medium-Term Canadian Perspective.* Toronto: Royal Trust Co., 1981, pp.31-62.

Langford, John W. and Kenneth Huffman. "The Uncharted Universe of Federal Public Corporations" in J.R.S. Prichard (ed.) *Crown Corporations: The Calculus of Instrument Choice.* Toronto: Butterworths, 1983.

Larkey, P.D., C. Stolp and M. Winer. "Theories of Government Size and Growth: A Literature Review." *Journal of Public Policy*, Vol. 1, No. 2, 1981.

Lermer, George and W.T. Stanbury. "Measuring the Cost of Redistributing Income by Means of Direct Regulation." *Canadian Journal of Economics* (in press).

Maxwell, Judith. "The Role of Government: Searching for a Framework." Montreal: C.D. Howe Research Institute, Staff Speeches No. 15, July 1977.

Olive, David. "Caisse Unpopulaire." *Canadian Business*, May 1982, pp.94–101.

Osberg, Lars. *Economic Inequality in Canada.* Toronto: Butterworths, 1981.

Reschenthaler, Gil et al. "What Ever Happened to Deregulation?" *Policy Options,* Vol. 3, No. 3, May/June 1982, pp.36–40.

Royal Commission on Financial Management and Accountability. *Final Report.* Ottawa: Minister of Supply and Services, 1979.

Schumpeter, J.A. *History of Economic Analysis.* New York: Oxford University Press, 1954.

Shepherd, John. "Hidden Crown Corporations." *Policy Options,* Vol. 2(2), 1981, pp.40–42.

Stanbury, W.T. and Jane Fulton. "Suasion as a Governing Instrument" in Allan Maslove (ed.) *How Ottawa Spends, 1984.* Toronto: Methuen, 1984, Ch.9.

Stanbury, W.T. and George Lermer. "Regulation and the Redistribution of Income and Wealth." *Canadian Public Administration,* Vol 26(3) 1983, pp.378–401.

Stanbury, W.T. and Fred Thompson. "The Scope and Coverage of Regulation in Canada and the United States: Implications for the Demand for Reform" in W.T. Stanbury (ed.) *Government Regulation: Scope, Growth, Process.* Montreal: The Institute for Research on Public Policy, 1980, pp.17–67.

―――. *Regulatory Reform in Canada.* Montreal: The Institute for Research on Public Policy, 1982a.

―――. "The Prospects for Deregulation in Canada: Political Models and the American Experience." *Osgoode Hall Law Journal,* Vol. 20, No. 4, December 1982b, pp.678–720.

Trebilcock, M.J. et al. *The Choice of Governing Instrument.* Ottawa: Minister of Supply and Services, 1982.

Tupper, Allen and G. Bruce Doern eds. *Public Corporations and Public Policy in Canada.* Montreal: The Institute for Research on Public Policy, 1981.

Tullock, Gordon. *Economics of Income Redistribution.* Boston: Kluwer-Nijhoff Publishing, 1983.

Vining, Aidan and Robert Botterell. "An Overview of the Origins Growth, Size and Function of Provincial Crown Corporations" in J.R.S. Prichard (ed.) *Crown Corporations: The Calculus of Instrument Choice.* Toronto: Butterworths, 1983.

Westell, Anthony. "Our Fading Political Culture." *Policy Options,* Vol. 3(1), Jan/Feb. 1982, pp. 8–11.

ROLF MIRUS

Rolf Mirus is Professor of Managerial Economics and International Finance in the Faculty of Business at the University of Alberta. He received his Pre-Diploma from the Free University of Berlin in 1963 and his M.A. and Ph.D. from the University of Minnesota. Professor Mirus completed his M.A. on a Fulbright Scholarship. In 1977 he was a Summer Fellow at the International Institute of Management in Berlin and in 1977–78 a Visiting Associate Professor at the University of Nairobi.

Professor Mirus has contributed articles to *Canadian Public Policy, Review of Economics and Statistics, Journal of International Business Studies, Journal of Finance, Journal of Banking and Finance* and has written a chapter entitled "The Unobserved Economy" for a forthcoming book with the same title (edited by Edgar Feige). In addition, he has presented major papers at various conferences in Canada and Germany.

His main areas of interest are macroeconomics and international financial markets.

CHAPTER 5

THE INVISIBLE ECONOMY: ITS DIMENSIONS AND IMPLICATIONS

Rolf Mirus

I. INTRODUCTION

The invisible economy is an international phenomenon. In Europe, *Economia Sommersa, travail noir,* and *Schattenwirtschaft* are some of the terms used to refer to it. There are two crucial reasons why the growth of the invisible economy is of concern. First, the existence of a large and growing sector of the economy that escapes taxation implies that taxes on the other sector must be higher than otherwise in order to finance the same level of government programs. We should find out why the invisible economy exists, what can be done to control its size, and how the tax base can be broadened. Secondly, a large and growing invisible economy distorts measures of economic performance, such as growth in real GNP, the inflation rate, the unemployment rate, and productivity advance. The measured indices may mislead economic policy-makers, likely resulting in their choosing overly expansionary policies. It is important to improve the measures on which policy is based by taking explicit account of the invisible economy.

In this paper I explore, first of all, the nature of the invisible or unobserved economy. Then I review the difficulties encountered when trying to measure its size. Notwithstanding those measurement problems, I present a range of estimates of the money-based unobserved economy in Canada. I conclude this paper with some speculations regarding the causes of the unobserved economy and some policy implications that follow from its growth.

II. UNOBSERVED ECONOMIC ACTIVITY — AN ATTEMPT AT CLASSIFICATION

Some actual examples of unobserved economic activity can help us grasp the nature of the phenomenon:

> It was discovered that ministry officials clocked in for a couple of hours, then left for the Capannelle racetrack, where they worked as (illegal) bookies. (*The* Economist, 1982, p.49).

> Teacher and Family from Lyon, France, are looking for trade of car and/or trailer with Edmonton person wanting to tour Europe from Lyon this summer. Call....... (*Folio*, March 8, 1982).

In the first of the above examples, bookmaking services are produced but their value is not recorded in GNP. The services are illegal and so, not surprisingly, operations are conducted in a way that makes impossible the "capture" of these transactions in the National Income and Product Accounts. Other examples of illegal economic activity would be the "street" value of illegal drugs (net of import content) and the income earned by prostitutes. As for legal activities, one might mention the tradesman who does repair work for cash, or the university professor who receives a cheque for a lecture abroad and uses it to pay his credit card balance. Again in these instances, there is economic activity that is unmeasured because those who engage in it have the ability and incentive to avoid reporting their legally earned income and it is then impossible for the official statistics to capture these transactions.

The second example above represents an exchange of services without use of money or cheques, i.e., a barter transaction. It may replace two market transactions, a car rental in Lyon and a car rental in Edmonton. Another example would be the provision of dental care in exchange for such services as tutoring, accounting, lawn-mowing, etc. Barter transactions, for the most part, are legal and result in income in kind which escapes taxation. Table 5.1 serves to illustrate the distinctions in transactions leading to unreported income.

TABLE 5.1

A Taxonomy of Types of Underground Economic Activities

	Monetary Transactions	Non-Monetary Transactions In Exchange	No Exchange
Illegal Activities	Trade in stolen goods, drugs; manufacture of drugs; prostitution, gambling, fraud	Barter, drugs, stolen goods, etc.	Produce or grow drugs for own use. Theft for own use.
	Tax Evasion	**Tax Avoidance**	
Legal Activities	Unreported income from self-employment, wages, salaries, and assets	Employee discounts, fringe benefits (cars, subsidized food, etc.)	Barter of legal services and goods	Do-it-yourself work

Source: This table was provided by Professor H.G. Grubel.

If, as Smith (1981) proposes, the invisible economy is defined as "GNP" that because of non-reporting or under-reporting is not measured by the offical statistics, there is still room for argument as to which transactions should be included or excluded when measuring it. Occasional neighbourly help with babysitting, for instance, is of course quite different from babysitting for a fee on a regular basis without reporting the income. When I help an Indochinese refugee with his first Canadian income tax return and in return he puts up a fence for me, this exchange activity is different in nature from that of a contractor professionally engaging in weekend construction for unreported cash payments. No doubt some may begin with casual neighbourly help and graduate to what amounts to professional work on a full-time basis. In practice, it may well be difficult to draw the line between these two levels of activity. This complexity in distinguishing non-market economic activity, such as work for cash, from more casual types of activity such as unpaid household work and home improvements has led to their exclusion from official GNP statistics.

There is no doubt about the existence of legal and illegal money-based and non-money-based economic activity in informal markets beyond capture by our official statistics. The question for us is the size and rate of growth of this sector. Perhaps the growth rate of real GNP has been low in recent years because resources are being diverted to the non-measured sector. Could it be that the widely used Consumer Price Index, by relying on prices in the measured sector, overstates inflation? As more and more people shift larger portions of their budget to purchase lower-priced substitutes in the informal markets, the true effect of rising prices is blunted, at least for those people finding it easy to shift out of traditional markets. Could it even be that reported unemployment rates overstate the degree of slack in labour markets? As more and more workers take full- or part-time jobs in the informal sector, they have a positive incentive to avoid telling anyone about it. The importance for economic policy-makers of finding answers to these questions depends less on the size of the invisible sector than on its growth trend.

III. MEASUREMENT OF THE INVISIBLE ECONOMY

There is by now a considerable body of both learned and popular writing on the subject.[1] Much credit is due to Professor Edgar Feige for having systematically addressed the measurement problems of transactions the participants intend to be hidden. Instead of reviewing in detail the various measurement methods in the literature, I limit myself here to an overview of the major approaches that might be used and outline their advantages and disadvantages.

Demoscopic approaches

One might, of course, begin by collecting a representative sample of the Canadian population and asking them about the extent of their informal economic activity. The results of this approach would almost certainly understate the volume of invisible transactions because each participant's vested interest is to disguise the truth. It is difficult, therefore, to interpret, for example, the Allensbach Institute's estimates (*Der Spiegel*, 1981) that 3.3 million German regularly pursue a paid job in their spare time, and on average work three hours extra per day. This is not to deny entirely the usefulness of using surveys to obtain insights into the availability of time for informal economic activity,[2] but to rely solely on surveys is to miss capturing the core of the issue.

Discrepancy method

In the United Kingdom and Belgium the central statistical offices publish the difference between national income estimates of GDP, as derived from tax information, and the national expenditure measure of GDP obtained from a family expenditure survey. There is little reason for people surveyed to exaggerate their expenditure. For tax avoidance purposes, however, they have every reason to under-report their income. Therefore, the difference between the expenditure and income estimate provides a clue as to the size and growth of the invisible economy. In the United Kingdom this discrepancy has been persistently positive, approaching 4 percent of GDP in 1974 but declining since (Macaffee, 1979). In Canada the necessary data are not readily available. Moreover, a problem with this approach is that concealed expenditures, for example those for purchase of illegal drugs, and income in kind go uncaptured. As a result, estimates based on the discrepancy method tend to be unrealistically low.

Monetary approaches

As the heading suggests, methodologies in this category limit themselves to the money-based segment of the invisible economy within which transactions are for cash rather than on a barter basis. This constraint again leads to an understatement of the invisible economy.

There are two variants to the monetary approach. One method studies the changes in the ratio of currency to deposits, attributing increase in the ratio over some base year to the need to hold additional cash for informal transactions.[3] The quality of estimates from this approach is influenced by improvements and innovations in financial services, such as corporate cash management and automatic transfers from savings to chequing accounts. These techniques have lessened the need for people to hold current account balances, so that an increase in the ratio of currency to demand deposits may be attributable to a decline in the usefulness of demand deposits rather than an increase in the usefulness of currency holdings. The consequence of omitting this factor would be an upward bias in the estimate of the size of the invisible economy.

A second approach is to study, to the extent data permit, the ratio of total monetary transactions – i.e., *all* cheque and cash-based transactions (except purely financial ones) – to measured GNP. The ratio of total economic transactions (cheques and cash) to final transactions (GNP) is historically rather stable, or perhaps a slightly declining ratio due to the relative growth of the service sector, which requires fewer intermediate transactions than the manufacturing sector. Use of the historical ratio of total to final economic transactions then permits an estimate of the level of GNP that would have been recorded if all final transactions had been properly observed by the official GNP estimates.[4] For the United States, on this basis, it was concluded that there exists a rapidly growing money and cheque-based unobserved sector of the economy.

One weakness of the latter approach is the problem encountered in estimating a turnover speed for banknotes. Another is the need to adjust the total value of cheques cleared to eliminate a possible bias due to the growth of purely financial transactions. If, for example, no adjustments are made for cheques written merely to obtain cash or transfer wealth from, say, stocks to deposits, one might capture financial fluff in the total transactions series. Confusing estimates of true "GNP" would follow from using an uncorrected figure for current monetary transactions in the historical norm of the ratio of total to final economic transactions.

Fiscal studies

As a result of some of the early estimates of the size of the invisible economy in the United States, the Internal Revenue Service undertook to estimate income unreported on individual income tax returns (U.S. Treasury, 1979). For 1976 their estimate of unreported monetary income from legal and illegal economic activity was $100 to $135 billion, or of 6 to 8 percent of GNP. Interestingly enough, 25 to 35 percent of this income was received by cheque rather than in cash. Since income from other sources – in kind from barter, from skimming in retail trade, or off expense accounts – is not included in this estimate, and since the IRS would not be expected to make an overly liberal estimate, it is safe to conclude that the magnitude of the invisible economy is significant.

Corroborating evidence

Since cash dealings are highly likely, particularly in illegal transac-

TABLE 5.2

Increase in Use of Currency and Larger Bills; 1979. 1980

	1979	1980
All Currency	8.1%	7.7%
$ 100 bills	12.7%	13.1%
$1,000 bills	12.5%	12.8%

TABLE 5.3

Indicators of Tax Compliance

Year	Prosecuted in Court	Investigations of Suspected Tax Evasions Completed by Revenue Canada
1975	122	722
1976	191	812
1977	145	847
1978	225	900
1979	196	949
1980	204	937
1981	158	684

tions, the growth in use of large denomination bills provides indication of the invisible economy (*Bank of Canada Review,* 1982). Table 5.2 illustrates the increasing use of larger bills.

An increase in the number of income tax evasion cases prosecuted in the courts and the number of investigations of suspected tax evasion cases completed by the Department of National Revenue, also suggests a growing invisible economy. These data are reported in Table 5.3

There is, of course, anecdotal evidence. For example, a person working at Revenue Canada's Edmonton office advised informally that the number of "complaints" regarding the involvement of people in "invisible" activities has been rising of late.

Canadian estimates[5]

In this section I present two new estimates of Canada's money-based invisible economy. The first of these is a point estimate, arrived at by viewing currency holdings as an inventory to meet ongoing transaction needs. Observation of the actual response of currency holdings to *price changes, interest rates,* and *real GNP growth* for the 1964–1981 period were compared with the response that could have been expected if people (a) had maintained their 1949–1964 pattern of currency holdings with respect to real GNP, or (b) had further economized on such currency holdings as a result of improved cash management. One would expect people to hold less currency, other things being equal (income, prices and interest rates), as they learn to be more sophisticated in their cash management and as more close substitutes, like credit cards, become readily available. Actually, however, the elasticity of currency holding with respect to real GNP was higher in the 1964–1981 than in the 1949–1964 time period. If behaviour patterns of the earlier period had continued throughout the later period, currency held in 1980 would have been $500 million below the actual level. Improved cash-management could easily explain another decline of $500 million in money in circulation. We assume that these have been accumulated for use in the money-based part of the invisible economy.

An important next step in going from cash balances to economic activity is to apply a rate of turnover to these cash balances. Because of the heavy concentration of the invisible economy in the service sector, which requires fewer intermediate transactions than the manufacturing sector, the turnover of cash balances is assumed to be 10 percent greater than in the formal economy. These considerations lead to estimates of at least $6.5 billion (more realistically, $13.2 billion) of cash-based final transactions in the invisible economy.

Considering that the IRS study revealed at least 25 percent of invisible economic activity to be cheque-based, a final adjustment is required to reflect this fact. The result is that from 1964 to 1980 there has been growth in the invisible economy such that in 1980 at least $8.7 billion (more realistically $17.6 billion) of additional output went unrecorded. The latter figure amounts to 6.0 percent of GNP in 1980.

However large the latter figure is, it represents only the addition to the invisible economy since 1964. Since it is safe to assume that some invisible economic activity existed in 1964, say 3.5 percent of GNP, for argument's sake, the size of our invisible money-based economy in 1980 can be placed at just under 10 percent of GNP.

A second estimate is based on the modified transactions method first suggested by Feige (1980). This method requires that the value of cheques cleared in Canadian clearing centres be adjusted for purely financial transactions. This was done by restricting the growth of cheque clearing in the financial centres — Toronto, Montreal, Calgary and Vancouver — to the rate exhibited in the rest of the banking system. Next, it is necessary to estimate a turnover speed for the stock of currency. Here I assume, with Feige, that on average, banknotes circulate 200 times before they wear out. For earlier years the average lifetime of banknotes was calculated from returned banknotes and for later years it was available in the *Bank of Canada Review* (1982).

The sum of adjusted cheque transactions and currency transactions can then be related to measured GNP. Were it not for the growth in the invisible economy, one would expect a fairly stable or slightly falling ratio of total to final (i.e., GNP) transactions. In fact, the ratio in Table 5.4. No doubt these estimates will strike many as quantitatively important, especially since non-monetary economic activity is excluded.

A noteworthy feature of these latter estimates is that they show a rapid growth of unobserved economic activity in the monetary sector during recent years. By applying a conservative 25 percent marginal federal tax rate to this unreported income, one arrives at $10.5 billion foregone revenue in 1980. By assuming the same productivity in the invisible as in the formal sector, namely $27,200.00 per employed person, there were another 1.5 million full-time job equivalents in the Canadian economy of 1980. If only one-tenth of these full-time job equivalents were actually held by persons reported as unemployed and collecting unemployment insurance benefits, the true unemployment rate was 6.2 percent, rather than the reported rate of 7.5 percent.

If indeed the invisible economy is as large as these estimates suggest, and if it is also growing faster than the measured sector, it is vital to improve the indicators of economic performance and to reform the tax system. We shall consider these points again below after first looking at the causes of the growth of the invisible economy.

TABLE 5.4

Estimates of the Invisible Economy Based on the Transactions Method
(assuming in 1964 3.5% of GNP was invisible)

Year	Invisible Economy in Billion $	% of GNP
1964	1.75	3.5
1965	1.88	3.4
1966	1.11	1.8
1967	2.32	3.5
1968	2.47	3.4
1969	.16	0.2
1970	.69	0.8
1971	1.13	1.2
1972	6.63	6.3
1973	12.97	10.5
1974	18.44	12.5
1975	28.44	17.2
1976	19.87	10.4
1977	20.87	10.0
1978	25.34	11.0
1979	33.27	12.7
1980	42.03	14.5

IV. CAUSES OF THE INVISIBLE ECONOMY

Though it is easy to speculate on why the invisible economy is growing, it is far more difficult to provide empirical documentation on
each of the various causes. There has, of course, been an escalation of
costs in the service sector, much of which can be explained by extensive economic and social regulation, sales and payroll taxes, and scarcity of some skills. For example, as the charge for an hour of car servicing rises to $35, it is not surprising that many people search for
substitute means of repairing their cars. The car mechanic working for
$15 per hour before taxes seeks opportunities to work evenings and
weekends for at least $15 but not necessarily $35; furthermore, the
time available for such extra activity has increased with the decline in
the average work week and the advent of labour-saving household
devices.

Whether money-based or non-money-based, the growth of the invisible sector is clearly a rational response to after-tax-related escala-

tion of prices in the observed sector. And indeed one could argue that our stock of housing would be in considerably worse condition than it is, were it not for the availability of craftsmen willing to participate in informal economic activity.

More generally, it is likely that progressive income taxation, and other taxes that we face in hidden form, have reached such burdensome proportions for many Canadians that they actively seek out tax-avoiding and tax-evading opportunities.[6] A simple regression of the estimated size of the invisible economy on the average personal income tax rate, shows that almost 50 percent of the variation of invisible economic activity can be explained by variation in the tax burden alone. An index of the Canadian public's trust in government, as exists for the United States, might very well explain the remainder of the variation.[7]

Attitudes towards government in general and the taxation authorities in particular appear to be changing. In Canada, the divisive wrangling between the federal and provincial governments probably contributes to a decline in respect for the political process. And the complexity of our tax system with its many special provisions that are difficult for the uninitiated to understand have apparently an effect on how average Canadians perceive the system's fairness. Consequently, income earners are reassessing their willingness to engage in a little "self-help" in order, as it is subjectively perceived, to offset inequities in the system.

V. IMPLICATIONS AND POLICY OPTIONS

It is always best to begin an assessment of the consequences of analysis with a note of caution. The measurement techniques employed here are not problem-free and I have made certain special assumptions that may not be accepted by everyone. But some healthy scepticism notwithstanding, the true size of the invisible money-based sector of the economy lies in the range of 10 percent to 15 percent of GNP, and this is too large to be neglected. Since the unobserved money-based economic activity is growing more rapidly than observed transactions, neglect may lead to irreversible social changes.

Should trust in government erode as the tax system increasingly becomes perceived as being unfair, fewer and fewer Canadians will be deterred from evading reporting taxable income by the risk of detection and any consequent penalties. The self-assessment feature of our tax system would be undermined. The size of the estimate of the invisible economy and the recent growth trend of the money-based unobserved economy make that outcome a very real possibility. Put differently, as tax revenues forgone rise, the tax burden in the shrinking observed sector is forced up. This further increases the incentive to avoid or evade taxation. Society starts inexorably following a vicious pattern leading to even greater tax evasion and eventual social decline.

One response to this would be to increase the resources available to the compliance division of National Revenue and raise the penalties for tax evasion. Germany recently increased the fines for "Schwarzarbeit." Additional resources for Revenue Canada might facilitate a study of the problem analogous to the one done by the Internal Revenue Service in the United States. Such a study, in helping to pinpoint whether invisible economic activity is practiced by all or only certain strata of society, would be useful in the design of measures to combat the problem. On the other hand, a survey of British taxpayers' attitudes towards tax evasion (Sherbaniuk, 1981) indicated that compliance was affected very little by perceptions as to the likelihood of detection and penalties.

There appear to be few quick remedies against a process that has slowly evolved. Instead, and in the medium term, we may have no choice but to re-evaluate even well-intentioned regulations which, nevertheless, create incentives for people to move into the invisible economy; certainly we will have to do away with special privileges for special groups—so-called tax expenditures—in order to broaden the tax base and lower direct and indirect taxes. Every possible step should be taken to lessen the perceived unfairness of the tax system. Instead of doing away with indexation of the personal income tax against inflation, for instance, a more complete program of indexation is advisable.

In the long term one might, with Professor Lipsey (see his article in this volume), derive comfort from the existence of the invisible economy: it seems to be a reflection of the resilience of markets. There are natural, corrective forces at work to counterbalance interferences with the market as an allocative mechanism. Nonetheless, the long run may be too long for many of us!

In the near term we need to learn more about the nature of the invisible economy, in particular its cyclical behaviour and its impact on income distribution. This will help policy-makers by providing them with more accurate measures of economic performance for the formation of macro-economic and tax policies.

Finally, this entire volume points toward the need to take a broader view on government intervention in the economy. The phenomenon of unobserved economic activity is not only an economic one causing relative prices and costs to change and thereby encouraging substitution from the observed to the unobserved sector. There are also significant psychological, sociological and political dimensions that have until recently received, at best, scant attention.

NOTES

1. For an informative summary see "The Underground Economy's Hidden Force," *Business Week,* April 5, 1982, pp. 64–70.
2. An example is John W. Kendrick's "Expanding Imputed Values in the National Income and Product Accounts," *Review of Income and Wealth,* December 1979, pp.349–363. For 1973 GNP would have been 63.5 percent greater if additional imputations had been made for unpaid economic activity.
3. This approach was pioneered by P. Cagan (1958) and used by P. Gutmann (1977).
4. This method was pioneered by E. Feige (1979).
5. For details of the estimates reported here, see R. Mirus and R. S. Smith (1982). For more details on the methods, see R. Mirus and R. S. Smith (1981).
6. See, for example, Pipes and Walker (1982). They show that the tax index has risen more than 500 percent since the mid-fifties while the income index has risen only 350 percent.
7. E. Feige (1980) explains 87 percent of the variation in his estimates of the unobserved economy with these two variables.

BIBLIOGRAPHY

Bank of Canada Review, January 1982, p. 17–18.

Business Week, "The Underground Economy's Hidden Force," April 5, 1982, pp. 64–70.

Cagan, Phillip, "The Demand for Currency Relative to Total Money Supply," National Bureau of Economic Research, Occasional Paper No. 62, 1958.

Der Spiegel, "Schwarzarbeit, Die Bluhende Wirtschaft im Untergrund," November 9, 1981, pp. 62–81.

The Economist, "Italy: Moonlighting in Public," February 20, 1982, p.49.

Feige, Edgar, L., "How Big is the Irregular Economy?" *Challenge,* November-December, 1979, pp. 5–13.

————,"The Theory and Measurement of the Unobserved Sector of the United States Economy: Causes, Consequences, and Implications," *A New Perspective on Macro Economic Phenomena,* (Unpublished Manuscript), 1980, p. 63.

Folio, Advertisement, March 8, 1982.

Gutmann, Peter, M., "The Subterranean Economy," *Financial Analysts Journal,* November-December 1977, pp. 26–28.

Kendrick, John, W., "Expanding Imputed Values in the National Income and Product Accounts," *Review of Income and Wealth,* December 1979, pp. 349–363.

Macaffee, Kerrick, "A Glimpse of the Hidden Economy in the National Accounts," *Economic Trends,* No. 316, February 1980, pp. 81–87.

Mirus, Rolf and Roger S. Smith, "The Unobserved Economy: Canada," paper presented at the International Conference on the Unobserved Economy, Wassenaar, June 1982.

————,"Canada's Irregular Economy," *Canadian Public Policy,* Summer 1981, pp. 444–453.

Pipes, Sally and Michael Walker (with David Gill), *Tax Facts 3: The Canadian Consumer Tax Index and You,* Vancouver: The Fraser Institute, 1982.

Sherbaniuk, D., "Canadian Tax Foundation, Report of the President," 35th Annual Report, April 1981.

Smith, Adrian, "The Informal Economy," *Lloyds Bank Review,* July 1981, pp. 45–61.

United States Treasury, Internal Revenue Service, "Estimates of Income Unreported on Individual Tax Returns," (Washington, D.C.: Department of the Treasury) Publication 1104, 1979, 166 pages.

APPENDIX TO MEASURING LEVIATHAN: THE SIZE, SCOPE, AND GROWTH OF GOVERNMENTS IN CANADA*

John L. Howard and W.T. Stanbury

The purpose of this Appendix is to identify and to discuss the nature, scope and growth of nine instruments used by governments in Canada to achieve their varied objectives. In succession we examine:

I.   direct expenditures (the most frequent measure of the size of government in the economy);

II.   public employment;

III. "tax expenditures" (revenues forgone in lieu of expenditure outlays);

IV.   regulation (perhaps the most ubiquitous governing instrument);

V.   Crown corporations;

VI.   loans and loan guarantees to the private sector;

VII. equity ownership in private sector firms or "mixed enterprises" (a relatively new form of intervention);

VIII. "chosen instruments" (private firms that effectively become instruments of public policy although the government has no equity interest); and

IX.   suasion, in which the government persuades private sector actors to alter their behavior without resort to legislation.

---

*We are indebted to the Word Processing Staff of the Faculty of Commerce at the University of British Columbia for superb quality work and to George Lermer and Michael Walker for their helpful comments.

I. EXPENDITURES

For most people "big government," which we have termed "Leviathan," is equated with large and growing government expenditures. For example, the federal estimates for 1983/84 total $89 billion or 23 percent of GNP. The estimates for 1984/85 total $98 billion. Among academics more effort has been devoted to analyzing the growth of government expenditures than to all other measures of government activity.[1] Perhaps this is because, as Bird (1970, p. 3) argues, "few aspects of economic policy are more important than public expenditure." However, more effort has been devoted to taxation and tax reform than to a systematic analysis of government expenditures. Stanbury (1972, p. 1) points out that prior to Bird's book, there was no comprehensive treatment of Canadian public expenditures—although Outer Mongolia's had been analyzed in 1957.[2] In any event, the gap has been filled and we now have considerable knowledge of government outlays in Canada.

The most common measure used to describe Leviathan is the ratio of government expenditures (G) to Gross National Product (GNP). Nutter (1978, pp. 1,2), like most writers on the size of government, notes that the concept is not easily quantified. He focuses on expenditures as a measure of "government's command over a nation's resources." While such a measure does not take account of "government lending or private spending that government mandates by law and regulation," he argues that "direct government spending as a fraction of national product is nonetheless a useful and widely used first approximation of the size of government." The particular measure he proposes is government spending as a fraction of net national product evaluated at factor cost.[3]

Total expenditures

In current dollar terms, since the mid-1970s the expenditures of all three levels of government ("G," which includes hospitals and the Canada and Quebec Pension Plans) have exceeded 40 percent of GNP (see Table A-1). This is an increase of 20 percentage points since 1950 and over 12 percentage points since 1965. In terms of constant 1971 dollars, the ratio of G to GNP increased from 26.5 percent in 1950 to 32.6 percent in 1960 to 36.9 percent in 1970 and then to 45.4 percent in 1982[4] (see Table A-2).

TABLE A-1

Government Expenditures in Canada, Selected Years, 1950-1982
(Millions of Current $)
National Accounts Basis

Year	Total Gov't Expend.	Transfers to Persons	Other Trans-fers*	Exhaustive Current (incl. Defence)	Capital Expend.	Federal	Provin-cial	Local	Hospi-tals	GNP	Gov't Current Expend. Deflator 1971=100	Personal Expend. Deflator 1971=100	GNP Deflator 1971=100	Gov't Expend. as a % of GNP
1950	4,080	1,023	632	1,928	497	2,370	1,230	913	na	18,491	35.9	61.2	54.8	22.1
1955	7,498	1,719	794	4,036	949	4,806	1,814	1,677	na	28,528	46.2	69.5	65.0	26.3
1960	11,380	3,090	1,498	5,281	1,511	6,746	3,532	2,827	779	38,359	57.3	76.3	72.1	29.7
1965	16,554	3,423	2,343	8,358	2,430	8,551	6,328	4,527	1,176	55,364	68.2	81.6	79.1	29.9
1970	31,148	6,985	4,373	16,630	3,160	15,262	14,124	8,100	2,395	85,685	94.2	97.7	96.9	36.4
1975	68,288	17,080	11,474	33,380	6,354	35,508	31,586	14,574	4,923	165,343	156.0	137.3	146.3	41.3
1980	121,851	30,204	24,763	58,538	8,346	60,799	56,997	25,068	8,596	291,869	257.0	205.3	223.7	41.7
1981	141,410	34,679	30,656	66,749	9,326	71,716	63,434	28,769	9,914	331,338	290.3	228.7	246.3	42.7
1982	165,557	42,630	36,485	75,748	10,694	85,957	72,020	32,839	11,243	348,925	327.3	252.8	272.6	47.4

* Includes interest on the public debt, subsidies, capital assistance and transfers to non-residents. In 1982 these amounts were 25,238; 7600; 2588; and 1059 respectively.

Source: Department of Finance (1983).

TABLE A-2

Government Expenditures in Canada in Constant 1971 Dollars,*
Selected Years, 1950-1982
($ Millions)

Year	Current Goods & Services	Gross Fixed Capital Form.	Total Exhaustive Expenditure	Total Transfers in Current Dollars	Personal Expend. Deflator	Total Transfer in 1971$	Total Gov't. Expend. (1971$)	Gross National Product	Total Gov't. Expend. ÷ GNP	Current Expend. ÷ GNP	GFCF ÷ GNP	Transfers to Persons ÷ Personal Income	Total Transfers ÷ Personal Income
1950	5,367	884	6,251	1,646	61.2	2,690	8,941	33,762	26.5%	15.9%	2.6%	7.1%	11.5%
1955	8,736	1,308	10,044	2,513	69.5	3,616	13,660	43,891	31.1	19.9	3.0	8.1	11.8
1960	9,218	2,142	11,360	4,588	76.3	6,013	17,393	53,231	32.6	17.3	4.0	10.4	15.5
1965	12,253	3,003	15,256	5,766	81.6	7,066	22,322	69,981	31.9	17.5	4.3	8.3	14.0
1970	17,650	3,329	20,979	11,358	97.7	11,625	32,604	88,390	36.9	20.0	3.8	10.5	17.0
1975	21,399	4,127	25,526	28,554	137.3	20,797	46,323	113,005	41.0	18.9	3.7	12.5	21.0
1980	22,782	3,591	26,373	54,967	205.3	26,774	53,147	130,467	40.7	17.5	2.8	12.6	22.9
1981	22,988	3,670	26,658	65,335	228.7	28,568	55,426	134,540	41.2	17.1	2.7	12.4	23.3
1982	23,145	3,748	26,893	79,115	252.8	31,295	58,188	128,057	45.4	18.1	2.9	13.9	25.7

* Except for columns 4, 5, and 8.

Source: Derived from Department of Finance (1983).

702-2
TA-2

As large as this fraction seems, it is not as large as the ratio for a number of Western European countries. For example, in 1980 the ratio of G to GNP was 44.6 percent for the United Kingdom, 45.9 percent for France, 45.2 percent for Germany, and 61.7 percent for Sweden. On the other hand, G/GNP was 35.1 percent for the United States and 31.7 percent for Japan.[5]

The rate of growth of government expenditures in constant dollars has been declining in Canada in recent years (Donner, 1981, p. 107) and the Economic Council's projections of governments' share of real GNP (*exhaustive* expenditures only)[6] suggest it will decline during the remainder of the 1980s (as cited in Donner, 1981, p. 113).

Well over a century ago, Adoph Wagner, a leading German economist of the day, formulated his now-renowned "law of expanding state expenditures" in "progressive states." Bird (1970, p. 70) offers the following modern formulation of Wagner's law: "As per capita income rises in industrializing nations, their public sectors will grow in relative importance." Canada certainly seems to offer confirmation of Wagner's law. Table A-3 indicates that total government expenditure in 1961 dollars increased from $61 million in 1867 to over $18 billion a century later. As a fraction of GNP, expenditures increased from 3.7 percent in 1867 to 13.2 percent in 1913 to 19.2 percent in 1926[7] and then to 31.3 percent in 1968. Bird puts real government expenditure at 7 percent of GNP in 1870, which is somewhat higher than Stanbury's estimate. Bird cites Creighton, who estimated that total government expenditures in 1866, the year before Confederation, were about 7 percent of national income.

In any event, we can confidently assert that the *ratio* of G to GNP in Canada has increased at least six times over a period of 115 years, i.e., from 4 to 7 percent of GNP in 1867 to 45 percent of GNP in 1982.

Expenditures by economic category

(a) *Methodology*

There are a number of obvious methodological problems with G/GNP as a measure of the relative size of government spending (in general see Stanbury, 1972, Ch. 2; Bird, 1970). First, as Nutter (1978) points out, capital is consumed in the process of production. Hence Net National Product is a better measure of the total value of output available for public or private use. Second, "G" includes both exhaustive expenditures and transfers to persons. While the former are

TABLE A-3

Canadian Government Expenditures in Current and Constant 1961 Dollars
Selected Years, 1867–1968

Year	Current Dollars		Constant 1961 Dollars		
	Government Expenditure ($ Millions)	% of GNP	Government Expenditure* ($ Millions)	GNP ($ Millions)	G/GNP
1867	20.6	5.6%	60.8	1,640	3.7%
1874	49.2	10.1	134.4	1,888	7.1
1913	409.0	15.5	1,155.4	8,743	13.2
1921	878.5	20.5	1,459.3	8,238	17.7
1926	859.3	16.7	1,559.5	10,727	14.5
1926**	810	15.7	1,954	10,203	19.2
1968**	23,824	33.3	18,141	58,041	31.3

* Deflated using the Wholesale Price Index from 1867 to 1926, then separate deflators for transfers and exhaustive expenditures.
** Derived from the revised *National Accounts* data; earlier years compiled from a variety of sources, see Stanbury (1972, Ch. 3).

Source: Stanbury (1972, Table 3-14).

included in GNP (and NNP), the latter are not — see Figure A-l. Therefore, as government's role as a redistributor of income grows, the ratio G/GNP grows even if government's share of GNP in terms of purchases of current goods and services and capital formation is unchanged. In fact, if government redistributive efforts are sufficiently great, the ratio of G to GNP can exceed one! In the post-war period a substantial part of the growth in G/GNP is precisely due to the changing structure of government expenditures. Bird (1970, p. 19), for example, shows that transfers to persons as a percentage of GNP (in 1961) have increased from about 8 percent in the 1950s to over 18 percent in the period 1975–77. The data in Table A-2 indicate that in constant dollars, total transfers for all three levels of government exceeded total exhaustive expenditures in 1980 while transfers were only 36 percent of exhaustive expenditures in 1955.

The third methodological problem has to do with the national income accounting convention by which the value of government's "out-

Figure A-1

Government in the Context of the Economy

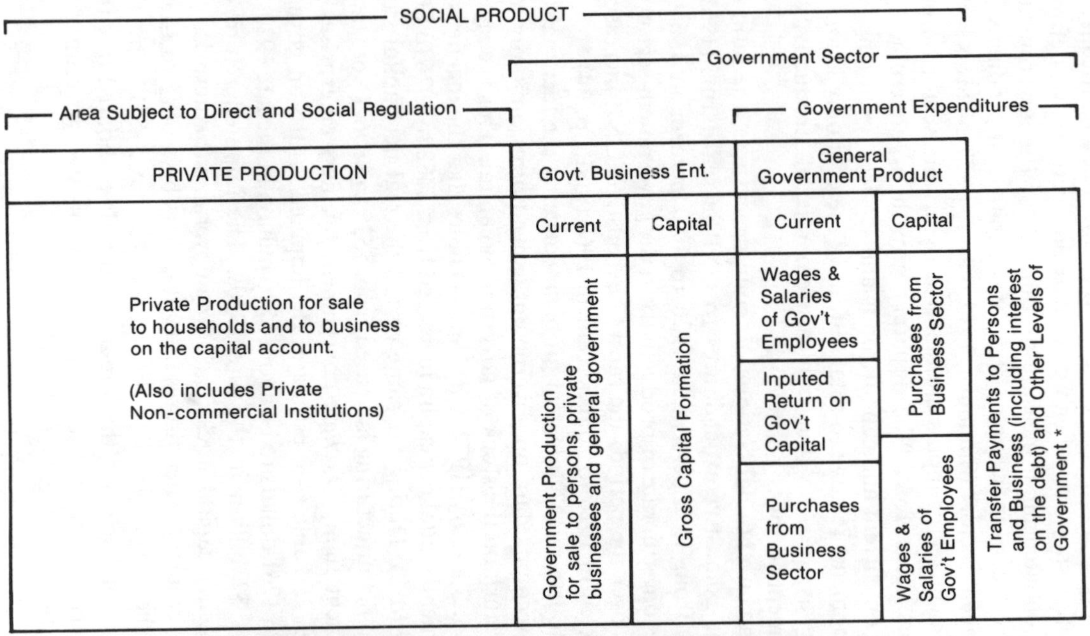

SOCIAL PRODUCT

Government Sector

Government Expenditures

Area Subject to Direct and Social Regulation

PRIVATE PRODUCTION

Private Production for sale to households and to business on the capital account.

(Also includes Private Non-commercial Institutions)

Govt. Business Ent.

Current — Government Production for sale to persons, private businesses and general government

Capital — Gross Capital Formation

General Government Product

Current — Wages & Salaries of Gov't Employees; Inputed Return on Gov't Capital; Purchases from Business Sector

Capital — Purchases from Business Sector; Wages & Salaries of Gov't Employees

Transfer Payments to Persons and Business (including interest on the debt) and Other Levels of Government.*

* Intergovernmental transfers net out to zero in the consolidated total of government expenditure.

Source: Stanbury 1972 (1972, Chart 3-1).

put" is held to be precisely equal to its expenditures on inputs, i.e., the value of its wage bill, plus the purchase of goods and services from the private sector (both current and capital). The significance of this assumption shows up when we estimate productivity. By definition, "a simply deflated input measure of 'output' for the government sector has the effect of indicating a zero rate of change of productivity in the government sector" (Stanbury, 1972, Ch. 2, p. 27). This is so because government sector inputs are deflated by private sector output price deflators. Therefore, "the apparent growth of government expenditures on current and capital goods and services (excluding transfers for a moment) relative to total output in the economy is *understated* so long as the *true* (but unmeasured) rate of productivity in the government sector is positive (ibid., p. 31).

Using conventional National Accounts measures, the ratio of government exhaustive expenditures to GNP in real terms (1961 $) increased from 13.2 percent in 1926 to 19.0 percent in 1968. If the average long-run rate of productivity in the government sector was 1.5 percent over the period, the ratio G exhaustive/GNP increased from 8.5 percent in 1926 to 20.6 percent in 1968 (ibid., p. 34).[8]

The fourth methodological problem concerns the fact that the National Accounts data on government expenditures omit any measure of the return on the stock of government capital. This is a significant omission. Stanbury (1972, Ch. 5, p. 21) notes that the real net stock of government capital per capita increased from $488 in 1926 to $1,412 in 1968 (1961 $). During the same period the real net capital stock per capita in manufacturing increased from $535 to $896. (Note that these government figures *exclude* government business enterprises.) Stanbury (1972, Table 6-6) estimates the imputed return on government capital in 1961 dollars to be about $220 million in the late 1920s, rising to about $2 billion in the late 1960s. The imputed return on the government's capital stock (excluding government enterprises) raised total government expenditures in 1961 dollars by from 5 to 14 percent during the period 1926 to 1968 (ibid., Table 3–85). The ratio is somewhat higher when the imputed return is compared to either the government's consumption expenditures or the government's net product (ibid., Table 3–86).[9]

(b) *Exhaustive expenditures*
As Bird (1979, p. 8) notes, "exhaustive expenditures are those which exhaust or use up goods and services (including labor services) which

would otherwise be available to be used in private sector activities." This type of government expenditure stands in contrast to transfer expenditures which shift the power to exert claims over resources (dollars) from one individual to another. While the government exercises its coercive power to determine who pays and who gets these transfers, it is the recipients who decide what these payments will be spent on.

At least two components of exhaustive expenditures should be distinguished:

1. expenditures on current goods and services; and
2. capital formation by governments.

In turn, it is important to distinguish in both (1) and (2) between the wages, salaries and benefits paid to government employees and *purchases* of goods and services from the private sector. (If we are interested in the size of the "government product," as Figure A-1 indicates, we must also add to (1) and (2) the imputed return on the government's capital stock.)

Bird (1979, p. 19) indicates that real exhaustive expenditures (1971 $) of all three levels of government in Canada increased from 17.7 percent of GNP in 1947 to 25.4 percent in 1952 (due to the Korean War) and then declined to between 21 and 23 percent of GNP from 1956 through 1977. If defense expenditures are excluded, we find that real civilian exhaustive expenditures were in the range of 14 to 15 percent of GNP between 1947 and 1957, rose in small increments to 20 percent of GNP in 1967 and remained at that level through 1977 (ibid.,p. 19).

The data in Table A-2 indicate that current real exhaustive expenditures (in 1971 $) rose from 15.9 percent of GNP in 1950 to 19.9 percent in 1955 and then fell to 17.3 and 17.5 percent in 1960 and 1965 respectively. The ratio rose to 20 percent in 1970, but fell thereafter, reaching 17.3 percent in 1981. Gross fixed capital formation (1971 $) by all levels of government in 1980 and 1982 was 2.8 percent of GNP, virtually the same ratio as 1955. In 1965 the ratio was 4.3 percent (see Table A-2).

Government has always played an important role in capital formation in Canada (Stanbury, 1972, Ch. 5). However, its significance has declined over the past two decades. Gordon (1981, p.250) indicates that government departments' and institutions' share of total public and private investment (in current dollars) decreased from 19.5 percent in 1960 to 16.0 percent in 1975 and to 12.5 percent in 1980. Bird

(1979, p.27) indicates that the public capital stock as a percentage of the total capital stock in Canada was essentially constant at 30 percent over the period 1961-1976. On the other hand, Stanbury (1972, Table 5-48) shows that between 1926 and 1968 the rate of growth of the real net capital stock of a variety of public sector entities far outstripped that of manufacturing or non-manufacturing excluding government and housing. Government's share of the real net capital stock (with government taken to include hospitals but *not* business enterprises) rose from 19.2 percent in 1926 to 31.9 percent in 1945 and then declined slightly to 28.1 percent in 1968 (ibid., Table 5-47).

The key component of government as a producer of goods and services in its own right (as opposed to being a purchaser of goods and services from the private sector) is its expenditures on wages and salaries, both civilian and military.[10] Bird (1979, p.23) indicates that total government wages and salaries as a percentage of all wages and salaries paid in Canada rose from 11.3 percent in 1947 to 16.3 percent in 1960, 23.1 percent in 1970 and 25.1 percent in 1977. These figures are in nominal dollars.

There is constant debate about the levels of pay in the private and public sectors. Proper comparisons, however, are very difficult to make. Bird et al. (1979, p.92) summarize their extensive analysis, in part, as follows:

> - Taxation data [i.e., from *Taxation Statistics*] show a sustained rise in relative public sector earnings throughout the post-war period. On the average, the earnings of public employees have exceeded those of private (sector) employees since the mid-1960's — but the differential has been almost unchanged since 1970.

> - Over the last decade wage increases in collective bargaining agreements have, on average, been almost identical in the public and private sectors. Since 1973 [to 1977] public sector wage increases have been slightly higher, but past experience suggests that this advantage may not persist.

> - Empirical studies show ... that there is a pure public sector wage advantage of 5 to 10 percent over the private sector, even after allowing for such factors as differences in education, age and experience of the two work-forces.[11]

The ratio of public sector wages and salaries to total wages and salaries in Canada will be overstated in real terms to the extent that public sector wages move ahead of those in the private sector. As we shall point out in Section II of this paper, public employment has been an almost constant percentage of total employment throughout the 1960s and 1970s. Therefore, a significant increase in the ratio of the government's wage bill to that of the total economy appears to be largely attributable to an increase in public sector wages relative to those in the private sector.

(c) *Transfers*
Transfers are unrequited payments to individuals, firms or other levels of government which alter the distribution of income but are not included in GNP (see Figure A-1). Government transfer payments include the following:

1. transfers to individuals, e.g., welfare payments, unemployment insurance;
2. interest on the public debt (assumed to be an unrequited payment in the National Accounts);
3. subsidies and capital assistance, e.g., regional economic expansion grants to business, subsidies paid to the railroads; and
4. transfers to other levels of government, e.g., contributions to finance, shared-cost programs or unconditional grants.

In general, the focus of most attention is on transfers to persons and to other levels of government. Bird (1979, p.23) shows that transfers to persons amounted to between 6.1 and 7.7 percent of personal income from 1947 to 1951, to between 8.1 and 9.0 percent from 1961 to 1966 and then rose from 12.5 to 13.0 percent in the period 1975–1977. He notes that these figures "understate the importance of government transfers to persons, since they exclude that portion of interest on the public debt paid to persons" (ibid., p.22).

Table A-2 indicates that transfers to persons (excluding interest on the public debt, subsidies, capital assistance and transfers to non-residents) in constant 1971 dollars increased from 7.1 percent of Personal Income in 1950 to 12.5 percent in 1975, the ratio it has maintained subsequently. All transfers as a fraction of personal income increased from 11.5 percent in 1950 to 25.7 percent in 1982. Therefore, the major growing component of government expenditures has been total transfers. In 1950, total transfers in 1971 dollars amounted to

$2,690 million. The comparable total for all exhaustive expenditures was $6,251 million. By 1980, as Table A-2 indicates, total real transfers were slightly larger (at $26,774 million) than exhaustive expenditures.

Just looking at the federal level for a moment we find that transfers to persons increased from 4.4 percent of GNP in 1965 to 6.8 percent in 1975 and then declined to 6.0 percent in 1980. Interest on the public debt increased from 1.9 percent in 1965 to 3.3 percent in 1980. (These were higher in 1981 and 1982 due to much higher deficits and higher interest rates.) Federal subsidies and capital assistance increased from 0.8 percent of GNP in the early 1970s to 2.2 percent in 1980.[12] The growth of federal transfers to persons (excluding interest) dates from World War I. Stanbury (1972, Table 3-8) shows that transfers to persons amounted to less than 1 percent of federal expenditures prior to 1915. On the other hand, interest on the debt typically absorbed from 16 to 25 percent of federal expenditures between 1867 and 1905.

Bird (1979, p.23) measures the "share of personal income originating directly in government" as government wages and salaries plus transfers to persons divided by total personal income. This ratio more than doubled between 1947 and 1977 — from 14.6 to 30.8 percent. Stanbury (1972, Table 3-19) indicates that this ratio increased from 7.5 percent in 1926 to 13.0 percent in 1939, and then to 23.4 percent in 1945. The ratio declined after World War II to 13.5 percent in 1948. It then began to rise steadily to 20.4 percent in 1958 and 24.7 percent in 1968.[13] Interest payments on all government debt ranged from about 5 percent of personal income in the late 1920s to 10 percent in 1933 to about 5 percent after World War II to as low as 3.1 or 3.2 percent between 1955 and 1958. They amounted to only 4 percent of personal income for most of the 1960s (ibid., Table 3-19).

Transfers to persons (and non-commercial institutions) as a fraction of personal income rose from 1.8 percent in 1926 to 6.9 percent in 1934, then fell to 2.5 percent in 1943. After World War II they amounted to about 7 percent of personal income. By the late 1950s they had increased to about 10 percent, but they declined slightly to 9.2 percent in 1967 (ibid., Table 3-19).

The growth of transfers, mainly transfers to persons, represents one of the principal structural changes in government expenditures in Canada. Total transfers per capita, including interest, increased from $64 in 1926 to $343 in 1968 in real terms (1961 $). During the same period, total government expenditures, including the imputed return on government capital, increased from $231 to $1,005 per capita in 1961 dollars. While real GNP per capita increased 2.6 times between 1926 and 1968, government transfers increased 5.3 times and total government expenditure increased 4.4 times (ibid., Table 3–81). Transfers, as a fraction of total government expenditure in constant 1961 dollars (including the imputed return on government capital), rose from 28 percent in 1926 to 39.4 percent in 1934 and fell sharply during World War II to 10.9 percent of total expenditure in 1942. They rose again after the war, for example, they were 36.6 percent of the total in 1948—but declined to 26.1 percent in 1952. They then rose fairly steadily to 34.1 percent in 1968 (ibid., Table 3–85).

The *composition* of total *real* transfers changed even more dramatically. In the late 1920s, for example, three-quarters of the total consisted of interest on the public debt while about 1.5 percent were subsidies to business. The remainder were transfers to persons. In the early 1950s, two-thirds of total transfers were transfers to persons. Subsidies to business were from 4 to 5 percent of the total. In the late 1960s, transfers to persons had declined to under 6 percent while subsidies to business had increased to 7 to 10 percent of the total, the remainder consisting of interest on the public debt (ibid., Table 3–87).

One of the hallmarks of Canadian federalism is the practice of higher levels of governments making large conditional and unconditional transfers to lower levels (Economic Council, 1982a). Bird (1979, p.57) indicates that federal transfers to the provinces were in the range of 1 to 2 percent of GNP between 1947 and 1958 but exceeded 4 percent between 1971 and 1977. These intergovernmental transfers were typically 8 to 10 percent of total federal expenditure between 1947 and 1957. In the 1970s they amounted to over one-fifth of federal expenditure. The *Main Estimates* (pI-91) indicate that in 1983–84 Ottawa will pay $16.5 billion to the provinces, or 19.3 percent of total budgetary expenditure.[14]

Looked at from the point of the receiving government, we find that federal transfers *declined* as a proportion of total gross general revenue for five provinces between 1957 and 1980. For Prince Edward Island, Nova Scotia and New Brunswick the ratio was high (over 50 percent for Prince Edward Island and about 45 percent for the other two) but trendless. In the case of Quebec the ratio increased from 13.0 percent in 1957 to 27.7 percent in 1962, but fell to 21.6 percent in 1980

TABLE A-4

Two Measures of the Relative Size of the Three Levels of
Government in Canada, Selected Years 1926–1982

Year	Federal		Provincial		Local	
	B	A	B	A	B	A
1926	39.6%	37.8%	20.5%	20.2%	39.9%	42.0%
1930	35.4	33.1	25.1	25.0	33.1	41.9
1935	41.4	34.7	28.1	33.8	30.5	31.6
1940	60.6	56.5	19.5	22.4	19.8	21.1
1945	83.9	82.3	8.9	9.3	7.3	8.4
1950	56.9	51.9	24.9	26.0	18.2	22.1
1955	60.6	58.1	21.5	19.8	17.9	22.1
1960	56.7	50.5	25.0	24.8	18.3	24.7
1965	51.8	43.1	30.0	29.6	18.2	27.3
1970	49.3	38.3	34.8	38.3	15.9	26.0
1975	52.7	41.3	35.6	37.1	11.7	21.6
1980	51.3	40.4	37.4	38.5	11.3	21.1
1981	52.3	42.0	36.1	31.7	11.6	20.9
1982	53.5	43.7	35.1	35.9	11.4	20.4

A = After intergovernmental transfers: transfers are subtracted from the expenditures of the paying government and added to the expenditures of the recipient government.

B = Before intergovernmental transfers: transfers are attributed to the level of government that makes them.

Source: Department of Finance (1983, pp. 201, 202).

(Economic Council, 1982a, p.1). Federal transfers increased the revenue capacity of the Maritime provinces and Quebec by from 10 to 55 percent in 1980/81 (ibid., p.18).

Some idea of the changes in the fiscal role of the federal government vis-a-vis the provinces and local governments can be found in Table A-4. If expenditures are measured as including transfers at the level of government making them (the columns headed "B"), the federal government's share of the national total has fallen from 60.6 percent in 1955 to 53.5 percent in 1982. If expenditures are calculated by subtracting them from the paying government and adding them to the expenditures of the receiving government (the columns headed "A"), then the federal government's share fell from 58.1 percent in 1955 to 38.3 percent in 1970 and then rose to 43.7 percent in 1982.[15] As Table A-4 indicates, regardless of which measure is used, the provincial share of total government expenditures in Canada has increased sharply from about 20 percent in 1955 to 36 percent in 1982.

Stanbury (1972, Table 3-65) shows that provincial transfers to local governments (including both conditional and unconditional grants) amounted to about 12 percent of gross provincial expenditures in the late 1920s, fell to about 6 percent in the mid-1930s, then rose to about 18 percent in the mid-1950s. By 1968 these intergovernmental transfers were 23.6 percent of provincial expenditures. These data show that between 1961, when hospitals were first identified in the National Accounts as a "level of government," and 1968 (ibid., Table 3-65) indicate that provincial transfers to hospitals amounted to between 16 and 17 percent of gross provincial expenditures. We note that the provinces, in turn, received a substantial fraction of the amount they transferred to hospitals from the *federal* government.

II. PUBLIC EMPLOYMENT

Bird, et al. (1979, pp.27-28) emphasize that "Public employment is ... at best a partial, and potentially misleading, indicator of the size, growth, and nature of total public sector activity." At the same time they state that "a principal reason for being interested specifically in measures of public employment is that such numbers provide a good indicator of the extent to which the public sector *produces* rather than simply *provides* public services (for example, through financing transfers or purchasing goods and services from the private sector)."

As with expenditure data, methodological problems abound in measuring the volume of public employment. Four principal measures are provided by Bird, et al.:

1. *Civil service employment* is comprised of "those who have been appointed to a government position on a full-time basis and whose entry into government service has been subject to final certification by a central personnel agency." This term is applied, therefore, only to the "hard core" of the *federal* and *provincial* bureaucracies and is the narrowest measure of public employment.

2. *Government employment* is comprised of (1) plus
   - regular employees of municipal governments, and
   - non-civil service but regular employees of federal and provincial governments.

3. *Public sector employment* is comprised of (2) plus
   - teachers and school board employees,
   - most hospital workers, and
   - employees of government enterprises
   This is the broadest concept of *direct* public employment.

4. *Indirect public employment* refers to the number of jobs generated in the private sector as a result of public purchases of goods and services, other than direct labour.

As Table A-5 indicates, in 1975 (the latest year for which we have complete and consistent data) federal and provincial civil service employment amounted to 533,000 persons, total government employment was double this figure (1.02 million) and total public sector employment amounted to 2.243 million. By level of government, we find that 24.2 percent of total public sector employment is at the federal level, 44.4 percent at the provincial level and 31.4 percent at the municipal/local level. It is important to recognize, however, that about half the expenditure on hospitals is financed by the federal government and that a good proportion of other provincial activities is financed in part by the federal government and that a good proportion of other provincial activities is financed in part by federal transfers or contributions to shared cost programs. Similarly, a substantial fraction of municipal government activity is financed by provincial governments, e.g., education, welfare, roads.

Bird, et al. (1979, p. 33) point out that data from *Taxation Statistics* indicate there were 2.4 million "public employees" in 1975. This figure includes employees of non-profit institutions and educational organizations (e.g., universities) that derive the bulk of their revenues from governments. A measure of *indirect public employment* (i.e., (d) above) in 1975 is 685,000 while a crude estimate of the number of casual government employees is 150,000 (ibid., p.34). This would bring the total number of direct and indirect public employees in 1975 to about 3.1 million persons.

In *relative* terms, total public sector employment—measure (c) as defined above—increased only slightly between 1961 and 1975. In the early 1960s public sector employment amounted to 22.2 percent of total employment in Canada. As of 1975, the proportion was 23.7 percent. The slight increase apparently occurred in the late 1960s (ibid., p.43).

TABLE A-5

Public Sector Employment in Canada, 1975

	Thousands	%
• Federal civil service	273.2	12.2
• Provincial civil service	259.9	11.6
Total civil service	533.1	23.8
• Other federal civilian	41.1	1.8
• Armed forces	79.8	3.6
• Other provincial	115.1	5.1
• Municipal	251.3	11.2
Total government employment	1,020.4	45.5
• Education	525.1	23.4
• Hospitals	369.5	16.5
• Government Enterprises	328.1	14.6
Total public sector employment	2,243.1	100.0

By Level of Government

• Federal		24.2%
• Civil service	12.2%	
• Armed forces	3.6	
• Enterprises	6.6	
• Other federal	1.8	
• Provincial		44.4
• Civil service	11.6	
• Other provincial employees	10.4	
• Hospitals	16.5	
• Enterprises	5.9	
• Municipal		31.4
• Employees	11.2	
• Local education	18.1	
• Enterprises	2.1	
Total public sector employment	100.0	100.0

Source: Bird, et al. (1979), pp. 30–32.

The composition of total public employment has changed noticeably, however. Between the early 1960s and 1975 federal government employment (excluding enterprises) fell by one percentage point while that for provincial government increased by 1.3 points. Employment in education and hospitals, as a percentage of total employment, increased by just over one-half a percentage point. As a fraction of total *service* employment in Canada, total public sector employment *fell* from 40.4 percent in 1961 to 36.6 percent in 1975 (ibid., p.45).

What happened to total public employment in Canada between 1961 and 1975 "appears to be very similar to what has happened in a number of other advanced industrial countries, namely, a very slow increase in what most consider to be an already large public employment share" (ibid., p.49). Bird indicates that public sector employment in Canada (which includes government enterprises) as a fraction of total employment was more than 3 percentage points *higher* than in the United States but 3.6 points *lower* than the United Kingdom. It is apparent that public employment in the United Kingdom has grown much more rapidly than in either Canada or the United States.

III. TAX EXPENDITURES

The concept

The expenditures are potential revenues the government chooses not to collect. Kesselman (1977, p. 161) defines them as "any form of incentive or relief granted via the tax system rather than via government expenditures." Smith (1979, p.1) defines tax expenditures as "indirect expenditures which generally take the form of 'special' exemptions, deductions, credits, exclusions, preferential rates or deferrals..."[16] Obviously, the use of the word "special" begs the question of what constitutes the normal or reference tax base. In the final analysis, there must be an element of arbitrariness in estimating the extent of tax expenditures, but so long as all the major assumptions are made clear, the concept is a useful one in analyzing the nature and extent of government.

Tax expenditures are sometimes called tax incentives, loopholes, tax subsidies and backdoor spending. The U.S. General Accounting Office's (1979, p. 1) "primer" in tax expenditures offers the following explanation of the idea that tax revenues forgone are analogous to expenditures:

The tax expenditure concept is based upon the idea that an income tax system can be divided into two parts. One part contains just the rules that are necessary to carry out the revenue-raising function of a tax on income: rules prescribing how net income is to be measured, what the tax unit is, what tax rates apply, and so forth. The other part contains exceptions to these rules that reduce some people's incomes but not others'. *These exceptions have the same effect as Government payments to favored taxpayers.* By identifying these provisions as tax expenditures, officials are better able to determine the total amount of government effort or influence in a program area.

The most obvious reason for identifying and measuring tax expenditures is the fact that "governments can choose to effect economic activity either through direct expenditures and transfers or indirectly through the tax system. Choice of the indirect route does not necessarily mean the government is less involved in an activity" (Smith, 1979, p.8).

Despite their substantial size and distributional consequences (discussed below), these "expenditures" receive very little scrutiny by the legislature beyond their initial authorization or when amendments are made to tax legislation. They are totally beyond the purview of the Auditor General, even though they "often thwart the government's own social goals" (Brooks, 1981, p.30). In the view of Neil Brooks, Osgoode Hall law professor and advisor to the federal Department of Finance,[17] "piecemeal adjustments under various forms of pressure have produced a tax system that would astonish and appal most Canadians if they fully understood it" (ibid.). These "adjustments" in recent years have largely taken the form of "tax expenditures" which amount to "giving by not taking."

This concept of tax expenditures has not gone unchallenged. For example, political columnist W.A. Wilson argues that "there is an implication in the new terminology that the state owns the money, and this is simply not true, although both politicians and senior officials constantly forget that reality." Wilson emphasizes that "the money belongs to the people who worked to get it, and who then necessarily contribute some of it to the official operation of the country.[18] This criticism," he notes, is "not just... nitpicking..., because the psychology is important." The idea that exemptions, deductions, and so forth, are "equivalent to spending programs" implies, in his view, "an extremely statist approach, suggesting that money left with the man or woman who earned it is in some way the same thing as the government spending it on him."

Although the concept has been well known in academic circles since the 1960s,[19] it was only in 1979 that the Canadian federal government produced the first official estimates of the amounts of revenues forgone in the form of tax expenditures.[20] The U.S. federal government published its first "tax expenditure budget" in 1968 and since 1974 Congress has required that one be submitted as part of the annual budget process (ibid., p.32).

Former Liberal Cabinet Minister Eric Kierans has described the tax expenditure concept as "the major innovation in tax and public finance during the past twenty or thirty years."[21]

Personal income tax expenditures

There are more than 100 tax preferences in the Canadian *Income Tax Act*. In Brooks' (ibid., p. 32) view, "whenever the government grants a tax concession or preference, for whatever purpose, it is paying a subsidy." The latest federal study of *personal* income tax expenditures estimated the revenue loss from five income exclusions, sixteen deductions, five exemptions, and six tax credit-type tax expenditures (Government of Canada, 1981, p.6). The benefits, i.e., revenue loss to the *federal* government, amounted to $6.2, $4.0, $2.1 and $1.3 billion respectively, for a total of $13.8 billion in 1979.[22] Because many tax expenditures also automatically reduce *provincial* taxes payable, the total value of personal income tax expenditures is about 50 percent *higher* than that indicated. Federal personal income tax actually collected in 1979 was $17.0 billion. Therefore, the amount of personal tax expenditures ($13.8 billion) is 81 percent of the total personal income tax received by the federal government (Government of Canada, 1981, p.1).

We note that almost one-third of the total value of the $13.8 billion in federal personal income tax expenditures in 1979 resulted from the non-taxation of imputed rent and capital gains on owner-occupied houses (ibid., p.5). This fact has been the focus of some controversy.[23] The idea of taxing imputed rent is hardly new or even unheard of in practice. In the United Kingdom it was taxed as personal income until 1962, when it was removed because of administrative difficulties. In Canada the taxation of imputed rent, however, was rejected by the

Carter Commission in the 1960s as impractical on administrative grounds (see Canada, 1966).

The Department of Finance estimates that for 1979 if tax expenditures embodied in the personal income tax were eliminated and the tax base thereby broadened, "a general cut of 45 percent in tax rates could have been provided and federal revenues would have remained unchanged." (Government of Canada, 1981, p.2). This estimate makes one recall the work of Blum and Kalven (1953), who argued that if a broad definition of income (e.g., Haig-Simons) was incorporated into the U.S. tax code, and if most loopholes were closed, a proportional rate of less than 20 percent would generate the same amount of revenue as the existing progressive rate structure.[24] An obvious benefit of such a system is that thousands of lawyers, accountants and other tax advisors would be liberated to do (more) productive work.

Earlier estimates of personal income tax expenditures

Bird (1970, Appendix A) estimated tax expendiures embodied in the personal income tax at $1,277 million in 1964 or 47 percent of the tax actually collected that year. The National Council of Welfare (1976), using a broad definition of tax expenditures, estimated that the revenue forgone from seventeen tax expenditures in the *Income Tax Act* was $6.4 billion in 1974. However, most writers in the field note that the Council included as tax expenditures items usually accepted as legitimate deductions (see Smith, 1979). Kesselman (1977) did the first detailed (although admittedly incomplete) estimate of tax expenditures embedded in the federal personal income tax system. By 1973, he found that they amounted to $1,723 million. He noted, however, that for the 1974 taxation year, two new tax expenditures were introduced: the Registered Home Ownership Plan and the exemption of the first $1,000 in interest income. If the effective tax rate forgone was only 25 percent, these two new tax expenditures past over $500 million in 1974. Kesselman (ibid., p. 167) notes that "with the elimination of all these 13 deductions, average tax rates on the new taxable income base could have been 19.5 percent lower — assuming no changes in economic behavior are induced." We should note that when provincial tax revenues forgone ($430 million) are included, Kesselman's total for personal tax expenditures in 1973 amounted to $2,153 million. For the same year, Maslove (1970, p.154) put the total at $2,436 million.

Smith (1979, p. 100) estimated that, using a 20 percent marginal rate, tax expenditures in the federal personal income tax were $5.7 billion in 1975; at a 30 percent rate they amounted to $9.3 billion. These two figures amount to 48 percent and 76 percent of personal income taxes actually collected in 1975.

Maslove's (1981) consistent, but conservative, estimates of federal tax expenditures indicate the following:

- Personal income tax expenditures increased from $2.2 billion in 1972 to $9.1 billion in 1978.

- The average annual rate of growth of personal income tax expenditures was 27 percent over the period 1972–1978.

- Personal income tax expenditures increased from 28 percent of personal income tax revenues in 1972 to 64 percent in 1978: as a proportion of total budgetary expenditures they increased from 14 percent to 20 percent over the same period.

Distributional aspects of personal income tax expenditures

Lipsey (1979, p.5) states quite correctly that "ordinary people have strong moral feelings about the distribution of income and these feelings are important determinants of attitudes toward state intervention into the market." The National Council of Welfare (1976), Fallis (1980), Kesselman (1977), Le Pan (1980), Maslove (1979), (1981), Smith (1979), and the Government of Canada (1981) all devote considerable space to the discussion of the distributional effects of personal income tax expenditures. For example, Maslove (1979, p.155) points out that "in 1976 the average tax expenditure received by a taxpayer reporting income under $5,000 was $75, between $15,000 and $20,000 of income it was $649, and to those reporting more than $50,000 of income, it was $6,613." He concludes that "tax expenditures are distributed heavily in favor of higher income groups, thus decreasing the progressivity of the personal income tax system" (ibid., p.157).

The Department of Finance's analysis of federal personal income tax expenditures in 1979 indicates that with the exemption of those

TABLE A-6

Personal Tax Expenditures
as a Percentage of Income, 1979

Income group,	% of tax filers	All tax expenditures incl. housing	excl. housing
under $5,000	30.7%	10.2%	8.5%
5,000 - 15,000	40.0	6.2	3.8
15,000 - 20,000	13.0	7.5	3.9
20,000 - 25,000	7.6	8.6	4.2
25,000 - 30,000	3.9	9.9	5.1
30,000 - 50,000	3.8	12.2	6.7
50,000 - 100,000	0.8	15.1	9.5
100,000 & over	0.2	23.1	19.7
Total or average	100.0	9.3	5.4

Source: Government of Canada (1981, p. 131)

with incomes under $5,000, these tax expenditures increase as a percentage of income in each income group. Consider the data in Table A-6. We should note that one percent of all tax filers in 1979, those with incomes over $50,000, obtained the following shares of the tax expenditures listed:

- 63 percent of exempt capital gains,
- 87 percent of income averaging annuity contracts,
- 41 percent of the dividend tax credits,
- 45 percent of gifts to the Crown,
- 66 percent of MURB investments,
- 77 percent of drilling fund investments, and
- 64 percent of film investments (Government of Canada, 1981, p.19)

It appears to us, particularly in light of the public reaction to the Budget of November 1981, that Canadians prefer a personal income system which is characterized by high nominal average and marginal tax rates and riddled with tax expenditures, most of which benefit only those whose incomes are well above the average. In this way, the illusion of progressively ("soak the rich" in vulgar terms) is maintained while the reality is only a mildly progressive effective rate (ibid., p.16).[25] The benefits of these special exclusions, deductions, exemptions and credits depend upon the advice of accountants, lawyers and other tax advisors. Obviously the latter group would have most to lose if the tax system were to incorporate a broad income base, very few tax expenditures and a much lower proportional rate. Perhaps that is why tax reform is so hard to achieve.

Corporate income tax expenditures

Bird (1970, Appendix A) estimated that in 1964 federal and provincial *corporate* tax expenditures were $545 million or 37 percent of the total corporate taxes actually collected. Perry (1976) analyzed federal and provincial corporation tax expenditures for 1972 and 1973 using effective tax rates of 51.6 percent (1971 and 1972) and 50.8 percent (1973), noting that his estimates do not represent the total potential revenue of the system. He estimates corporate tax expenditures to be $1,309 million in 1971, $1,623 million in 1972 and $2,368 million in 1973.

Just three categories accounted for the great bulk of corporate tax expenditures: the difference between capital cost allowances for tax purposes and economic depreciation; differences in the treatment of exploration, development and depletion expenses; and the non-taxable element of capital gains.

Bird (1979, pp. 118, 120) showed that in the period 1971-1973 corporate tax expenditures amounted to 15 percent of corporate profits before income tax. Actual corporate taxes amounted to between 34 and 40 percent of pre-tax profits. Smith (1979, p.17) extended Perry's analysis of corporate tax expenditures to 1974 and 1975 and estimated that they amounted to $4.9 billion and $4.8 billion respectively, or 75 and 69 percent of actual corporate tax revenues. Note that in 1973 such tax expenditures amounted to 67 percent of federal and provincial corporate taxes. Smith's (1979, p.101) estimate of federal corporation income tax expenditures was $3.9 billion for 1975, or 75 percent of taxes payable in that year. He noted that total federal tax expenditures in Canada in 1975 amounted to 27 to 38 percent of federal direct expenditures. This compares with 25 percent for the U.S. federal government in fiscal 1977.

The latest estimate of federal corporate tax expenditures places the total at $6,184 million in 1980 (Government of Canada, 1980).[26] By comparison, federal corporate income tax collections in 1979 were $7.2 billion. Brooks (1981, p.34), who placed the total at $6 billion in

1979, notes that such tax expenditures have more than doubled since 1976 when they were $2.4 billion. He also indicates that actual corporate tax revenues have declined from 29 to 13 percent of federal revenues between 1951 and 1977. On the changing role of the corporate income tax in general, see Bird (1980).

The most consistent series on tax expenditures embedded in the corporate income tax has been compiled by Maslove (1981). He found that:

1. Corporation income tax expenditures increased from $1.9 billion in 1972 to $4.7 billion in 1975 and then decreased to $4.4 billion in 1977.
2. As a proportion of corporate tax revenues, corporate income tax expenditures rose from 50 percent in 1972 to 67 percent in 1974, then fell to 59 percent in 1976, but rose to 66 percent in 1977.
3. As a proportion of total budgetary expenditures, corporate income tax expenditures declined from 13.8 percent in 1972 to 12.9 percent in 1973, then rose to 14.5 percent in 1974, but fell to 10.4 percent in 1977.

Brooks (1981, p.35) argues that "there is astonishingly little evidence that these tax breaks [for corporations] are effective." He notes that while corporate tax incentives in manufacturing alone cost the government $2.5 billion between 1972 and 1975, the additional amount of investment generated ranged between $340 million and $846 million.

Overview

Brooks (ibid., p.34) states that in 1979 federal tax expenditures through the corporate tax system amounted to $6 billion.[27] The Department of Finance estimates the value of tax expenditures in the federal sales and excise tax system to be $4.5 billion in 1979 (Government of Canada, 1980).[28] Taken together with tax expenditures embedded in the personal income tax, federal tax expenditures amounted to over $24 billion in 1979. Since total direct federal expenditures in 1979 were $52.4 billion (on the National Accounts basis), tax expenditure amounted to 46 percent of actual outlays. In other words, if cash subsidies had been employed instead of forgone revenues, the federal budget would have been almost half again as large as it actually was in 1979.

How do Canadian federal tax expenditures compare to the U.S. expenditures? Maslove (1981, Table 4) shows that as a fraction of budgetary expenditure, the sum of personal and corporate income tax expenditures in the United States ranged from 25.5 percent in 1974 to 23.5 percent in 1975 and steadily increased to 29.8 percent in 1981. Using Maslove's figures and other data collected by the authors, we find the comparable figures for Canada were 27.6 percent in 1972, 25.8 percent in 1973, 30.1 percent in 1975, 26.5 percent in 1976 and 1977, 33.0 percent in 1979 and 29 percent in 1980. In other words, corporate and personal income tax expenditures are about equally important in the fiscal systems of the two countries in relation to budgetary expenditures. Compared to the United Kingdom, however, they are vastly more important. Maslove (ibid., Table 5) indicates that for 1973/74 to 1975/76 personal income tax expenditures amounted to only 5.4, 4.0 and 4.0 percent respectively.

The central point, however, is that tax expenditures as an instrument of government intervention have grown more rapidly than have direct expenditures in the 1970s. Why?

There are three technical reasons why tax expenditures have outpaced budgetary expenditures. First, "since most of the [personal income] tax preferences are in the form of deductions or exemptions from income (rather than tax credits), as incomes rise and individuals move into higher marginal tax brackets [despite indexing of personal exemptions], each deduction translates into a larger tax expenditure" (ibid., p.13). Second, as incomes rise, there is a greater propensity for higher income earners to take advantage of the available deductions or to arrange to receive their income in the form of capital gains, Moreover, as Maslove (ibid., p.13) points out, "As incomes rise people have greater financial capacity to set aside funds in RRSPs, RHOSPs and the like ...." Third, the federal government has increased the number and generosity of specific tax expenditures. Two notable examples are RRSP and RSPs, and the $1000 investment income deduction. In 1979 these two tax expenditures cost $2,000 million and $650 million respectively (Department of Finance, 1980).

IV. REGULATION

Douglas Hartle (1979, p.1) has recently reminded us that "regulation, in the broadest sense, is the essential function of government." Taxes and expenditures, he argues, are special cases of regulation. Therefore, "to examine government regulation is to examine the role and function of government itself — no small task."

Despite its being the most pervasive instrument of government policy, until the Economic Council's Regulation Reference from the First Ministers in 1978,[29] there was almost no effort devoted to defining and measuring the size and scope of government regulation in Canada. This may be because regulation is so hard to measure. Priest, Stanbury and Thompson (1980, p.5) define economic regulation as the "imposition of rules by a government, backed by the use of penalties, that are intended specifically to modify the economic behaviour of individuals and firms in the private sector." Economic regulation is primarily aimed at narrowing certain choice sets. The choices affected are typically in the following areas:

1. prices, e.g., airline fares, minimum wages, certain agricultural products, telephone rates;
2. supply, e.g., broadcasting licences, occupational licensing, agricultural production quotas, pipeline certificates "of public convenience and necessity";
3. rate of return, e.g., public utilities, pipelines;
4. disclosure of information, e.g., securities prospectuses, content labelling;
5. methods of production, e.g., effluent standards, worker health and safety standards;
6. attributes of a product of services, e.g., automobile fuel efficiency standards, safety of children's toys, quality of food products, "Canadian content" requirements in broadcasting;
7. conditions of service, e.g., requirements to act as a common carrier, or not to discriminate in hiring or selling goods and services.

Priest, et al. (1980, p.4) emphasize that the areas affected by economic regulation include not only the traditional forms of "economic" or "direct" regulation, but also what has been called the "new regulation" or "social regulation" (Lilley and Miller, 1977). Direct regulation is industry-specific and affects price, output, rate of return and entry or exit. Social regulation typically affects a broad range of industries although its impact may be much greater on some than on others. It includes environmental regulation, consumer protection legislation, "fairness" regulation, health and safety regulation and cultural regulation.

Table A-7 gives some indication of the enormous scope and coverage of regulation in Canada. The problem is vastly complicated by the fact that Canada is a federal state. Stanbury and Thompson (1981,

TABLE A-7

Types of Regulation in Canada

DIRECT REGULATION

- airlines
- buses
- taxis
- railroads
- trucking
- pipelines
- marketing boards
- commercial fisheries
- broadcasting (radio, t.v.)
- telecommunications (telephone, cable t.v., telegraph)
- energy:
  - oil/natural gas
  - coal
  - nuclear
  - electricity
- financial markets/institutions:
  - banks
  - finance co.
  - trust co.
  - insurance
  - pension plans
  - co-ops/caisse populaires
- occupational regulation (licensure/certification/registration)
- business licensing
- liquor regulation
- rent controls
- minimum wage

SOCIAL REGULATION

- occupational health and safety
- pure food and drug
- hazardous (consumer) products
- transportation safety:
  - airlines
  - railroads
  - marine
  - road/auto
- environmental protection
- culture/recreation regulation
  - language
  - content
- horse racing
- gambling
- land use regulation
- building codes
- human rights

FRAMEWORK REGULATION

- competition policy
- patents
- trademarks
- registered industrial designs
- corporation laws
- securities regulation
- foreign investment
- anti-dumping provisions
- bankruptcy
- labour standards
- collective bargaining

Table 1) indicate that in 38 of the 58 types of regulation listed in their table, two or more levels of government are involved.

Stanbury and Burns (1982) described the Department of Consumer and Corporate Affairs (CCA) as a regulatory department par excellence. For example, in 1982/83 it will spend about $105 million administering and enforcing about 60 statutes and more than 70 sets of regulations, many in conjunction with other departments. It has *primary* responsibility for nine consumer protection statutes, eight corporate affairs statutes, five intellectual/industrial property statutes and the *Combines Investigation Act*.

In constant (1971) dollars, CCA's budget doubled between 1967/68 and 1974/75 and has remained roughly constant since that time. In terms of authorized person-years, CCA increased from 1,470 in 1967/68 to 2,688 in 1977/78 and then declined somewhat to 2,371 in 1982/83. Between 1970 and 1978, when more new regulatory statutes were enacted by the federal government than in the previous thirty years, CCA accounted for one-quarter of the total. Only the Liberal government's failure of political will prevent CCA from doubling this large legislative output (see Stanbury and Burns, 1982).

How do we measure the amount of government regulation? A variety of proxy measures have been used:

1. *The proportion of economic activity subject to direct regulation,* i.e., the value of output subject to some form of price and/or output (including entry) control. This measure, we must note, gives no indication of the stringency of such controls.
2. *The government's budgetary outlays to conduct its regulatory activities.* These, as we shall see, are small and give no indication of the costly larger *indirect* effects of regulation on private sector activity, e.g., the administration of pollution control regulations may cost only a few million dollars but the capital and operating costs of the emission controls to firms may amount to hundreds of millions of dollars.
3. *The number of statutes and pieces of subordinate legislation (e.g., regulations) by which economic regulation is effected.* It should be obvious that this is the crudest proxy of all because it says nothing about the actual economic *effects* of these pages of legislation.

We will now provide estimates for each of these measures.

Economic activity subject to direct regulation

Stanbury and Thompson (1980) have estimated that in Canada 29 percent of Gross Domestic Product at factor cost was subject to *direct* regulation in 1978. (Note, this is before the imposition of the National Energy Program which greatly increased regulation of the petroleum industry.) The comparable figure for the United States was 26 percent. To determine the scope of direct regulation, they first identified the contribution to real domestic product at factor cost (GDP) made by each industry or activity in both the United States and Canada. Next, they identified all industries subject to price and/or supply controls and estimated the proportion of industry output subject to these controls in 1978. In addition, they made a qualitative judgment as to the predominant type of control exercised with respect to to each industry or activity. Finally, these estimates were summed to produce an estimate of the proportion of total economic activity subject to direct regulation (see Stanbury and Thompson, 1980, Table 5).

They note that the most frequently cited estimate of the size of the regulated sector in the United States (17 percent of GNP) is given by Posner (1975, pp. 818–819). The difference between their estimate and Posner's primarily reflects the fact that Posner ignores a number of industries and activities that are subject to price and supply control of greater or lesser severity than those included in his list.

Stanbury and Thompson (1980) indicate that in nearly every industry group, either the scope or the coverage of regulation (sometimes both) is broader or more comprehensive in Canada than in the United States. While these were not dramatic differences, they were consistent. They found also that about half of the difference in the two estimates is explained by differences in the weights of the industry groups in the two countries. They also found that virtually all industries or activities subject to these controls in one country were also subject to direct regulation in the other. These include transportation, energy (notably electricity and petroleum), telecommunications, broadcasting, insurance, banking, securities, and a substantial proportion of the agricultural sector, as well as a large number of licensed occupations and businesses. Moreover, Stanbury and Thompson (1980) found that the same industries tend to be subject to the same *type* of controls in both Canada and the United States.

Regulatory effort

(a) *Federal expenditures*
In 1977/78 Stanbury and Thompson (1980) estimated that the federal government in Canada spent $678 million on the administration of regulatory programs.[30] This amounted to only 1.6 percent of total budgetary expenditures. For the same year U.S. federal regulatory expenditures were $4,862 million or slightly less than 1.1 percent of total federal expenditures. Such expenditures, of course, are the mere "tip

of the iceberg." Their economic impact may be many times greater. For example, Weidenbaum and DeFina (1978, p.2) estimate that the private sector's cost of complying with federal regulation in the United States is almost 20 times the government's budgetary outlays.

While not all of these compliance costs are costs to society (they include some transfers, for example), Weidenbaum and DeFina's estimates make us aware that the social costs of regulation far exceed the government's "administrative costs." It should be noted, however, that Green and Waitzman (1979) have challenged Weidenbaum and DeFina's methodology and their results. In turn, Miller (1979) has extensively criticized Green and Waitzman's analysis. In our view, private sector compliance costs with respect to Canadian federal regulation are far below those in the United States because of the latter's more extensive and more stringent health and safety and environmental regulations. They could well amount to 10 to 15 times the government's budgetary outlays.

Stanbury and Thompson (1980) note that in 1970/71 U.S. federal expenditures on regulation were 5.6 times those of Canada and 7.2 times Canadian expenditures in 1977/78. However, the total volume of economic activity in the United States potentially subject to regulation (GNP less the government sector) was 11.6 and 9.3 times as large as that in Canada in 1970 and 1977 respectively. Therefore, in proportional terms, Canada's federal regulatory effort, measured in terms of expenditures, was *twice* that of the United States in 1970/71 and 30 percent greater in 1977/78.

(b) *Federal regulatory employment*
In 1977/78 regulatory employees in Canadian federal departments and agencies accounted for 5.9 percent of total federal employment (ibid.,). In the United States the comparable figure was 3.1 percent. Although the ratio of total federal government employment in the United States and Canada 1970/71 was 9.5 to 1, that for federal *regulatory* employment was only 3.3 to 1. In that year, federal regulatory activities accounted for 5.3 percent of total federal employment in Canada. The comparable figure for the United States was 1.84 percent.

By 1977/78 the ratio of U.S. to Canadian federal regulatory employment had increased slightly to 3.7 to 1, while the ratio of total federal government employment fell to 7.0 to 1. Total U.S. federal employment actually fell slightly over the 1970s. During the same period,

Canadian federal employment grew by 30 percent. Therefore, in terms of the "number of regulators," it seems clear that at the federal level Canada makes a considerably larger regulatory effort than does the United States.

(c) *Number and pages of regulations*

There are just under 10,000 pages of regulations and other statutory instruments stemming from federal regulatory statutes in the 1978 *Consolidated Regulations of Canada.* The total number of pages of regulations, orders and other statutory instruments pursuant to all federal statutes is about 14,420 (Priest and Wohl, 1980). This may be contrasted with the 75,000 pages in the 1977 U.S. *Code of Federal Regulations.* Furthermore, the U.S. Code is set in even finer print and is unilingual, while the Canadian is bilingual, which more than doubles the number of pages.

It does not appear, however, that the number of pages of regulatory statutes is a very good index of the extent of regulation. Consider, for example, the American and Canadian consumer product safety statutes. Stanbury and Thompson (1981) found that, in terms of function and jurisdiction, the two bodies of regulation are remarkably similar. Yet the U.S. regulations contain five or six times the number of pages as the Canadian. For example, Canadian federal hazardous products statutes total 10 pages in length while the consolidated U.S. statutes are 93 pages long. The same holds for other statutes in this area of regulation: motor vehicle safety, 24 pages v. 81 pages; food, drugs, and cosmetics, 25 pages v. 145 pages; etc. These differences seem to be largely attributable to differences in drafting practices.

Regulatory growth

The same measures that have been used to indicate the scope and coverage of regulations have also been used to indicate its *growth:* pages of regulations, number of programs, important legislative initiatives, and public expenditures. Stanbury and Thompson (1980) conclude that while it is difficult to make precise comparisons using similar measures, the growth of federal regulation in Canada in the 1970s in general terms was about as great as it was in the United States.[31] Federal regulatory expenditures in Canada increased by 212 percent between 1970/71 and 1977/78 as compared with 298 percent in the United States. Regulatory expenditures as a proportion of total federal expenditures in Canada, however, remained the same — 1.6 percent. Canadian federal regulatory employment increased by 45 percent between 1970/71 and 1977/78, somewhat above the increase in total federal employment of 30 percent, but only slightly more than the 39 percent increase in real GNP. In contrast, the total population only increased by nine percent over the same seven-year period.

The stock of new or re-enacted regulatory statutes increased more than did federal regulatory employment in the 1970s. Of the 140 federal economic regulatory statutes at the end of 1978, twenty-seven were enacted between 1970 and 1978. An additional ten had been passed earlier but were re-enacted in the 1970s (Priest and Wohl, 1980). More new federal regulatory statutes were passed between 1970 and 1978 than were passed between 1940 and 1969.

Twenty-one new regulatory statutes and ten re-enactments were passed between 1970 and 1975. The new regulatory statutes were concentrated in a few areas:

1. environmental protection: *Arctic Waters Pollution Prevention Act* (1970), *Clean Air Act* (1971), *Environmental Contaminents Act* (1975), *Ocean Dumping Control Act* (1975);
2. health and safety: *Motor Vehicle Safety Act* (1970), *Radiation Emitting Devices Act* (1970), *Railway Relocation and Crossing Act* (1974); and
3. consumer protection: *Textile Labelling Act* (1970), *Consumer Packaging and Labelling Act* (1971), *Investment Companies Act* (1971).

Between 1950 and 1970 the number of new regulations amendments or revocation of existing federal regulations (i.e., subordinate legislation) ranged between 98 and 143 annually. In the 1970s, the number increased in every year except 1972, reaching 352 in 1977 (ibid., 1980 p.91).

The growth of provincial regulation in the 1970s in Canada, as measured by the volume of statutes and pages of regulations, appears similar to that of the federal government. For example, 262 of the 1,608 provincial regulatory statutes on the books in 1978 were enacted between 1970 and 1978. The *increase* in the volume of regulations pursuant to regulatory legislation in three provinces, including the two largest, was as follows:

	% Increase in Number of Regulations	% Increase in Number of Pages
Manitoba, 1971 to 1978	71	222
Ontario, 1970 to 1978	103	78
Quebec, 1972 to 1978	148	78

Source: Economic Council, (1978, p.16)

The regulatory instrument

Courchene (1980, p.563) argues that "the real battle over the future role of government and, therefore, the future role of markets, will be fought on the regulatory front." While public attention is focused on the more visible manifestations of government activity, notably taxes and direct expenditures, expansionist governments are more likely to reach for the regulatory tool. Its fiscal implications, in terms of the dollars in the Estimates or Public Accounts, are very small. Probably 95 percent of its costs are borne in the private sector in the form of higher prices, lower incomes or slower economic growth. Doern (1978, p.17) argues that governments will seek to adopt the least coercive instrument. Becker (1956, 1981) argues that they choose the most efficient one, the one whose cost is lowest given the desired level of effectiveness. Trebilcock et al. (1982) argue that the choice of instruments is based on the politician's calculus of marginal voters, constitutional constraints and the existence of imperfect information. In our view, in an era of fiscal stringency, governments will opt for those instruments of intervention that are *least visible* to the general population. If this is the case, the growth of governments will be expressed in terms of more regulation, but other instruments as well, e.g., tax expenditures.

V. PUBLIC ENTERPRISES/CROWN CORPORATIONS

Gordon (1981, p.1) emphasizes, and we concur, that "any discussion of the role of government that excludes [state-run commercial enterprises] provides an increasingly less representative view of the way governments affect the lives of all Canadians." Langford (1979, p.239) puts the matter very simply when he states that "throughout Canada's history as a nation, Crown corporations have been used at the federal level as instruments of public policy." They have also been fundamental instruments of provincial public policy. Herschel Hardin (1974, p.54) expresses the idea more strongly when he states that public enterprises are "one of the most vibrant expressions of the Canadian character." In fact, he argues that Canada is a "public enterprise country" — a fact that was "forced on us by American expansionism" (Hardin, 1974, p.55).

Our first public enterprise, which built the Lachine Canal, was owned by the Government of Lower Canada. It came into existence in 1821 when a private firm failed to get the job done (Hardin, 1974, p.56). The Privy Council Office (1977, p.11) suggests that the first Crown corporation in Canada was established in 1841, also to construct a canal system. It argues that "the creation of the Canadian National Railways in 1919 has generally been seen as the first major venture into public enterprise.[32] The second was the creation of the Canadian Broadcasting Corporation in 1932. As Borins (1982) notes, World War II resulted in the creation of about three dozen federal Crown corporations, (FCCs) only some of which were discontinued after the war. The Privy Council Office (1977, p.12) put the number of FCCs in operation in 1951 at 33. In 1950 the *Financial Administration Act* was passed. It was "intended to lay the foundation for a more uniform and systematic financial relationship between the ministry and Parliament on the other" (ibid., pp.12–13).

In the first decade of the twentieth century the foundations of Ontario Hydro were laid. It is now the second largest non-financial corporation in Canada in terms of assets. In addition, the Governments of Manitoba and Saskatchewan took over the Bell Company's operations while the Province of Alberta started a competitive telephone company. In the 1970s there was a tremendous boom in provincial Crown corporations (PCCs). Vining and Botterell (1983) estimate that of the 233 PCCs in existence in 1980, 48 percent had been created between 1970 and 1979 and 75 percent since 1960.

Gracey (1978, p.25) attributes Canada's reliance on public enterprise as a major instrument of public policy "to the Canadian situation: a vast country, rich in natural resources but small in population, bordering on the United States, the most dominant economic power in the world." In his view, Crown corporations have been used primarily to provide essential services (transportation and communication), to develop natural resources, and to operate public utilities, e.g., hydroelectricity. In contrast to Gracey, a recent policy document emanating from a federal central agency began its discussion of the philosophy behind the Crown corporation policy as follows:

> Crown corporations have been established by successive govern-
> ments for an almost bewildering array of purposes. In addition,
> individual Crown corporations may have been established with
> one purpose in mind but governments have added additional ob-
> jectives to the corporations' mandates or, in some extreme cases,
> the original purpose for incorporation has been lost sight of com-
> pletely.

It then emphasizes the public policy objectives of such enterprises.

> ..., however, it is clear that every Crown corporation has been
> created to attain a public policy objective or set of public policy
> objectives. Although the specific objectives may change over
> time, the fact remains that Crown corporations' primary *raison
> d'etre* is the achievement of stated government policy objectives.[33]

Despite the number and importance of public enterprises in the Canadian economy, "little sustained attention has been paid to the
behaviour and performance of public enterprises, the politics of nationalization, the political and economic impact of government business, or the dynamics of decision-making" (Tupper, 1979, p.124). This
situation, however, is changing.[34]

How many?

(a) *Federal Crown corporations*
Nobody knows precisely how many federal Crown corporations
(FCCs) there are. Like the begetting and begats in the Bible, one
Crown corporation creates others. While everyone knows the names
of the largest FCCs, e.g., Air Canada, NCR, AECL, CBC, CMHC,
Petro-Canada and the Federal Business Development Bank, not even
Ottawa specialists can provide the names of *all* federal Crown corporations. For example, in 1977 the Privy Council Office published a
list of 366 "government-owned and controlled corporations." A revised list in January 1978 put the total at 383 and in August 1979 the list
was extended to 401 (Langford and Huffman, 1983).

In the next year, the Comptroller General (1980) identified 464
FCCs. The *Financial Administration Act* records 56 FCCs on its
various "schedules." The Comptroller General's list included 23
wholly-owned FCCs excluded from the FAA schedules, 25 corporations in which the federal government holds an interest, 213 sub-

sidiaries and subsubsidiaries of previously named corporations and 126 "associated" corporations (Gordon, 1981, pp.3–4). Revisions by the Comptroller General (1981) produced a list of 306 corporations "in which the federal government has an interest."[35] This figure excludes all subsidiaries or associated corporations of the 22 mixed enterprises corporations. The latter are corporations with share capital owned jointly with other governments and other organizations or both.

The 306 corporations[36] are classified as follows:

1. Crown corporations
   - Departmental corporations   14
   - Agency corporations   20
   - Proprietary corporations   23
                                                                  ———
                                                                   57

   - Associated corporations of Departmental corporations   1
   - Subsidiaries of Agency corporations   2
   - Associated corporations of Proprietary corporations   58
                                                                  ———
                                                                  175

2. Other corporations
   - Other government corporations   22
   - Mixed enterprises   22
   - Other entities and associates   27
   - Subsidiaries of other government corporations   7
                                                                  ———
                                                                   78

Departmental corporations include the Economic Council of Canada, the Atomic Energy Control Board and the National Museums of Canada. They are treated as departments under the *Financial Administration Act* and are responsible for "administrative, supervisory or regulatory services of a governmental nature." Agency corporations are "responsible for the management of trading or service operations on a quasi-commercial basis, or for the management of procurement, construction or disposal activities...." They usually have their own Act and include AECL, Canada Post Corporation, the Canadian Dairy Commission and Loto Canada Inc. (now disbanded). Proprietary corporations include Air Canada, CMHC, CBC, Farm Credit

Corporation and Petro-Canada. Proprietary corporations are "responsible for the management of lending or financial operations or for the management of commercial and industrial operations involving the production of or dealing in goods and the supplying of services to the public." They are "ordinarily required to conduct [their] operations without appropriations" (Privy Council Office, 1977, pp.82, 83).

"Other corporations" are owned or controlled solely by the federal government but have not been designated as Crown corporations. They include the Bank of Canada, the Canadian Wheat Board, de Havilland Aircraft of Canada Limited and the nine Harbour Commissions. Mixed enterprise corporations include the Canada Development Corporation, Canarctic Shipping Company Limited, the Caribbean Development Bank and Telesat Canada. Associated corporations are those in which Crown and other government corporations hold a minority interest. For example, the CNR has a minority interest in 19 companies and its subsidiaries have a minority interest in 14 others. In terms of subsidiaries and subsubsidiaries, the Comptroller General (1981) indicates Air Canada has five subsidiaries and six subsubsidiaries. The CNR has 23 of each.

The data on the number of federal Crown corporations are confusing. For example, according to the Royal Commission on Financial Management and Accountability (1979), there were 54 FCCs and another 25 "shared enterprises." (The former number includes 8 marketing agencies.) These numbers do not include subsidiaries of FCCs, which, as we have noted, greatly swell the number.[36] The gross understatement of the number of FCCs is also found in Gracey (1978, p.27) who states that there were 55 in existence in 1977 as opposed to 32 in 1950. Statistics Canada's compilation on the finances of government enterprises recorded 28 federal and 58 provincial enterprises in 1958. By the end of 1977 these numbers had increased to 50 and 106 respectively (Gordon, 1981, p.11).

Although the federal government's own counts of the number of Crown corporations increased between May 1977 and March 1980 from 366 to 464, Langford and Huffman (1983, p.225) state that "there are still a large number of corporations unidentified."[37] Their own list records 454 federal public corporations as of May 1980.[38] In 81 of these the government is the sole owner. In another 38 the government is a joint owner or has a membership interest. The remaining federal Crown corporations are subsidiaries or subsubsidiaries. Indeed, the CNR, Petro-Canada and the Canada Development Corporation[39] jointly had over 200 subsidiaries in early 1980.

The number of federal public corporations has increased greatly in the last two decades. Langford and Huffman (1983, p.274) state that 58 percent of the 119 on their list (excluding subsidiaries) were created between 1960 and 1980, while 27 percent were created between 1940 and 1960.

(b) *Provincial Crown Corporations*
Vining and Botterell (1983) identified 233 Provincial Crown corporations (PCCs) operating in 1980. The number by Province was as follows:

Nfld.	42	Sask.	25[40]	P.E.I.	10
B.C.	36	Alta.	20	N.B.	9
Que.	35	Man.	13	N.W.T.	2
Ont.	27	N.S.	10	Yukon	2
Regional	2				

While 75 percent of all PCCs were created since 1960, less than half this proportion (33 percent) of assets were created since 1960. Since 1970 some 48 percent of PCCs were created, but since that year only 13 percent of total assets were created (ibid., p.320).

Vining and Botterell (ibid., pp.308–17) grouped the 233 PCCs in 1980 into 24 "functional" categories:

— Agricultural development (13)
— Banking, saving, investment (5)
—-Forest development and manufacturing (13)
— Government buildings (3)
— Government computer services (4)
— Housing (18)
— Industrial development (31)
— Insurance: general and automobile (5)
— Liquor distribution (12)
— Lotteries (4)
— Marketing & brokerage facilities (18)

— Mining and development (10)
— Manufacturing (10)
— Municipal finance (5)
— Oil and gas (5)
— Power utilities (11)
— Research and development (13)
— School and hospital financing (17)
— Shipyards (2)
— Steel (3)
— Telephones & communications (8)
— Transportation facilities (7)
— Transportation services (14)
— Water supply (2)

Distinguishing characteristics

Christopher Green (1980, p.249) emphasizes that "it is probably impossible to provide a single unambiguous and generally accepted definition for the term 'public enterprise' which can clearly differentiate among the numerous activities governments undertake." What are the distinguishing characteristics of government-owned enterprises? Gordon (1981, p.6) emphasizes the point that they operate in a market setting and undertake activities similar to those of their private sector counterparts. They may or may not operate in competition with privately owned firms. They usually have a corporate form or organization and are *not* subject to statutory requirements concerning civil service employment. Most importantly, they depend *largely* (but not exclusively) on the sale of their outputs to cover their cost and finance expansion.

Vining and Botterell (1983, p.307) indicate the crucial characteristics of a public enterprise: it is expected to pay its own way through the sale of goods and services in the marketplace. Yet FCCs are not simply commercial enterprises owned by the federal government. As the Royal Commission on Financial Management and Accountability (1979, p.329) stated, "most are created as instruments of national purpose and that purpose, as expressed in their mandates, extends beyond the business at hand." The Commission continues, "indeed, if this were not true, there would be little to justify government involvement in them."

Gordon (1981) classifies federal and provincial government business enterprises in terms of their rationale or circumstances of creation as follows:

1. "natural monopolies," e.g., electricity and gas distribution, telephone systems and transit utilities;
2. "nation builders," e.g., CNR, Air Canada, CBC, PWA, Alberta Energy Co., Petro-Canada and the CDC;
3. "regional development," e.g., B.C. Railway, Alberta Resources Railway, provincial development corporations (most of which were created in the 1960s and 1970s);
4. "bailouts," e.g., Cape Breton Development Corp., Canadian Cellulose, Minaki Lodge, Sydney Steel Corp.;
5. "pioneer ventures," e.g., Polysar Ltd., Eldorado Nuclear, Panarctic Oils, Syncrude, AECL, Urban Transportation Development Corporation; and

6. "rent collectors," e.g., Potash Corporation of Saskatchewan, B.C. Petroleum Corp.

Economic significance

Unfortunately we have no simple measure of the economic significance of Crown corporations, such as the fraction of GNP produced by federal and provincial enterprises. Because so little is known of their activities, the Auditor General (1982, p.13) was moved to describe federal Crown corporations as follows: "It may be helpful in visualizing the scale of the problem to think of the whole group as an enormous iceberg, floating lazily in the foggy Atlantic; silent, majestic, awesome."

Some data, however, are available to assess the economic significance of Crown corporations. Walter Block (1982, pp.38–39) compiled a list of the largest corporate employers in Canada and found that Crown corporations occupied seven of the top 50 places. They ranked number 2, 12, 14, 21, 28, 45 and 46, respectively. In terms of assets in 1979/80, Block (1982, p.36) found that the largest federal and provincial non-financial Crown corporations ranked in the largest 87 of all non-financial corporations. In fact, the first and second largest non-financial corporations (by assets) in Canada in 1983 were Hydro-Quebec and Ontario Hydro.[41] Petro-Canada ranked number 6 and CN ranked number 12. In terms of financial enterprises, eight Crown corporations ranked in the top 35 as measured by assets in 1983. Four of the eight ranked in the top 20 financial corporations. In 1983, 16 federal and 23 provincial non-financial Crown corporations were among the 500 largest enterprises in terms of sales (*Financial Post 500,* Summer 1984; *Report on Business 1000,* June 1984).

Table A-8 summarizes some of the salient characteristics of the largest 35 Crown corporations in Canada. It indicates that just over one-half are provincially owned. A similar proportion is subject to direct regulation. These are the power utilities, the telephone companies, the airlines and the railroads. Canada, it seems, feels the need to layer government regulation on top of government ownership in much the same way that some terribly insecure men wear both belt and suspenders.

Of the top 35, eight Crown corporations are electric power utilities and a similar number are financial institutions. Like Block's tally, ours indicates that Crown corporations in Canada rank well up in the *Financial Post*'s list of the largest non-financial corporations. Seven-

TABLE A-8

Characteristics of the 35 Largest Canadian Crown Corporations, 1980

Crown Corp.	Prov. owned	Regulated**	Hydro	Financial Corp.	Monopoly	Capital intensive**	F.P. 400 (rev.)	Rank Among Fin. Inst. (assets)
Hydro-Quebec	X	X	X		X	X	26	
Bank of Canada				X	X			6*
Ontario Hydro	X	X	X		X	X	20	
Caisse de Dépôt... (Quebec)	X			X				7
Can. Mtge & Housing Corp.				X				8
B.C. Hydro	X	X	X		X	X	74	
Alberta Heritage Fund	X	X		X		X		10*
Can. Nat. R.R.							11	
Petro-Canada							64	
Export Dev. Corp				X				12*
Farm Credit Corp				X				15*
Manitoba Hydro	X	X	X		X	X	153	
Can. Wheat Board		X			X		10*	
New Brunswick Electric	X	X	X		X	X	138	
Atomic Energy Can. Ltd.		X				X	115	
Fed. Business Dev. Bank				X				19
Alta. Gov't Telephones	X	X			X	X	91	
Air Canada	X	X					35	
Sask. Power	X	X	X		X	X	128	

							in top 200
Nfld. Hydro	X		X		X	X	239
Canada Dev. Corp.****	X				X		29
Royal Can. Mint	X			X	X		63
Societe Generale...(Quebec)	X			X			41
Sidbec (steel)	X					X	104
Potash Corp. of Sask.	X	X			X	X	142
Nova Scotia Power	X						170
De Havilland	X	X				X	202
Alberta Energy Co.****	X	X					210
Pacific Western Airlines	X	X					212
Sask. Tel.	X	X			X	X	221
Man. Tel.	X	X			X	X	224
B.C. Railway	X	X			X	X	297
Nordair						X	321
Canadair					X	X	337
Teleglobe	X	X			X	X	345
n = 35	19	18	8	8	15	18 of 27	17/27

* not on *Financial Post's* 400 list, ranked by author.

** includes Cabinet regulation.

*** assets at least twice sales — excludes financial enterprises, n = 8.

**** should be classified as a mixed enterprise, see section VII.

Source: Compiled by W.T. Stanbury.

teen of the 27 largest federal and provincial Crown corporations were in the top 200 in 1980. Of the 27 non-financial public enterprises, 18 are capital intensive in that their total assets amount to at least twice their annual revenues. Fifteen of the 35 are essentially monopolists in their industry.

The Auditor General (1983, p.52) has remarked that, "Many of the Crown-owned corporations, large and small, have monopolistic or significant positions in a segment of the economy." Of particular concern was the degree to which such corporations are accountable to Parliament. If such economically important entities are not accountable to Parliament on behalf of their owners, the people of Canada, and if they are in a position to exercise considerable market power, their effective exemption from the *Combines Investigation Act* is of even greater significance.[42] The same proposition applies to provincial Crown corporations. Where such entities are engaged in commercial activities they should be subject to the same laws of general application as are privately owned firms.

Langford and Huffman (1983, p.288) categorizes 61 of the 119 federal Crown corporations (excluding subsidiaries) on their list as being "corporate enterprises." These firms (and their 213 subsidiaries) operate in the following sectors: communications; culture and recreation; financing, insurance and business services; industrial development; manufacturing; marketing, wholesaling and trading; resource development; and transportation systems and facilities. Only 29 would be included in Statistics Canada's definition of "government business enterprises," i.e., the production of economic goods and provision of services for sale to the consumer at a price intended to wholly or largely cover costs. Its definition also includes the notion of being in competition with privately owned firms or operating as a monopoly for the sale of goods and services that would otherwise be provided by a privately owned enterprise. Langford and Huffman's broader definition focuses on the "production of generally marketable goods and services" by government-owned enterprises. The point is that while not all federal Crown corporations produce and sell goods and services in competition with privately owned firms, a great many do.

Langford and Huffman (1983, p.296) note that their list of 61 federal "corporate enterprises" in 1978/79 represented roughly 68 percent of the total assets of the federal government; 32 percent of total federal government employment (departments, armed forces and federal government enterprise employment); and had revenues equal to 37

TABLE A-9

Measures of the Size of Federal Crown Corporations

Date	Source	Assets	Revenues	Employees	Comments
Mar. 31, 1979	Langford (1983)	$53.5 billion	$14.7 billion (net income $1.7 billion)	183,000	61 "corporate" enterprises & their 213 subsidiaries
Mar. 31, 1979	Statistics Canada, fed. gov't enterprises	$35.1 billion	$10.5 billion	149,000	as given in Langford and Huffman (1983)
Mar. 31, 1982	Auditor General (1982)	$66.8* billion	$28.5 billion	263,225	261 agency, proprietary corps. (incl. Canada Post, 69,457 employees)
Mar. 31, 1982	Auditor General (1982)	$7.5 billion	$6.1 billion	not available	48 mixed enterprises and other federal gov't corp.

* excludes Canada Post, which became a Crown corporation on 16 October 1981, because valuation was not completed. Canada Post was, however, included in the revenues figure.

percent of federal tax and fee revenues. In terms of both assets and revenues, federal corporate enterprises in 1978/79 accounted for 12 to 13 percent of total public and private sector activity in the eight sectors listed above.

Bird (1979, p.102) indicates that the revenues of federal Crown corporations increased from $2,087 million in 1961 to $5,477 million in 1975 while the comparable figures for provincial corporations were $1,374 million and $8,302 million respectively. Bird (1979, p.4) notes that between 1961 and 1975 the sales revenue of federal and provincial government enterprises declined as a proportion of government revenues—from 30 percent in the early 1960s to 20 to 22 percent in the first half of the 1970s. Except for a dip in the late 1960s, government enterprise revenues stayed at just over 8 percent of GNP. Using a more inclusive definition of Crown corporations (see Table A-9), we find that the revenues of federal Crown corporations were $14.7 billion in 1978/79 and almost doubled to $28.5 billion in 1981/82, 12 percent of which was received from the federal government.

The total assets of the 233 provincial Crown corporations amounted to $62.3 billion in 1977 or 10.1 percent of all corporate assets and 26.2 percent of corporate *fixed* assets.[43] The PCCs assets were substantially larger than the total assets of the federal and provincial governments (Vining and Botterell, 1983, p.318). The Royal Commission on Financial Management and Accountability (1979, p.328) states that in 1977/78, the assets of federal Crown corporations amounted to $29 billion out of a total of $75 billion in federal government assets.

As a measure of their relative importance, Vining and Botterell (1983, p.326) calculated the ratio of total PCC assets to Gross Domestic Product for each of the provinces. The result was as follows:

Nfld.	123%	N.B.	33%	Ont.	23%
Man.	47	B.C.	32	N.S.	19
Que.	47	Alta.	25	P.E.I.	13
Sask.	33				

We should note that Vining and Botterell (1983, p.341) put the total assets of the provincial power utilities at $34.5 billion or 55 percent of the assets of all PCCs. They also indicate that the assets of the 11 provincial power utilities amounted to 81.5 percent of the assets of both publicly and privately owned firms in that sector.

The Auditor General (1982, p.51) states that the 261 federal agency, proprietary and government corporations (the others are mixed enterprises and "other entities") had assets of $66.8 billion on March 31, 1982. Their revenues in 1981/82 totalled $28.5 billion. Mixed enterprises and "other entities had assets of $7.5 billion and revenues of $6.1 billion (see Table A-9).

Gordon (1981, Appendix A), using Statistics Canada data, notes that the assets of federal enterprises grew from $6.5 billion in 1958 to $35.1 billion in 1978. Provincial enterprises grew even more rapidly, from assets of $5.1 billion in 1958 to $55.6 billion in 1978. At the end of 1977 the assets of federal and provincial enterprises totalled $87.8 billion or 14 percent of total corporation assets of $620 billion (Gordon, 1981, p.110). The government enterprises' share of *fixed* assets (reflecting the enormous capital investment of the provincial hydros) was even higher—28 percent.

Tupper and Doern (1981, p.7) indicate that of seventeen major federal Crown corporations, twelve more than doubled their assets between 1970/71 and 1979/80 while eight trebled in size. The most rapid growth was experienced by the Export Development Corporation, whose assets swelled from $348 million in 1970/71 to $3,175 million in 1979/80. The assets of Petro-Canada increased from $721 million in 1976/77, its first year of operation, to $3,411 million in 1979/80. With the takeover of Petrofina Inc. in 1981, the oil company's assets as of December 31, 1983 were $8.2 billion.

The importance of government business enterprises in the nation's capital formation is illustrated by the following data in Gordon (1981, p.250). Business enterprises of all three levels accounted for 15.0 percent of all public and private investment in Canada in 1980. In total, governments accounted for 27.5 percent of domestic capital formation. The *share* of total investment attributable to government departments decreased between 1960 and 1980 while that of government enterprises increased. (It was 8.9 percent in 1981.) The result was that the total government share of capital investment in Canada decreased slightly from 30.4 percent in 1960 to 27.5 percent in 1980.

The Auditor General (1982, p.51) noted that the 261 federal agency, proprietary and government corporations had 263,225 employees in March of 1982. Canada Post, which became a Crown corporation on October 16, 1981, alone had 69,457 employees on March 31, 1982. By comparison, all the federal departments on the same date had 221,000 employees while the Armed Forces and the RCMP had another 83,000 and 18,000, respectively. Bird (1979, p.4) noted, however, that federal and provincial enterprise employment appears to have declined slightly as a fraction of total employment in Canada between 1961 and 1975. In the early 1960s it amounted to 3.2 to 3.4 percent while in the early 1970s it was 2.8 or 2.9 percent of total employment.

In terms of employment, the 17 major federal Crown corporations in Tupper and Doern's list grew far less rapidly than they did in terms of assets. They grew from 116,426 in 1970/71 to 122,587 in 1977/78, an increase of only 5.3 percent. We might note that the CNR accounted for the great bulk of employment on this list of 17 FCCs: 82,400 in 1970/71 and, 78,700 in 1977/78 (Tupper & Doern, 1981, p.8).

VI. LOANS AND LOAN GUARANTEES

Economic significance

The Economic Council of Canada (1982b, p.3) points out that "through its financial intermediation activities, government ranks second to the chartered banks among Canada's financial institutions." Federal and provincial agencies accounted for 18.1 percent of the assets of the major financial institutions in Canada in 1980 (ibid., p.2). The value of federal and provincial loans and investments, loan guarantees and credit insurance[44] extended to the private sector amounted to 18.5 percent of GNP in 1980. In contrast, the ratio was 4.3 percent in 1950, but 13.2 percent in 1930 and 15.6 percent in 1939 (ibid., p.3).

The federal government accounted for 74 percent of all government loans and investments and 95 percent of all guarantees and credit insurance in force in March 1980 (ibid., p.5). Government financial assistance in 1980 was concentrated in four sectors: business, 13.6 percent; exports, 11.1 percent; housing, 60.0 percent; and agriculture, 10.9 percent (ibid., p.6). This assistance was provided through some 42 agencies and boards as well as through a number of ad hoc arrangements. While the federal government's aid was concentrated in the four sectors listed above, the provinces were more active in natural resources, housing and agriculture.

Some idea of the significance of federal and provincial financial activities for specific sectors can be adjudged by the following. In agriculture, governments account for 30 percent of all credit outstanding and 58 percent of long-term loans. In export financing, the federal government is the major lender and the only supplier of some forms of credit insurance, through the Export Development Corporation. Governments are the sixth largest supplier of residential mortgages, but they supply one-half the mortgage insurance. In business financing, government is the fourth largest institution, but accounts for only 4.3 percent of the outstanding credit (ibid., p.8).

The financial activities of governments vis-a-vis the private sector accounted for a large part of the public debt for several provinces in 1980: Alberta, 57 percent; B.C., 42 percent, Nova Scotia, 25 percent. Financial aid to the private sector accounted for 25 percent of the federal government's total debt (ibid.,).

The Council does not refer to a more nebulous form of loan guarantee which is troubling to the Auditor General.[45] This is the "letter of comfort." through which, for example, over $1 billion was guaranteed to the creditors of Canadair Ltd. A letter of comfort is:

> ...a device under which a minister is authorized by the Cabinet to support the credit of a corporation. Even when they contain a disclaimer, the moral obligation of the Government is clear. Thus, although the guarantee of money drawn down from a bank under a Letter of Comfort must later be authorized by Parliament in the Main or Supplementry Estimates, the obligation is already firm, either legally or morally (Auditor General, 1982, p.12).

The problem, of course, is that all money bills must be introduced by the government and passed by the House of Commons. Letters of comfort are a "backdoor" method of providing loan guarantees in the form of undisclosed contingent liabilities that are only later sanctioned by Parliament.

Indirect subsidies embodied in government loans

How large are the subsidies inherent in federal and provincial loans to the private sector? This is not easy to measure. Do we use only the "financial costs"—the difference between the lending rate and the government's borrowing rate? Do we add to this the government's costs of administering its loan programs, which can be substantial? These two elements the Economic Council (ibid., p.131) calls the "cash cost" of such loans. Or do we measure the subsidy based on the social opportunity cost of capital? For one year only, 1978/79, the Economic Council (ibid., p.133) estimated that subsidies amounted to $196 million on a "cash cost" basis or $906 million on social opportunity cost basis. On the other hand, the Council estimated that loan guarantee programs produced a slight financial surplus of $8.9 million. By sector, the subsidy in federal and provincial loans to the private sector (on an opportunity cost basis) in 1978/79 was $176 million to business, $118 million to exports, $345 million to housing and $267 million to agriculture.[46]

In thinking about the indirect subsidies involved in government financing schemes, it is useful to focus on a recent, well-publicized, example. In June 1982 Bombardier Ltd. of Quebec obtained a contract to sell 825 subway cars to New York City.[47] In order to clinch the deal, valued at $822 million ($663 million U.S.), the federal Export Development Corporation agreed to lend the buyer $563 million (U.S.) at 9.7 percent interest over 15 years. The OECD's minimum terms for such financing were then 11.25 percent for a maximum term of 8.5 years. American officials estimated that the value of the subsidy amounted to $230 million (U.S.) over the term of the contract. The irony of this deal is that Bombardier agreed that the subway cars would have at least 40 percent American content and from 16 to 20 percent New York state content. However, the five-year contract was expected to create 15,000 to 20,000 man-years of work for a depressed area of Quebec for a company not in the best of financial shape. An *ex post* analysis by the U.S. Treasury indicated that New York would have awarded the contract to Bombardier even if the cheap loan had *not* been offered. If Canada had only offered the OECD rate of 11.5 percent it would have saved $53 million (U.S.) or $67 million (Canadian).[48] If New York had borrowed at 14 percent to finance the contract, its costs would have been $135 million (U.S.) greater than by accepting the 9.7 percent rate from Canada's Export Development Corporation.

Recent guarantees and bailouts

In the last few years the federal government has extended loan guarantees to a number of companies in economic difficulty. The results have been surprising in some cases, as the following examples illustrate. Ottawa guaranteed $125 million of preferred shares of Massey Ferguson. When dividends were not paid the federal government received 7 percent of the common shares for its $125 million.[49] The Province of Ontario's guarantee for $75 million in preferred shares was similarly called and it received 3.6 percent of Massey's common shares.

In the case of Chrysler Canada Ltd., the federal government offered loan guarantees of $200 million to be used in the period 1982–84 in exchange for Chrysler agreeing to spend $681 million on new plant and equipment in Canada through 1985. In addition, Chrysler was to establish a new van plant in Windsor, to produce K-cars in Canada in 1984, and to maintain at least 11 percent of its labor force in Canada.[50] However, in early 1983 Chrysler announced that it was not proceeding with its new diesel engine plant in Ontario, for which it had obtained another $105 million in loan guarantees.[51] As of mid-1983

Chrysler, which began to make a profit, had not taken up the loan guarantee.

In mid-1982 the federal government moved to bail out Maislin Industries Ltd., a trucking firm with 2,000 jobs in Canada, largely in Quebec. The deal involved a $34 million loan guarantee. In exchange, the company agreed to abide by the August 1982 "6 and 5" guidelines for wage increases. The family owners agreed to increase their equity by $2.5 million and to find a new chief executive. The government was given an option to acquire 15 percent of the common shares for $1. In addition, the government guaranteed up to 90 percent of the potential losses of a new bank loan of $21 million.[52] Maislin subsequently went bankrupt in July 1983.

In the case of Consolidated Computer Inc., the federal government began guaranteeing the company's loans in 1971. By 1976 it had extended $30 million in loan guarantees and acquired 49 percent of the equity. CCI piled up cumulative operating losses of $69 million over its life and federal loan guarantees increased. The final result was that Ottawa lost over $119 million ($125 million in some estimates) by the time CCI was sold off to the private sector in November 1981 for $100,000 plus an "earn out" payment of $6 million based on future sales.[53]

A report on CCI by a special advisor to the Treasury Board found that the company, "except for the first two years ... had few assets, tangible or otherwise, that would support the investment decisions made." From 1970 onwards the company had a negative worth. In fact, according to the consultant, at no time was CCI ever a financially viable company. Through a tangled web of relationships the federal government became the firm's owner, banker, and manager. While the Treasury Board continually sought to end government support for CCI, the Department of Industry, Trade and Commerce was able to keep the company going through its Enterprise Development Board. The final irony is that a year after the government acquired 65 percent of CCI, Nabu Manufacturing reported making $2.3 million on its $100,000 investment.[54]

In July 1983 the federal government announced, following the report on the Atlantic fishery by a special committee headed by Michael Kirby (1983), that it would spend $75 million to acquire control over three of the largest fish processing firms in the industry.[55] Other examples of federal "bailouts" are given in Table A-10.

TABLE A-10

Progress Report on Bailouts

COMPANIES	BAILOUT PLAN	STATUS (Aug. 6/83)
Dome Petroleum Ltd., Calgary	September, 1982 — offer by Ottawa to lend Dome $500 million in convertible debentures which could be converted to common shares and ultimately provide government with up to 40% of Dome equity. (Dome's Canadian bankers would contribute an equal amount as part of a large debt restructuring package.)	Offer has not yet been taken up by Dome. There is as yet, no liability for Ottawa. Dome is still in business looking for an alternative way of raising money.
Chrysler Canada Ltd., Windsor	May, 1980 — offer of $200 million in loan guarantees conditional on Chrysler making certain capital investments and maintaining certain employment levels. The federal offer was part of a larger North American financial bailout, including the U.S. and Ontario governments.	To date, Chrysler has not taken up the Ottawa loan, and has since returned to profitability.
Maislin Industries Ltd., Montreal	July, 1982 — offer by Ottawa of $33.4 million loan guarantee through the Enterprise Development Program of the Industry department.	Maislin, which had losses of $20 million in 1982, borrowed the guaranteed loans and recently went into receivership. Ottawa lost the full amount of the loan.
Massey-Ferguson Ltd., Toronto	February, 1981 — Ottawa offers to guarantee $125 million of a preferred share issue, which is part of a larger $715 million financial package. In July, 1982, Massey failed to pay a required dividend and triggers the guarantee. Ottawa ends up with 62% of the non-voting share issue.	Company today remains in business, continues to sustain losses and waits for a revival of the farm implement business.

TABLE A-10 (Continued)

COMPANIES	BAILOUT PLAN	STATUS (Aug. 6/83)
Co-op Implements Ltd., Winnipeg	February, 1982 — Ottawa loaned a further $5.5 million, and forgave $7.5 million in previous loans. The federal aid was part of a larger $35 million refinancing package involving Prairie provincial governments and co-operative farm groups.	The company continues business, is losing money and, like Massey-Ferguson awaiting recovery in the farm implements business.
Consolidated Computer Inc., Ottawa	The company received a total of $94 million in federal loan guarantees over the past decade, plus additional aid — all of which has been lost.	Total federal losses were about $125 million and, in 1981 Ottawa sold remaining assets of the computer firm to Nabu Manufacturing Corp. of Ottawa for $100,000.
CCM Inc., Toronto	In the late 1970s, Ottawa made direct loans and loan guarantees totalling $22 million to the bicycle company.	The company declared bankruptcy in October, 1982, and losses to the government totalled $15.5 million.
White Farm Equipment Canada Ltd., Brantford, Ont.	March, 1981 — Ottawa guaranteed $10.5 million in loans to help resurrect the company which had been placed in receivership by its bankrupt U.S. parent, White Motor Corp. of Michigan. An additional $2.5 million grant was made by the Enterprise Development Board.	The company sustained major losses since the loans and was placed in receivership in June. The government will lose its money.
Pioneer Chain Saw, Peterborough	In 1978, FDB approved $6.5 million in guaranteed loans as part of a larger restructuring package.	The company was sold to Sweden's Electrolux AB in 1979 and Ottawa was repaid.

TABLE A-10   (Continued)

COMPANIES	BAILOUT PLAN	STATUS (Aug. 6/83)
Lake Group Inc., St. John's	June, 1982 — Ottawa authorized $13 million in loan guarantees to help restructure the fish products firm. The money has been all taken up.	The company had a $22.5 million loss in 1982, but reported a $1.5 million profit in second quarter 1983. It is also part of a planned Newfoundland fishery reconstruction program announced recently by federal Fisheries Minister Pierre de Bane.
St. Anthony's Fisheries Ltd., Nfld.	June, 1982 — Ottawa approved $8 million in loan guarantees to refinance the company.	As of March, 1983, the company has taken up $1.3 million of the total.
Electrohome Ltd., Kitchener	Ottawa, in 1977, insured loans worth $15 million to help in the financial restructuring of the company.	The company's fortunes reversed and it was able to repay the loan by 1980. Because of the risk, Ottawa took an option on a block of shares as a condition for the loss. It made $10 million when it exercised the option.
Petromont Inc., Montreal	March, 1983 — Ottawa offered the hard-pressed oil-based petrochemical firm $25 million in repayable contributions over the two years if Quebec matched the offer.	Quebec has agreed to the matching condition, and the first payment was approved last week. At presstime (Aug. 1/83) there has been no acceptance of the offer.
Petrosar Ltd., Sarnia	March, 1983 — Ottawa offered the oil-based petrochemical firm $25 million on loan guarantees over two years if Ontario matched the offer.	At presstime (Aug. 1/83) there has been no acceptance of the offer.

Source: Hyman Solomon, "Progress Reports on Bailouts," *Financial Post,* August 6, 1983, p. 102 (This list omits Canadair and de Havilland, both Federal Crown corporations which have had enormous losses.)

VII. MIXED ENTERPRISES: EQUITY OWNERSHIP IN PRIVATE SECTOR FIRMS

Canadians are long familiar with Crown corporations. Recently, however, we have witnessed a rise in government holdings of equity in private-sector firms. Most Crown corporations were "created from scratch" (e.g., Petro-Canada, Air Canada) and some were created by "nationalizing" existing firms (e.g., CNR, Canadair, B.C. Hydro, Quebec Hydro). The "equity route" has now been used in some cases to obtain legal or de facto control of previously privately owned firms through the stock exchange and by other means—see Elford and Stanbury (1984). In this section we review the holdings of the Caisse de Dépôt of Quebec and of the Alberta Energy Corp. and Alberta Heritage Fund.

The Caisse

The outstanding example of the equity approach to government intervention is the Caisse de Dépôt et Placement du Quebec. Its primary function is to invest the funds collected by the Quebec Pension Plan and thirteen other public agencies in the province. As of March 31, 1982 its total assets were $14.5 billion and its equity portfolio, said to be the largest in Canada, amounted to $2.6 billion.[56] (A year later total assets were $16 billion and the equity portfolio was $3 billion; at the end of 1983 the Caisse had total assets of $18.2 billion.) Among the 183 companies in which the Caisse had equity holdings in March 1982 were the following:

* 43.9 percent of Gaz Metropolitain Inc., Montreal, the natural-gas distributor;
* 30 percent of Provigo Inc., Montreal, Quebec's big grocery chain;
* Brascade Holdings Inc., which owns 30 percent of Brascade Resources Inc. which owns 42 percent of Toronto-based Noranda Mines Ltd.;
* 27.9 percent of Prenor Group Ltd., Montreal, a financial holding company;
* 23.8 percent of Domtar Inc., Montreal, the forest-products producer;
* 15.2 percent of Dofor Inc., which owns 21.6 percent of Domtar;

- 15.10 percent of Quebec-Telephone, which provides phone service outside Montreal;
- 14.1 percent of La Verendrye Management Corp., La Sarre, a holding company in air and land transport;
- 13.2 percent of Dominion Textile Inc., Montreal;
- 13 percent of Logistec Corp., Montreal, a cargo handler;
- 10.8 percent of Domco Industries Ltd., Lachine, a flooring producer;
- 9.8 percent of General Trust of Canada, Montreal;
- 9.2 percent of Canadian Pacific Ltd., Montreal, the nation's largest company;
- 7.1 percent of Alcan Aluminium Ltd., Montreal, the world's second-largest aluminum maker.[57]

By November 1982 the Caisse had increased its interest in Canadian Pacific to 9.976 percent. This move prompted the federal government to introduce Bill S-31 in November 1980, to prevent any provincial government or its agent from owning more than 10 percent of the voting shares of any company engaged in interprovincial road, rail, water or pipeline transport. This move prompted a furious reaction from Quebec.[58]

Canadian Business ranked the Caisse as the fourth largest federal or provincial Crown corporation in terms of assets in 1981.[59] If it was inserted in the list of the largest private-sector *financial* institutions, it would rank seventh. The magazine put the Caisse's assets at $13.9 billion at the end of 1981. By comparison, the Alberta Heritage Savings Trust Fund had assets of $8.6 billion on March 31, 1981 and was ranked sixth on the list of Crown corporations. As of March 31, 1983 the Caisse's assets were $16 billion while those of the Heritage Fund were $13 billion.

The Province of Quebec has another entity with significant equity holdings in the private sector. The *Financial Post* indicates that in 1981 the Societe Generale de Financement du Quebec (SGF) had revenues of $801.1 million (#95 on the F.P.'s list) and assets of $977.4 million (#80).[60]Among its major holdings are (i) 55 percent of Donahue Inc., a forest products company with sales of $289.9 million in 1981; (ii) 50 percent of BG Checo International Ltd., a chemical firm, with sales of $108.4 million in 1981,[61] (iii) 22 percent of Domtar Inc., with 1981 sales of $1.76 billion. Early in 1982 it was announced that the Caisse and SGF were jointly forming a new company to hold

SGF's interest in Donahue and Domtar.[62] By December 1982, the two Quebec agencies had 45 percent of Domtar.[63]

Note that SGF, the province's equivalent of the Canada Development Corporation, acquired about 20 percent of Domtar in the summer of 1981.[64] The Caisse obtained its first major interest in Domtar by buying Argus Corp's 18 percent block which had first been sold to MacMillan Bloedel Ltd. The *Financial Post* questioned whether the acquisition of control of Domtar was part of a larger strategy of transforming "the province's industrial base into an integrated and sustaining whole":

> Bernard Landry, the province's influential Minister of State for Economic Development, doesn't try to hide the pattern: "Part of our global strategy is to be less dominated. We don't deny that many corporations have done well for the province but it is a matter of proportion — that's the key word" ... "We don't want to own everything", Landry adds, "but we want to have real power in some firms. It is not that we want the power in government hands, we want it in Quebecers' hands."[65]

The *Financial Post* states that only about two dozen companies of its top 500 can be said to be Quebec-owned. It also says that the Quebec government "believes its ownership of the Canadian economic base should be in proportion to its population vs. the total population of Canada."[66]

In addition to the Caisse and SGF, the Province of Quebec has other vehicles through which to acquire equity interests in existing enterprises:

> Quebec already has investment, development and holding companies such as Soquem (for mining), Soquip (petroleum) and Sogefor (forestry). Furthermore, the rules will be changed for financial institutions, allowing these companies more freedom to invest in equity.[67]

Beyond acquisition of equity interests, the use of holding companies and traditional Crown corporations, the Province has undertaken other actions to "patriate" its economy.[68]

The Caisse's equity interests in Canadian corporations are enormous. *Canadian Business* states that it is the largest *single* shareholder in the seven largest banks, Canadian Pacific Ltd., (Canada's largest enterprise in terms of sales), Alcan Aluminum, Prenor Group Ltd., Domtar, Gaz Metropolitain, Provigo Inc. and probably the largest shareholder in Bell Canada with 3 percent of the shares.[69] Although the Caisse does not hold *de jure* control (i.e., 51 percent of the voting shares) in any company, it obviously has effective control in several (e.g., Domtar, Gaz Metropolitain). This raises the question when the Caisse will be able to *exercise* control with its minority holdings.[70] Two conditions would appear to be necessary for this to occur. First, that the Caisse actively seeks to exercise influence on a firm's board. Second, that the remaining ownership of voting shares is widely distributed and hence less capable of organizing into larger blocks. When one thinks of effective control by a minority shareholder, one automatically thinks of the old Argus Corp. prior to its takeover by Conrad Black.

The question is whether the Caisse (or its ultimate controller, the Government of Quebec) sees itself as a passive portfolio investor or as an owner actively seeking to control the firms in which it has invested. In its 1982/83 annual report the Caisse's chairman said it "may occasionally, for reasons inherent to a corporation or to the nature of the investment, propose staff" [changes].[71] In dealing with the matter of active control, the Caisse's managers must recognize the interests of current and potential pensioners whose funds they hold in trust. Presumably they must live within the statutory pension fund constraints both on the percentage of equity holdings to total assets and the maximum equity investment in any one firm (30 percent). They must also, despite their avowed and, on occasion, demonstrated independence, be sensitive to the interests of the government of the day.

Alberta Energy Company Ltd.

Although much smaller than the Caisse in Quebec, AEC is an interesting example of a joint enterprise which, in turn, holds equity interests in private sector corporations. Formed originally in September 1973 as a Crown corporation owned by the Province of Alberta, AEC became a public company in December 1975 when one-half its shares were sold to the public. At March 31, 1983, the Province of Alberta held a 45 percent interest in AEC while 55,000 individuals held the balance. The company has grown rapidly: its 1983 sales were $469.1 million and its net income was $62.4 million. In 1980 its net income was $57.5 million on revenues of $232.5 million. At the end of 1983

AEC had total assets of $1,613 million, up from $703 million at the end of 1980.

AEC's purpose is to develop the industrial and resource bases of the Canadian economy, particularly in Alberta. In addition to its extensive operations in its own right, AEC has equity interests in a considerable number of other companies:

- 10 percent equity interest in Syncrude and a 7 percent royalty interest at a net cost of $205 million;
- 28 percent of B.C. Forest Products Ltd. (which cost $215 million in June 1981);
- joint venture with Esso Chemical and HBOG to build a world-scale ethylene plant ($700 million) announced in January 1982;
- joint venture with Deminex (Canada) Ltd. to develop heavy oil deposits northeast of Cold Lake, Alberta (initial investment: $27 million in 1983);
- 67 percent of the $262 million Syncrude Utilities plant through AEC Power Ltd.;
- 100 percent of the 270–mile Alberta Oil Sands Pipeline;
- 25 percent of a coal mine at Coal Valley with long-term sales contracts for 2 million tonnes per year of thermal coal;
- 33 percent of a 550–mile ethane collection pipeline system;
- 40 percent of a lumber mill at Whitecourt, Alberta;
- 50 percent of Steel Alberta Ltd.;
- 50 percent Pan-Alberta Gas Ltd.;
- joint venture partner in the Petalta project to produce benzene and by-products using a condensate feedstock; and
- 50 percent of Zimpro-AEC Ltd. which markets a wet air oxidization boiler.[72]

In 1982 AEC made an offer of $24 per share ($168 million in total) for up to 51 percent of Chieftain Development Ltd.[73] AEC eventually acquired 57 percent of Chieftain. The deal raised the Canadian ownership of Chieftain sufficient to make that company eligible for the highest rate on the federal government's Petroleum Incentive Payments under the NEP.

The Edmonton *Journal* reported that Premier Lougheed supported

AEC's bid for Chieftain, although the Province had not been consulted in advance.[74] The premier stated that the government was not involved in the management of AEC. He also stated that AEC operates under guidelines which prohibit hostile takeovers. He had earlier contrasted Petro-Canada's approach of being in close touch with Energy Minister Marc Lalonde and engaging in hostile takeovers.

Editorially, the Edmonton *Journal* argued that the Alberta Heritage Fund, which holds the Province's AEC shares, should be sold off to the highest bidder.[75] The editorial described AEC as "a bastard organization with a slippery relationship to the government that may satisfy neither its 60,000 private shareholders nor the Alberta public."[76]

Alberta Heritage Savings Trust Fund

The Alberta Heritage Fund is potentially the most important single vehicle by which a government could acquire equity in privately-owned corporations. It was established in 1976 as a collective savings organization in recognition of the non-renewable nature of the petroleum and natural gas resources in Alberta. Thirty percent of the province's revenues from non-renewable resources are deposited in the Fund.

As of March 31, 1983, the Fund had assets of $13.0 billion, up from $11.0 billion the year before. (As of December 31, 1983 total assets were $13.5 billion, including $2.0 billion in "deemed assets" in the capital projects division.) In 1982/83 the Fund had total revenues of $2,838 million as compared with $2,441 million in 1981/82.[77] In 1980 the Fund's governing legislation was amended to permit it to establish a commercial investment division which could acquire equities. Like the Caisse, the Fund has said that it does not plan to file insider trading reports to the OSC.[78]

The Fund began to buy equities in the first quarter of 1982 with a ceiling of $200 million for the year. Under its general guidelines, the Fund cannot purchase more than 5 percent of the outstanding shares in any company. No more than 10 percent of the Fund's resources can be invested in any one company. The executive assistant to Provincial Treasurer Lou Hyndman stated that the Fund did not propose to seek an active management role in the companies in which it invested.[79] If the Fund limits itself to 5 percent of the voting shares, it is unlikely to be able to do so. Unlike the Caisse, which for the first fifteen years of its life refused to publish a list of its equity holdings, the Heritage Fund proposes to do so annually. By March 31, 1983 the Fund had acquired $156 million in equities (at cost) while the market value was $203 million.

Let us consider the economic potential of the Alberta Heritage Fund by exploring the implications of the following assumptions:

1. The value of the Fund at January 1, 1984 is $14.0 billion.
2. The Fund earns an average of 10 percent per year on its total assets.
3. The Province transfers $1.4 billion each year to the Fund (at the end of each year).

Then as of January 1, 1989 (i.e., five years later) the Fund would have total assets of $30.1 billion. If just *10 percent of the increment* in the assets is used to acquire shares in private corporations, some $1.6 billion would be available over the next five years. If these funds are used to acquire minority interests in corporations whose shareholdings are widely diffused, the possibilities for government influence are enormous.

As the data cited above indicate, the Heritage Fund has started slowly in acquiring equities. Perhaps the greatest potential constraint on an aggressive equity ownership policy for the Heritage Fund is the conservatism of Alberta voters. They are not anxious to see more government intervention, particularly if it would involve the acquisition of control over existing private sector enterprises. It should be noted that there was much opposition in Alberta when the Province acquired control of Pacific Western Airlines in 1974 (see Tupper, 1981). The government did not set up the airline as a Crown corporation. Rather both the government and the firm's managers emphasize the independence and profit-oriented nature of the airline. (In 1983, the Province sold off 85 percent of their shares of PWA.)

In conclusion, several points should be made about the "equity route" or mixed enterprises as a tool of intervention. First, it creates the opportunity to either benefit or hurt the private shareholders of firms in which the government has a substantial interest. Second, unlike many other forms of intervention, the economic effects of doing so are immediately apparent as the stock market will capitalize the change in expectations induced by the government's action. Third, and this characteristic makes the instrument less attractive to politicians, the cost of adverse changes in government policy are not only widely apparent because of changes in stock market prices, but are also *concentrated*. The private shareholders (and of course the government as shareholder) bear all the costs of the adverse effects of a change in policy (see Eckel and Vining, 1982). This violates the basic rule of instrument choice, which says that costs should be diffused (and not widely known) while benefits are concentrated (Trebilcock et al., 1982). To illustrate the previous point, it should be noted that when it was revealed that the Caisse and SGF had obtained more than 40 percent of Domtar Inc., the market price of the company's common shares fell 16 percent immediately.[80]

VIII. CHOSEN INSTRUMENTS

The concept

Chosen instruments are privately owned corporations which are systematically favored by government in order to achieve public policy objectives. While there is no clear and comprehensive definition of a chosen instrument, the following characteristics are associated with the term:

1. It is a privately-owned firm, *not* a Crown corporation.
2. It is "accepted as a lead company in the industrial sector, to which it belongs" (Shepherd, 1981, p. 41).
3. Its position is consciously reinforced by government with the eventual objective of replacing imports, and of penetrating export [markets] (ibid.).
4. Favorable treatment by government may take a variety of forms: sole or preferred source procurement, tariffs, import quotas, subsidized financing (e.g., loans, guarantees), or special tax treatment.
5. "They are indeed 'instruments of state' and as such are expected to be the catalyst for growth, the practitioners of advanced technology, and nowadays the inspirers of stock markets" (ibid.). Above all, they are expected to penetrate export markets.
6. Firms may become chosen instruments by positioning themselves to attract policymaker's attention of they may be chosen by government.

Shepherd (ibid.) asserts that, "Because the chosen instrument is not enshrined, it represents a status and a position which has to be continually earned, supported and buttressed." This proposition is questionable. The systematic favoritism of one firm in an industry through such means as R&D grants, procurement and loan guarantees, will have the effect of severely weakening its competitors or driving them into other industries. As a result, the government's options are sharply reduced. This becomes particularly important if the chosen instrument performs poorly. Shepherd (ibid.) is of the view that "because the status of chosen instruments can be abrogated at any time, there is a constant, persuading influence which shapes the chosen instrument to the dictates of government policy." If this were true, how many owners or managers would want to play the role of supplicant to what most people would find to be a tyrannical patron, even if the patron can be generous. Many businessmen can testify that getting something from government is a time-consuming, emotionally-exhausting task. While economic markets can be tough, the rules of the game are moderately well specified. That is *not* the case in dealing with government. Government has the capacity — which it exercises all too frequently — of changing the rules to suit immediate, narrow political considerations. In general, changes in government policy are the enemy of good planning.

Are chosen instruments a more flexible instrument of policy? Shepherd (ibid.) argues that by "the simple expedient of diverting one major order, or redirecting a significant grant," government can imbue the chosen instrument with "a flexibility rarely found in a Crown corporation." If that is true, then the primary skill required of management is political, i.e., being able to predict with tolerable accuracy the twists and turns of government policy and of constantly reshaping the firm's substantive efforts to coincide with such changes.

It is argued that chosen instruments can be better controlled by the government, whereas Crown corporations have, in the view of some, a lamentable habit of moving toward greater independence. One thinks of Robert Bandeen's efforts as president of the CNR and Anthony Hampson's strategy at the CDC. In the former, it appears Bandeen was forced out by the board of directors who disagreed with this approach to major policy questions.[81] The federal government's failure to obtain its appointments to the board of CDC resulted in an announcement that it would gradually sell off its 49 percent equity interest.[82]

Referring to Dome Petroleum, Lumonicas (in laser technology) and Mitel (in chip technology), Shepherd (ibid., p.42) states that, by virtue of their favored position, such chosen instruments have a "unique capacity to attract the support of capital from the private Canadian investor." In the case of Dome, however, several Canadian banks have relied so much on its role as a chosen instrument of federal energy policy that they may end up controlling the company along with the federal government, if Dome is unable to re-finance itself from private sector sources.

Identifying chosen instruments

It is difficult to identify and document the growth of "chosen instruments" as a technique of government intervention. Certain companies are frequently mentioned in this regard. They include Dome Petroleum, Nova Corp., Northern Telecom, Spar Aerospace (maker of the Canadarm used in the space shuttle), Mitel Corp., Consolidated Computer (now bankrupt), CAE (flight simulators), Lumonicas (laser technology), Norpak Ltd. (major licensee of the government-produced Telidon videotex technology) and Connaught Laboratories (owned by CDC).

The firms that might be called chosen instruments are generally in the energy, communications, high-technology (chips, lasers) and aerospace industries. The forms of government assistance are varied. Shepherd's long-term, sole-source procurement model is not much in evidence. Government aid is largely subsumed under the rubric of a "national industrial strategy" or the National Energy Program, although assistance to Dome and Nova Corp. (then Alberta Gas Trunk Line) predate the NEP of October 1980. In general terms, the strategy is highly interventionist, discretionary, nationalistic and "high-tech" oriented. Some might apply the label "corporatism" to the relationship between the favored firms and the government.

Financial Post reporter Fred Harrison, in a series of articles on chosen instruments, found that "officials of every company contacted by the *Post* in recent weeks steadfastly denied their own firms were chosen instruments.[83] For example, the president of Northern Telecom said a chosen instrument was a knife. The president of Norpak "admits to a close relationship with Ottawa but rejects, quite passionately, any suggestion of favoritism." A senior official of the Department of Communications said that while the possibility of assigning the manufacture of Telidon to a single chosen instrument was discussed, this route was rejected. Instead, about seventeen companies were involved in Telidon development without government help.

This may illustrate another attribute of chosen instruments for the calculus of instrument choice—"deniability" on behalf of the private sector firm. They can claim to be quite independent of the government. Harrison quotes Shepherd as saying that chosen instruments will develop as natural spin-offs of other interventionist policies regardless of the label used.

Dome Petroleum and Nova Corp. are widely perceived to be chosen instruments in the energy field. But, as one wag cracked, "they chose the federal government." What is clear is that these companies, far more than others in the petroleum industry, have been attuned to the energy policy objectives of the federal government. Harrison quotes an oilman as saying "Gallagher [then chairman of Dome] is the smartest man in Canada, he knows which side his bread is buttered on—both sides."[84] The allusion is to the idea that he makes advantageous deals with his free enterprise colleagues *and* with the "socialist" federal government. The *Financial Post* has described both Robert Blair and Jack Gallagher as "politicians par excellence."[85] It was said they have a "sometimes uncanny ability to sense changing political winds and shift their companies' positions so as to make it seem it was they, and not the government, who changed first." The article referred to Blair's skills in leading the Foothills consortium to victory over Canadian Arctic Gas, which was backed by several large multinationals (see Bregha, 1979).

It was pointed out that one of Gallagher's lobbying techniques is to provide Cabinet ministers and backbenchers with details on the benefits of Dome's activities on a regional basis. He also is "always taking pains to ensure that [his plans] complement federal policy." (see Lyon, 1983, Ch.5)

Dome's extraordinary ability to respond to federal initiatives and obtain help from Ottawa is best illustrated by its creation of Dome Canada Ltd. shortly after the NEP was announced on October 28, 1980. For a company to get the highest ratio of grants to exploration expenses incurred on Canada Lands (80 percent), 70 percent of its shares must be owned by Canadian residents. Dome Petroleum was far from qualifying as over half of its equity is held by Americans. Dome needed the money in a hurry to support its large-scale Beaufort Sea exploration in the summer of 1981. (Foster, 1984, Ch. 7)

Dome and its legal and financial advisors set to work furiously. Within about a week the Canadian-owned subsidiary idea evolved.

Then a target was set to float the new company by the end of 1980. That was impossible, but the draft prospectus was ready by mid-December. In fact, Dome moved so fast it got ahead of the regulation writers in Ottawa. How the problem was resolved shows the close linkages between Dome and the highest levels of the federal government.

> Dome's headlong rush to the market was checked during December. "We had to run the thing by the Ottawa people responsible for the Canadianization program and they were still writing the rules," explained Mr. Richards [President of Dome].
>
> They still are. There was also the ticklish problem that the legislation authorizing the exploration incentive grants has not yet been passed by Parliament. Just possibly, it might never be. [They were passed in mid-1982.]
>
> The impasse was resolved by written assurances from Mr. Lalonde, contained in a letter to Mr. Gallagher dated January 29. Mr. Lalonde said he could not commit Parliament, but said he intends to "exercise the discretion which I expect the legislation to provide" to exempt the proposed Dome arrangements even from some of the terms of the draft rules that were published in January. In return, he obtained a commitment from Dome Petroleum to become at least 50 percent Canadian-owned over the next few years.[86]

Dome Canada Ltd. became the largest new equity financing in Canadian history.[87]

A symbiotic relationship

Fundamental to understanding the nature of the privately-owned firm as a chosen instrument of public policy is the symbiotic nature of the relationship. Both sides must benefit. While Dome spent a very large part of its exploration budget looking for oil and gas on the "Canada Lands" in the high Arctic (a federal priority), Ottawa gave Dome the super depletion allowance.[88] The top people at Dome and Nova actively cultivate a supportive relationship with government. The corporations' plans are described and responses are noted. Information is exchanged. Aspirations are explored — what can't be made public is made known to each other. The overall objective is to create a mutually supportive, reciprocal relationship. Both sides stand to benefit by the exchanges. Harrison argues that in part, Dome's ambitious plans are based on confidence in government, confidence that if adjustments to the investment framework are required, Ottawa will be persuaded to make them.[89]

Blair has been able to make friends in Ottawa by reason of his demonstrated Canadian nationalism.[90] A cynic might suggest that when a businessman wraps himself in the cloak of nationalism it is precisely because it is profitable to do so.

IX. SUASION

The least obtrusive instrument used by the governments to effect their purposes is that of suasion. Ideally, the relevant private sector actors "voluntarily" change their behavior in the desired direction, but the whole operation "leaves no official tracks." Politicians do not have to commit themselves by going to Parliament for new regulations, taxes, or expenditures. Yet their bidding gets done. Suasion offers enormous opportunities for deception, reversibility, redirection and the selective use of information for what may be short-term political purposes. It is government by executive action without all the troublesome details of Parliament. It can be the ultimate in the exercise of discretion by the politicians and bureaucrats involved.

It should be pointed out, however, that there are limits to the use of suasion. If the sacrifice required is too great relative to the positive or negative inducements offered (hinted at) by government, the desired behavior will not be obtained. Or a maverick will publicly declare — "to hell with you — if you want me to do that bring in legislation to require me to do your bidding."

Stanbury and Fulton (1984) identify six types of suasion. "Pure political leadership" involves "the use of exhortation by politicians to persude citizens to alter their beliefs and ultimately their behavior on the basis of emotional and/or logical appeals without any explicit or implicit inducements to do so." "Suasion with inducements" consists of exhortation by politicians or bureaucrats which is designed to produce an involuntary change in behavior with the aid of positive or negative inducements involving the powers of government other than actions approved by the legislature. This form of suasion may be seen as immoral because of the absence of the use of *legitimate* coercion, i.e., the exercise of constitutionally valid powers approved by the majority of the legislature. "Mass suasion" is defined by Stanbury and Fulton

(1984) as "intentionally persuasive advertising or other forms of communication paid for by a government from tax revenues." Advertisements may be designed to alter behavior directly (e.g., "Stop Smoking," "Drive at 55") or they may be designed to alter perceptions about the performance of the government (e.g., "Complete energy security for Canada is this close.").

The fourth type of suasion is "monitoring and information disclosure." Here a government agency monitors the behavior of targeted actors and "encourages the mass media to publicize the activities of those deemed to be behaving in an 'undesirable' way." Although the monitoring agency has no sanctions to, for example, control wages or prices, "the moral force of adverse public opinion is supposed to encourage compliance with the guidelines suggested by government." The most obvious example is that of the Food Prices Review Board which operated between 1972 and 1975. "Consultation leading to co-optation" is another form of suasion. Actual or potential opponents of government policy are drawn into the decision-making process with a view to co-opting them and "turning them into advocates or at least defenders of what the government intended to do all along." When Peter Ittinuar, the country's first Inuit MP crossed the floor from the NDP to the Liberals in November 1982, he was described as a "tragic victim of high-powered Liberal manipulation." A vocal critic became silent, but found it easier to get money for projects in his riding and to get the government to act on specific problems.

Finally, the sixth type of suasion is the "discreet use of confidential information" or the planned use of "leaks." Stanbury and Fulton (1984) argue that "politicians may 'leak' confidential information (i) to help create a climate of opinion to facilitate planned subsequent actions, or (ii) to obtain 'feedback' concerning a possible course of action without having it attributed to them." Bureaucrats may use "leaks" to influence other departments in battles over policy matters or to alter the behavior of their own political master.

We now provide two examples of the use of suasion by the federal government.

Wage and price guidelines: toward a "6 and 5" world

Because government is now so large and so intertwined with private sector economic activity, it has myriad opportunities to exercise "leverage" on private sector actors. Such leverage was used to obtain numerous "volunteers" for the "6 percent this year and 5 percent next year" wage and price ceilings associated with the federal budget of June 28, 1982.[91] For example, on July 23, 1982 the Minister of Employment and Immigration hinted that the federal government "might use its economic aid programs to entice, arm twist or otherwise cajole the private sector into a six-and-five world." When asked about this approach at his news conference the same day, the Prime Minister stated:

> Twist the arms is not an expression that conveys our thinking. I mean, I would hope that every grant and every accord and every subsidy that the government is paying out of taxpayers' money would be negotiated with this in mind; that it be used as leverage...
> I make no bones at all about that... Maybe that is twisting arms, but I think it is just using the powers of persuasion.[92]

In the case of the 6 and 5 percent guidelines, there appeared to be two parts to the iron hand inside the velvet glove. First, there is the prospect of the loss of present or future "goodies" from the government. Second, there is the possible imposition of mandatory controls, perhaps along the lines of the Anti-Inflation Board between 1975 and 1978 (see Maslove and Swimmer, 1980). It is the prospect of these undesirable outcomes that helped to persuade labour and management to go along.

Ottawa then turned its attention to the provinces. On July 27, the Prime Minister stated that provincial governments "will be asked to comply with Ottawa's wage and price guidelines if they want federal money for programs." The newspaper report continues:

> While Mr. Trudeau stopped short of saying federal money will be withheld from provinces that do not accept the guidelines, he told the House of Commons that his Government intends other governments and private companies to live with the limits on prices and wages "as much as possible" in return for financial aid.[93]

The Leader of the Opposition, Mr. Clark, described Mr. Trudeau's statement as a "threat." The Minister of Employment and Immigration described his discussions concerning jointly financed projects for economic development as "friendly persuasion."

The federal government's 6 and 5 campaign had the distinct odour of corporatism about it. Peter Newman noted that "a squad of some of Canada's most powerful industrialists has sprung to the defense of the Trudeau government's six-and-five percent wage guidelines. Calling itself the Private Sector 6/5 Committee, the group is headed by Ian Sinclair, chairman of CP Enterprises." Its members consist of a number of other well-known business leaders. Newman described their role as follows:

> They are determined to swing their fellow entrepreneurs behind the notion that despite the strong antipathy toward Trudeau, the Liberal government has set a worthy example with its wage guidelines. Not only that, but the 6/5 Committee has taken upon itself the task of persuading the business community to apply the same set of rules to prices and profits. "It would be a hell of a thing if we didn't give it a real effort," says Sinclair, the burly CP chief who is known as Big Julie and who has spent the past 40 years fighting government intervention. "Besides, if we don't succeed, the guidelines will become compulsory."[94]

Labor, predictably, was unhappy about the employers' support for the 6 and 5 guidelines. A CLC spokesman described the government's policy as a "convenient cop-out for companies which want to hold down wages." But he pointed out, "at least it only has suasion behind it ... the collective bargaining process is still in place."[95]

Business leaders began to realize the implications of linking government subsidies and other benefits from government to adherence to the guidelines. A CMA spokesman said he hoped the government "would not hold it against a company receiving a subsidy if the company had to settle with a union for 8 or 9 percent in order to avoid a strike...." The newspaper story pointed out that before extending a $34 million loan guarantee to the Maislin trucking firm, the government obtained assurances from the Teamsters Union that wage increases would be within the guidelines. Suncor Inc. (25 percent owned by the Province of Ontario) said it would aim to abide by the guidelines in exchange for tax concessions, but indicated that it had already signed agreements above the guidelines. Bombardier Ltd., which had received at least part of the benefit of over $200 million in government concessionary financing, said it planned to stay as close as possible to the guidelines, but noted that competitive considerations would also have to be taken into account.[96]

In order to sell the program the government organized a substantial effort by MPs throughout the summer recess.[97] They were provided with a "resource book" which tied 6 and 5 to the Liberal Party's recovery strategy. Their performance was evaluated at the end of the recess by party strategists.

The 6 and 5 program lasted for two years—see Swimmer (1984).

Reining in the banks

Another example of the use of suasion by the federal government occurred in mid-1981. On July 29 the Minister of Finance, "worried about the damage Canadian takeovers of U.S. companies is doing to the sagging Canadian dollar, told reporters he has asked chartered banks to 'reduce substantially' the money they lend to finance the deals."[98] The newspaper story continued:

> MacEachen said he is aiming mainly at non-energy related takeovers and said the government remains committed to its goal of 50–percent Canadian ownership of the petroleum industry by 1990.
> But he added that energy takeovers — estimated at over $6 billion since the energy program was announced Oct. 28 — are also hurting the Canadian dollar and should "proceed somewhat more slowly."
> MacEachen, calling his move prudent, said it should ease downward pressure on the Canadian dollar and help keep the lid on inflation and interest rates.[99]

The Minister of Finance denied that the suggestion made to the banks stemmed from pressures by the U.S. government, whose unhappiness with the NEP and other manifestations of Canadian nationalism was well known. He said it was a "made-in-Canada policy." He did, however, state that the federal government had no intention of extending the Canadianization program to other industries.

The economics department of the Bank of Montreal, in a study dated August 18, 1981, estimated that $9 billion worth of mergers/takeovers occurred in the period January to July 1981.[100] It also noted a very sharp increase in capital outflows during the same period. The Bank estimated that takeover-induced outflows reduced the value of the Canadian dollar, *ceteris paribus*, by 1.25 cents between October

1980 and June 1981. It appears that the NEP prompted a faster rate of Canadianization than was anticipated by both politicians and their advisors. It should be noted, however, that the NEP should not be blameded (or praised) for all the takeovers of oil companies by any means.[101]

Mr. MacEachen's efforts at suasion worked promptly. Within two days, "the banks agreed to support this request." But, in the words of the president of the Canadian Bankers Association, it would be left up to each bank to work out individual plans for its implementation. The vice-chairman of the Royal Bank said his bank welcomed the Finance Minister's request because "the magnitude of the takeover trend has probably reached unhealthy proportions....it has put strains on the banking system and financial markets generally."[102] Obviously, suasion works more easily when the self-interest of those subject to it coincides with the direction the government wishes to go.

The *Globe and Mail* editorially attacked Mr. MacEachen's action, saying that the curb could "affront" the banks' "best borrowers" and thereby "injure their shareholders." The *Globe* continued:

> The request itself was improper. The banks are not, and should not be, an extension of the Government. Apart from their behaving like good corporate citizens, do we want banks in politics, responsive to political requests rather than the law? Mr. MacEachen's request, moreover, comes from a Government which 67 percent of Canadians, according to a Gallup Poll, believes is not running the economy properly. Do we want its incompetence extended to the banks?[103]

This case illustrates almost perfectly the nature of suasion. A whole series of federal economic policies produced a mini-crisis.[104] Rather than reassess and directly alter the policy, politicians deny they are wrong and move to "plug various leaks in their dam." But a second point is more important, and that is that the government did not have the political will to go to Parliament or even to have the Cabinet approve a regulation to *compel* the change in behavior it sought. Instead, the Minister of Finance calls in the heads of the banks to "register a request" that they "voluntarily" take an action that appears to be inimical to their self-interest.

NOTES

1. See, for example, Bird (1970, 1979); Auld (1976); Rosenfeld (1972, 1973); Stanbury (1972); Canadian Tax Foundation, *Provincial Finances* (biennial) and *The National Finances* (annual); Doern (1980, 1981, 1982, 1983); Hodgetts and Dwivedi (1969); Hartwick (1967); Dominion Bureau of Statistics (1952).

2. Stanbury (1972, pp.2-3) does point out that some earlier works do deal with government expenditures in a larger context. See, for example, Firestone (1958), Hood and Scott (1956). Three specialized studies prepared for the Royal Commission on Dominion-Provincial Relations (1940) examined certain aspects of government expenditures.

3. GNP consists of the sum of expenditures on goods and services, gross fixed capital formation, the value of the physical change in inventories, and exports (less imports). Net national product (NNP) consists of GNP minus capital consumption allowances to reflect the using-up of part of the capital stock in producing the nation's output. NNP at factor cost consists of NNP minus indirect taxes less subsidies.

4. Constant dollar estimates for current expenditures were obtained by deflating exhaustive expenditures by the government expenditure deflator and by deflating total transfers (including interest) by the personal expenditure deflator.

5. See Department of Finance (1983, p.178).

6. Exhaustive expenditures are those that utilize goods and services in the public sector and hence are not available for use by the private sector. Total exhaustive expenditures consist of current expenditure on goods and services plus gross fixed capital formation by government.

7. We use the ratio derived from the revised *National Accounts*. As Table A-3 indicates, the early expenditure series, based on a variety of sources (see Stanbury, 1972 Ch.3) produces a substantially small ratio. The difference lies almost entirely in the estimate of total government expenditures ($1,560 millions versus $1,954 millions) rather than in the GNP estimates.

8. Note that both the numerator and the denominator are adjusted in making these calculations.

9. Real government consumption expenditures are the sum of expenditures on current goods and services plus depreciation of the stock of government capital plus the imputed return on the government's net capital stock. The net government product is the sum of expenditures on current goods and services plus the imputed return on government capital plus net capital formation by government (Stanbury, 1972, Ch.3, pp.30-31).

10. Both the "payroll intensity" and capital intensity of various government functions of the federal and provincial governments are discussed in Bird *et al.* (1979, pp.115-123). Typically, government wages and salaries in government gross fixed capital formation amount to 10 to 15 percent of the total expenditure on capital investment (see Stanbury, 1972, Table 3-24).

11. For more detail see Chapters 6 and 7 in Foot (1978) and Chapter 1 in Bucovetsky (1979). A newspaper report of a study of the public sector in Quebec indicates that the wages and salaries of provincial public sector employees were on a par with private sector employees in 1974/75. However, by 1979-80 Quebec public servants, on average, earned 20 percent more than private sector employees. The excess in 1982 was estimated to amount to $1.7 billion. This is the amount by which Quebec taxes exceeded the average of other Canadians, (William Johnson, "The high cost of a runaway public service." *Globe and Mail*, February 19, 1982, p.5). The study referred to is by Pierre Fortin and Pierre Frechette and in English is entitled *The Challenges of Quebec's Socio-Economic Development in the Eighties* (Quebec Planning and Development Council, 1982).

12. Government of Canada, *Estimates, 1982-83 Part I*, Table 5.2, p.56.

13. We note that Bird (1979, p.23) puts the ratio in 1968 at 25.4 percent. The difference is negligible.

14. The level of federal transfers to the provinces in the first sixty years after Confederation was as follows:

Period	% of total federal expenditures
1867 − 70	15.4%
1871 − 80	11.2
1891 − 95	10.0
1906 − 10	8.0
1920 − 25	4.5

Source: Stanbury (1972, Table 3-58)

15. Stanbury (1972, Ch.3, p.77) emphasizes that all the main sources of information on intergovernmental transfers "completely fail to recognize the substitution of tax abatements for unconditional grants to the Provinces which has taken place since the early 1950s." For example, in 1968 federal conditional and unconditional grants to the provinces amounted to $1,903 million and $1,003 million respectively. The estimated value of federal tax abatements was $1,961 million (Stanbury 1972, Table-3-57). In 1981/82 federal transfers to the provinces in the form of tax abatements totalled $5.1 billion, including just over $1 billion to Quebec for contracting out transfers. Cash transfers totalled $13.8 billion, of which $3.6 billion was for fiscal equalization. Data from Task Force on Federal-Provincial Fiscal Arrangements (1981). See also Economic Council (1982a).

16. A more comprehensive definition can be found in Government of Canada (1980). See also the U.S. *Congressional Budget Act of 1974*.

17. Brooks apparently had a hand in the November 1981 Budget. See Deborah McGregor, "Four men behind the budget," *Financial Times of Canada*, January 18, 1982, p.5.

18. W.A. Wilson, "Bureaucrats forget who owns 'public' money," *Calgary Herald*, January 13, 1982, p.A6. For a similar view, see Weidenbaum (1978).

19. The concept appears to have been the work of Stanley Surrey of the Harvard Law School, who was Assistant Secretary for Tax Policy in the U.S. Treasury (see Surrey, 1970, 1973).

20. See Government of Canada (1979). We note that estimates by academics had been produced in the 1970s — see Bird (1970), Perry (1976), Kesselman (1977), Maslove (1979, 1981), and Smith (1979). See also the National Council of Welfare (1976) estimates which gained considerable publicity. More generally, see Fallis (1980), Fiekowsky (1980), McLoughlin and Proudfoot (1981), Tamagno (1979), Woodside (1979), Le Pan (1980), and Brown (1982).

21. As quoted in Brooks (1981, p.32).

22. We should note that for 1980 the Department of Finance estimated the total of personal income tax expenditures at $23.4 billion (Government of Canada, 1980). The total was calculated by the authors while the Department (p.7) emphasizes that "the revenue impact of simultaneously eliminating two tax expenditures is generally not the same as the sum of their individual revenue impacts...." Five items accounted for 66 percent of the

1980 total: RPP/RRSPs ($2,600 million), the marital exemption ($1,055 million), non-taxation of capital gains on principal residences ($3,500 million), non-taxation of imputed income on owner-occupied houses ($5,000 million), and transfers of "income tax" room to the provinces concerning shared-cost programs ($275 million).

23. Columnist W.A. Wilson, for example, has said that such an estimate indicates that the bureaucrats' "thinking has become wholly detached from the social implications of their ideas and the realities of politics." He went on to say that "no finance minister would attempt to impose that sort of scheme unless he were certifiably insane." (Wilson, *supra*, note 18). Yet the idea gained some currency and Mr. MacEachen was forced to "state categorically that no plans whatsoever exist to tax imputed rent, now or in the future." (as quoted in a *Globe and Mail* editorial, March 17, 1982, p.6).

24. There has recently been some discussion of this idea in Canada. See Arthur Drache, "Flat taxers out of touch with reality," *Financial Post*, December 4, 1982, p.7, and "Flat tax can work," *Financial Post* editorial, February 12, 1983, p.9.

25. Lipsey (1979, p.7) points out that "some measures such as the progressive income tax may not really be intended to redistribute income but only to salve consciences by appearing to do so." More generally, see Tullock (1983).

26. This total was compiled by the authors from Government of Canada (1980). As indicated in note 22, the Department of Finance deliberately omits a total because of the interactive effects of eliminating various tax expenditures.

27. Brooks (1981, p. 34) states that in 1976 corporate tax expenditures were $2.4 billion.

28. This total was compiled by the authors from Government of Canada (1980). The caveat in note 22 applies here also. We note that almost half of the total ($2,110 million) arises from the exemption of food and non-alcoholic beverages from federal sales tax. Another $495 million is attributable to the exemption of clothing and footwear.

29. See Economic Council of Canada (1979) and (1981).

30. The authors emphasize that this is a conservative estimate. Although the Economic Council's regulation reference staff made considerable efforts

to determine a similar figure for provincial governments, they were unsuccessful because of differences in the provinces' public accounts and the inability to separate expenditures on regulatory activities from expenditures on other functions. It seems reasonable to believe that provincial expenditures on their regulatory activities are at least as large as those of the federal government. Priest and Wohl (1980) report that the ten provinces had some 1,608 regulatory statutes on the books in 1978 as compared to 140 for the federal government. The number ranged from 112 in Prince Edward Island to 206 in Ontario. Overall, what Priest and Wohl (1980, p. 93) defined as "regulatory statutes" amounted to 32 percent of all provincial statutes. In addition to these statutes each province has many hundreds of pages of regulations or subordinate legislation. For example, in 1978 Ontario had over 6,600 pages of regulations on the books.
In general, the number of pages of regulations exceeds the number of pages in the regulatory statutes themselves. See Priest and Wohl (1980, p. 107). We note that the number of pages of economic regulations in Quebec and Ontario exceeds that of the federal government (9,475 in double-column, bilingual format). Ontario's are double-column, unilingual so each page contains about twice as many words as the federal *Consolidated Regulations of Canada*, 1978 (Priest and Wohl, 1980, p. 87).

31. Stanbury and Thompson (1980) state that regardless of the measure used, the growth in federal regulation in the United States from 1970 through 1975 was dramatic. The number of pages published annually in the *Federal Register* more than tripled. The number of pages in the *Code of Federal Regulations* increased by a third. The number of "major" regulatory agencies increased by 35 percent. Thirty important regulatory laws were enacted by Congress (Lilley and Miller, 1977, pp. 49–52). More recent and more comprehensive figures than were available to Lilley and Miller indicate that American federal expenditures on regulatory programs increased from $866 million in fiscal 1970 to $3,268 million in 1975 to $4,862 million in fiscal 1978 (Chilton, 1979, p. 3). These data indicate an increase in expenditures of 277 percent in expenditures between 1970 and 1975 and one of 49 percent between 1975 and 1978.

The one area where American federal regulatory growth in the 1970s appears to be far higher than in Canada is in the number of employees of regulatory departments and agencies. The "raw figures" taken from Wallace and Penoyer (1978, p. 101) indicate an increase of 168 percent between 1970/71 and 1977/78. The comparable figure for Canada is 45 percent. Stanbury and Thompson's (1980) analysis of Wallace and Penoyer's figures indicates that the number of regulatory employees in 1970/71 is understated by about 18,000. If this correction is made, federal regulatory employment in the United States grew by 63 percent between 1970/71 and 1977/78, as compared to 45 percent in Canada.

32. Although the CPR was nominally a private enterprise, Hardin (1974, p. 56) notes that as of 1913 the estimated value of public subsidies and land grants (at $20 per acre) to the railroad amounted to $1.32 billion or $50,000 per mile.

33. From a confidential federal document.

34. See, for example, Beatty (1981); Berkowitz (1979); Borins (1982); Gordon (1981); Graham (1976); Langford (1979, 1981, 1982, 1983); Royal Commission on Financial Management and Accountability (1979); Stanbury and Thompson eds. (1982); Treasury Board Secretariate (1977); Privy Council Office (1977); Tupper (1978, 1979, 1981); Tupper and Doern (1981); Vining and Botterell (1983); Prichard (1983); Maclean (1981); Boardman et al. (1982); Trebilcock and Prichard (1983).

35. These data are used by the Auditor General (1982) in his recent discussion of federal Crown corporations.

36. The total adds to 310, but four corporations qualify in more than one place.

37. Gracey (1978, p. 26, n. 2) indicates that the CDC's subsidiary, Polysar Limited, has established 46 subsidiaries located around the world. The CDC itself is a mixed enterprise in which the federal government now owns 49 percent. It is not, strictly speaking, a Crown corporation. For its origins and early years see Graham (1976); for the last few years, see Foster (1983).

38. In his latest report to Parliament, the Auditor General (1982, p. 49) puts the total number of corporations in which the federal government was whole or part owner at 306 in November 1981. This total included 178 subsidiary or associated corporations. The principal difference between Langford's total and the Auditor General's is due to the former's inclusion of the CDC and its many subsidiaries.

39. The federal government owns 49 percent of the issued shares of the CDC. Technically, CDC has not been a Crown corporation since the time it began to sell shares to the public. Presumably, Langford and Huffman (1983) included the CDC in their list of "federal public corporations" because the enterprise is widely regarded as a Crown corporation. It should be noted that the Government has announced that it plans to sell off its shares in CDC. See "Ottawa plans to sell its 48.5 percent of Canada Development Corp.," Toronto *Star*, May 28, 1982, p. A3.; "Sale of CDC shares will hinge on Market," *Globe and Mail*, November 26, 1982 p. B4.

See also Foster (1983) and "Canada Development Corp.; A Shopping Spree Leaves It Owing a Bundle," *Business Week*, September 5, 1983, pp. 58–59.

40. Saskatchewan's seventeen Crown corporations held by the Crown Investments Corp. recorded a profit of $115 million in 1981 and a loss of $125 million in 1982. CIC paid a dividend of $142 million to the government in 1982. See Edward Greenspan, "Crown's dividend eases government deficit," *Financial Post*, May 21, 1983, p. 6.

41. According to the *Financial Post 500* (Summer 1984, p. 70), at the end of 1983 these two had total assets as follows: Hydro-Quebec $25,199 million and; Ontario Hydro $23,194 million.

42. See the judgment in *R. v. Uranium Canada et al.* (1983) 39 O.R. (2d) 474; 68C.C.C. (2d) 200; 66 C.P.R. (2d) 207 (Ontario C.A.) which was upheld by the Supreme Court of Canada on December 15, 1983. Note that in Bill C-29, introduced on April 2, 1984, the government proposed to make the commercial activities of federal and provincial Crown corporations where they are in actual or potential competition with other firms subject to the *Combines Investigation Act*. That bill, however, died on the order paper on July 9, 1984 – see Stanbury (in press).

43. We note that authors had to rely on asset data primarily for 1976 and 1977 – see Vining and Botterell (1983). Therefore, the ratio is understated.

44. Loan guarantees are for specific transactions (e.g., export contracts) while credit insurance is available to a class of leaders (e.g., the Canada Deposit Insurance Corporation). Loans by the federal and provincial governments increased from $6.7 billion in 1970 to $19.1 billion in 1980 (Economic Council, 1982b, p. 3). For an examination of the role of federal financial assistance in the United States, see; Break (1965) and Larkens (1972).

45. Loan guarantees by the federal government are rising rapidly. They increased from $6.9 billion at March 31, 1980, to almost $9 billion at the end of 1981. But the latter figure excludes a variety of loan guarantees including those made to Canadair Ltd. (over $1 billion). See Deborah McGregor, "Ottawa worried about loan guarantees," *Financial Times*, June 14, 1982, p. 8; "Guarantees raise fears," Vancouver *Province*, April 6, 1982, p. C8; and "Crown backing to apartment-flip firms tops $460 million," *Globe and Mail*, August 18, 1983, p. 3.

46. Note that the Economic Council (1982b, pp. 132–133) was able to include agencies and programs that accounted for "almost 80 percent of public

loans outstanding to the four sectors under consideration, as of March 31, 1979."

47. See "A bonanza for Bombardier," *Maclean's*, May 31, 1982, p. 43; Carl Mollins, "Canadian taxpayers save N.Y. commuters a nickel a day," *Vancouver Sun*, June 2, 1982, p. B5; "A subway collision over export credits," *Business Week*, June 14, 1982, pp. 30–31; and "U.S. Treasury chief approves Bombardier deal," Ottawa *Citizen*, July 14, 1982, p. 33.

48. John King, "Bombardier loan called waste," *Globe and Mail*, July 17, 1982, p. 4.

49. See Gillian MacKay, "Sowing a seed for survival," *Maclean's*, February 23, 1981, pp. 42–43; Nicholas Hunter, "Governments must take Massey shares Monday," *Globe and Mail*, July 3, 1982; "Massey-Ferguson needs more financial help," Vancouver *Sun*, August 9, 1982, p. B9; Nicholas Hunter, "Massey offers bankers shares in lieu of money," *Globe and Mail*, August 7, 1982, p. B14. More generally, see Cook (1981).

50. See Les Whittington, "Government's bailout attempts often end in disaster," Ottawa *Citizen*, August 31, 1982, p. 5; Hyman Soloman "Why a save-Dome deal could be in the making," *Financial Post*, July 31, 1982, pp. 1–2; Robert English, "Chrysler, Massey strike 11th-hour deal," *Financial Post*, August 21, 1982, p.4.

51. "Chrysler imperils the bailout deal," *Maclean's*, January 10, 1983, p. 26; "Chrysler in reverse," *Globe and Mail*, January 21, 1983, p. 6.

52. See Robert Gibbens and John Gray, "Ottawa to provide loan guarantees for Maislin rescue," *Globe and Mail*, July 31, 1982, p. B14; Robert Gibbens,"Maislin reveals rescue package with CIBC, Ottawa is $55 million," *Globe and Mail*, October 22, 1982, p. B1. Many of Maislin's competitors, also suffering economically because of the severe recession, were not pleased by the government intervention. Opposition critics claimed that the deal involved a bailout of the politically well-connected Bronfman family. One columnist argued that the structure of the Liberal Party's support explained why the government acted: "If Maislin were a Calgary company with 2,000 U.S. employees, the federal government wouldn't have considered a bailout... the Liberal government is protecting nearly 2,000 jobs in its political stronghold of Quebec." The *Financial Post* said the bailout was not a way to build business confidence, and the Ottawa *Citizen* said it was not justified. See Robert English, "Concern over Maislin spreads," *Financial Post*, August 14, 1982 p. 7; "As many truckers

back aid to Maislin as oppose it: government," Ottawa *Citizen*, August 11,1982, p. 29; Hyman Soloman, "Ottawa trying to draw bailout blueprint," *Financial Post*, October 23, 1982, p. 2; "Tories believe they can smell a political pork barrel," *Globe and Mail* August 3, 1982, pp. 1–2; John Gray, "Bronfman called minister on Maislin, Tory says," *Globe and Mail*, August 4, 1982, p. 1; Jamie Lamb, "Keeping them rolling in Quebec," Vancouver *Sun*, August 3, 1982, p. A4; *Financial Post* editorial, August 14,1982, p. 9; Ottawa *Citizen* "Maislin bail-out not justified," August 4, 1982, p. 8. For subsequent developments, see Amy Booth, "Questions hang over Maislin," *Financial Post*, August 27, 1983, p. 7.

53. Ian Anderson, "A greedy grab that risks new plays," *Maclean's*, January 11, 1982, James Rusk; "Report indicts Government over $125 million loss," *Globe and Mail*, February 20, 1982, p. 13; Bert Hill, "Johnston takes CCI blame," Ottawa *Citizen*, February 26, 1982, p. 11; "Red ink, red faces in the bureaucracy," *Maclean's*, March 1, 1982, pp. 42–43. The original $125 million figure was later revised.

54. See Douglas Yonson, "How Nabu is making big profits from CCI," *Financial Times*, December 6, 1982, pp.3, 11.

55. Amy Zierler, "Fishing company shakeup runs into troubled waters," *Financial Post*, August 27, 1983 p. 7, Patrick Roche, "Atlantic fish plan just stays afloat," *"Financial Post*, September 3, 1983, p.7. 107

56. Harvey Enchin, "Caisse de dépôt owns up to some of what it owns", Montreal *Gazette*, June 10, 1982, p.E1. As of June 30, 1982, the Canada Pension Plan Investment Fund had assets of $21.6 billion earning an average of 9.92 percent *(Globe and Mail*, September 13, 1982, p.6).

57. Ibid. As of October 1982 the Caisse had acquired 19 percent of Rolland Paper and 6.6 percent of Westburn International Ltd.

58. In response to the Quebec business community and the Quebec caucus, the federal government dropped the Bill.

59. *Canadian Business*, July 1982, pp.96–97.

60. *Financial Post 500*, June 1982, p.70.

61. Ibid., p.98.

62. *Globe and Mail*, January 14, 1982, p.87. More generally, see Robert Gib-

bens, "SGF digesting implications of its joint Domtar control," *Globe and Mail*, April 13, 1982, p.B1; and Wendie Kerr, "No merger talks held with Donahue, Domtar reports," *Globe and Mail*, May 12, 1982, p.B6.

63. "Board reflects equity of SGF, Caisse," *Globe and Mail*, December 27, 1982, p.B3. See also Amy Booth, "Quebec's big affair with Domtar," *Financial Post*, February 12, 1982, pp. 1, 6.

64. "Patriating Domtar first step in nationalization," *Financial Post*, September 19, 1981, p.S14.

65. Ibid.

66. Ibid.

67. Ibid.

68. *Financial Post* (September 19, 1981, p.S14) states:

> The linking pieces of the government's grand design were set in place in the past two years: A stock savings plan was established, whereby investments in new issues of Quebec-based companies, meeting certain criteria of provincial dominance, could be sheltered from provincial taxes; in last year's budget, state companies, including Hydro-Quebec, which had been excused from traditional income-based taxes, were required to remit to Quebec all income in excess of prudent requirements.

In addition, in 1981 the province purchased 54.6 percent of Asbestos Corp. from General Dynamics and has set up Societe Nationale de l'Amiante to develop the primary and secondary asbestos industry in Quebec. See Wendie Kerr, "Quebec takes long term view of Asbestos Corp." *Globe and Mail*, June 17, 1982. In general on the politics of Asbestos Corp., see Fournier (1981).

69. Quoted in David Olive, "Caisse unpopulaire," *Canadian Business*, May 1982, p.96.

70. The importance of the Caisse's 30 percent interest in Brascade Resources, 70 percent of which is owned by Brascan Ltd., which now effectively controls Noranda Mines through its 42 percent equity holding, should not be understated. Noranda is itself an enormous enterprise which combines both operating companies and conglomerate holdings. For example, in 1981 it had sales of $3.03 billion, (ranked 19th in the *Financial Post 500*)

and had assets of $5.254 billion. But these data understate Noranda's economic reach. Consider the following partial list of Noranda's holdings: 49.8 percent of MacMillan-Bloedel Ltd., Canada's largest forest products company and #36 on the F.P. 500; 100 percent of Maclaren Power and Paper; 75 percent of Canadian Hunter Exploration (one of Canada's largest holders of natural gas reserves); 42 percent of Tara Exploration; 33 percent of Placer Development (#227); 20 percent of Craigmont Mines; 51 percent of Brenda mines; 50 percent of Wire Rope Industries; 100 percent of Canada Wire and Cable; 44 percent of Kerr-Addison Mines; 64 percent of Fraser Inc. (#155); 64 percent of Brunswick Mining (#246); and 49 percent of Pamour Porcupine Mines. Note that Brascan, the Caisee's partner in Brascade, is controlled by Edper Equities which is controlled by only two men — Edward and Peter Bronfman (see Newman, 1982).

71. *Financial Post*, May 21, 1983, p.60. See also "Investments get major change in orientation," *Financial Post*, September 10, 1983, p.19. The Caisse in 1982 was the seventh ranked firm on the *Financial Post's* (June 1983, p.119) list of financial institutions.

72. Data from the annual reports of the Alberta Energy Company Ltd. We note that in 1982/83 the Fund spent $867,000 to advertise the activities of the fund and for public opinion polls. See Robert Sheppard, "Some cracks in the nest egg?" *Globe and Mail*, September 6, 1983, p.4.

73. Anthony McCallum, "Price of Chieftain shares jumps $3 after AEC announces plans for bid," *Globe and Mail*, June 18, 1982, p.B1. See also Jane Becker, "Chieftain directors to tender 30 percent of holdings to AEC," *Globe and Mail*, June 18, 1982, p.B14. The AEC bid for Chieftain at $24 per share was about a 50 percent premium over the price two days before the bid was announced.

74. Dennis Hryciuk, "AEC bid on Chieftain supported by premier," Edmonton *Journal*, June 22, 1982, p.D6.

75. Editorial, Edmonton *Journal*, June 22, 1982, p.D6.

76. The paper pointed out that in April 1981 the premier had written AEC's president to say that "AEC will not at this time actively pursue a program of attempting to acquire other petroleum companies." Apparently the premier did not want AEC taking advantage of the bargains created by the NEP and thereby having the petroleum industry liken the premier to Marc Lalonde. The editorial (Edmonton *Journal*, June 22, 1982, p.D6) correctly identified the dilemma created by joint public-private ownership of business enterprises:

When the government is the only shareholder of a Crown corporation, it can bring political pressure to bear against the company at an economic price because only the government pays that price. The morality of doing this at the cost of 60,000 private shareholders is another matter.... As troubling as this negative intervention, is the possibility of favoritism towards AEC because of partial government ownership. This penalizes the shareholders of competing energy firms to the benefit of AEC's private investors

77. Alberta Heritage Savings Trust Fund, *Annual Report*, 1982–83. About four-fifths of the Heritage Fund was committed to long-term investment. On March 31, 1983, the Heritage Fund had $11.39 billion in financial assets plus $1.61 billion in the form of capital assets. It held $7.6 billion in debentures in provincial Crown corporations. In his 1980/81 *Annual Report*, Treasurer Lou Hyndman pointed out that the Fund's income-earning investments (then $7.4 billion) amounted to a little more than one year's budgetary expenditure by Alberta, one-third of the assets of all trusteed pension plans in Canada, one-half the assets of the Canada Pension Plan and only about 2 percent of the total stock of assets that constitute the Canadian capital market. Note that the provincial Cabinet (through a resolution of the Assembly) has *direct* control over specific investments of the Fund with the very broad guidelines set out in the statute. See Diane Francis, "Blind Trust: We All Contribute to Alberta's Heritage Fund; Only 12 People Know How It's Invested," *Quest*, April 1982, pp.20–22.

78. Anthony McCallum, "Alberta buys shares in companies on TSE," *Globe and Mail*, May 20, 1982, p.B4. The Caisse de Dépôt has similarly refused, arguing that as an agent of the Crown it is not bound by the insider trading provisions of the *Canada Business Corporations Act*. See "OSC rules Caisse's bid for Domtar was illegal," *Globe and Mail*, November 11, 1982, p.B1.

79. *Globe and Mail*, May 20, 1982, p.B4.

80. More generally, see Eckel and Vermaelen (1983).

81. See, for example, Anderson Charters, "Jobs vs. profits dilemma at CN Express," *Financial Post*, December 20, 1980, p.16; Alan D. Gray, "Will Ottawa call shots at CN?" *Financial Times*, September 27, 1982, pp.18–19;

82. See Ronald Anderson, "Plan Subverting CDC Would be a Betrayal," *Globe and Mail*, May 13, 1981, p.B2; Roger Newman, "Directors of CDC

Return Sellers, Hampson to Posts," *Globe and Mail*, May 22, 1982, p.B7; and "The Seedy Assault on the CDC," *Maclean's*, June 1, 1981, pp.46–47. See also Foster (1983).

83. Fred Harrison, "Chosen instruments of public policy," *Financial Post*, July 18, 1981, pp.1–2; "In oil and gas it pays to be among the chosen," *Financial Post*, July 25, 1981, pp.1–2; "First get chosen, then be protected," *Financial Post*, August 1, 1981, pp.1–2.

84. July 25, 1981, p.1. For a useful discussion of Dome's strategy see Michael Bliss, "The Great Gamble," *Saturday Night*, July 1982, pp.13–21.

85. "The business leader as politician, *Financial Post*, December 13, 1980, p.18.

86. Hugh Anderson, "Dome's daring set up record issue," *Financial Post*, March 14, 1981, p.B1.

87. Its total initial capitalization was $1.06 billion comprised of 46 million shares at $10 sold to the public, netting Dome Canada $435 million for 52 percent of the common shares; 48 percent of the common shares to Dome Petroleum in exchange for 24 percent of the equity of TCPL and $150 million in cash; and $225 million loan from Japanese interests to be paid back with oil or, if no oil was found, with only the principal paid back.

88. See Foster (1980, pp.201-202).

89. Harrison, *supra* note 83 p.2. This point may have to be revised in light of the harsh terms of Ottawa's bailout of Dome. See Jennifer Lewington, "Ottawa and 4 banks may get 65 percent of Dome," *Globe and Mail*, October 1, 1982, p.B1. But Dome may find a way to survive without direct financial help from the federal government. See Jack Hanna, "Smilin' Jack bounces back, Jack Gallagher is out to save Dome from its rescuers," *Financial Times*, December 27, 1982, p.11 and p.18. Gallagher has since resigned as chairman of Dome. See Foster (1984), Lyon (1983).

90. Blair was the co-chairman, with Shirley Carr of the CLC, of the consultative Task Force on Industrial and Regional benefits from Major Canadian Projects. Their report, *Major Canadian Projects, Major Canadian Opportunities* (Ottawa: June 1981) advocated that premiums be paid to Canadian suppliers of inputs used in mega projects. More generally, see David Thomas, "Nationalists in the boardrooms," *Maclean's*, December 7, 1981, pp.54–56.

91. Generally see Swimmer (1984); Peter Cook, "6-and-5 controls: dramatic half measures," *Globe and Mail*, September 25, 1982, p.B1; Deborah McGregor, "MacEachen's 6 percent solution: Broader controls are likely if the new package fails," *Financial Times*, July 5, 1982, p.104, "6/5: The new politics of pain," *Maclean's*, August 16, 1982, pp.18–24.

92. Quoted by Jamie Lamb, Vancouver *Sun*, July 26, 1982, p.A4. See also "PM using 'leverage' to enforce restraints," *Globe and Mail*, July 24, 1982, p.1; and Ann Silversides, "Blais 'sells' 6/5 to supportive suppliers," *Globe and Mail*, September 2, 1982, p.B1.

93. "Ottawa's purse tied to provincial restraint," *Globe and Mail*, July 28, 1982, p.1.

94. *Maclean's*, August 2, 1982, p.3. See also Allan Fotheringham, "Bill, Big Julie and Pierre," *Maclean's*, September 20, 1982, p.64; Richard Spence, "Sinclair seeks restraint — 6/5 style," December 27, 1982, p.15.

95. "Policy linking subsidies to curbs questioned," *Globe and Mail*, August 7, 1982, p.B1.

96. Ibid. See also "Planned subsidy restraints tie irritates business," *Globe and Mail*, July 27, 1982, p.B1.

97. See Giles Gherson, "Liberal's restraint-selling helps keep them afloat," *Financial Post*, August 14, 1982, p.5; Thomas Walkom, "A day in the selling of 6–5 lands MP in grapes, gripes," *Globe and Mail*, September 16, 1982, p.8; Jamie Lamb, "Behind the restraint campaign; a most cynical man," Vancouver *Sun*, August 19, 1982, p.A4; Bruce Hutchison, "The motives are mixed in the senator's red book," Vancouver *Sun*, August 26, 1982, p.A4; "Chairman Keith's Big Red Book," *Maclean's*, August 16, 1982, p.21; Thomas Walkom, "MPs 6–5 homework graded," *Globe and Mail*, August 26, 1982, pp.1, 8. For more recent developments, see "The problem with 6-and-5 is its dangerous inflexibility," *Financial Times*, August 1, 1983, p.7; Bill Levitt, "Government hit for breaking 6–5 guides," Ottawa *Citizen*, August 3, 1983, pp. 1,5; Arthur Donner, "Government 6 and 5 program a vital boost in war on inflation," Toronto *Star*, July 22, 1983, p.A20; Joe O'Donnell, "Firm run by 6 and 5 champion gives workers 24 percent wage hike," Toronto *Star*, July 28, 1983, p.1; Robert Gibbens, "Mulholland urges long term policy for limiting wage, price increases," *Globe and Mail*, August 3, 1983, p.B1: "Ottawa has double standard," Montreal *Gazette*, July 28, 1983, p.B2.

98. A list of such takeovers can be found in Newman (1982, Appendix).

99. "Ottawa puts brakes on energy program," Vancouver *Sun*, July 30, 1981, p.D1.

100. The Standing Committee on Finance, Trade and Economic Affairs (1982, p.69) further notes that the purchase of financial assets of associated businesses totalled $2.6 billion in 1977 $3.7 billion in 1978, $7 billion in 1981. Canadian absorption of foreign-owned firms in the energy business totalled $5.57 billion in 1981, in the *private* sector alone. See also Foster (1982) and Crane (1982) re federal energy policy during the period. For the latest developments, see Jack Hanna, "PIP grants: Is it the beginning of the end?" *Financial Times*, August 22, 1983, p.3; Christopher Waddell, "PIP: Ottawa changes rules in mid-game," *Financial Post*, August 13, 1983, p.102. A Gallup poll released in April 1983 indicated that 45 percent of Canadians think that the federal government should sell Petro-Canada to the private sector. The Crown corporation is now Canada's fourth largest retailer of gasoline. See "Petrocan's costly push," *Maclean's*, August 8, 1983.

101. "Energy program not to blame for all oil takeovers," Vancouver *Sun*, July 25, 1981, p.H8. We note that energy firms participating in the takeover boom subsequently performed worse than those which did not acquire other companies. See "Takeovers costly for oil firms: Report," Toronto *Star*, July 27, 1983, p.B-12.

102. "Banks to curb takeover loans," *Globe and Mail*, July 31, 1981, p.B3.

103. *Globe and Mail*, July 31, 1981, p.6.

104. See, for example, "The Ottawa mess," August 1, 1981, p.6.

REFERENCES

Auld, D.A. *Issues in Government Expenditures Growth*. Montreal: C.D. Howe Research Institute, Canadian Economic Policy Committee, 1976.

Auditor General of Canada. *Report to the House of Commons: Fiscal year ended 31 March 1982*. Ottawa: Minister of Supply and Services, 1982.

Beatty, G.H. "Bridling the Beasts: How Saskatchewan combines accountability and management freedom in its Crown corporations." *Policy Options*, Vol. 2, No. 3, July/August 1981, pp.35-38.

Becker, Gary. "Competition and Democracy." *Journal of Law and Economics*, Vol. 1, 1958, pp.105-120.

————. "A Theory of Political Behaviour." University of Toronto, Law and Economics Workshop Series, October 22, 1981.

Berkowitz, S.D. "Form of State Economy and Development in Western Canada." *Canadian Journal of Sociology*, Vol. 4, No. 3, 1979, pp.287-312.

Bird, R.M. *The Growth of Government Spending in Canada*. Toronto: Canadian Tax Foundation, 1970.

————. "The Growth of the Public Service in Canada." In (ed.) *Public Employment and Compensation in Canada: Myths and Realities*, pp.10-44, ed. by D.K. Foot, Toronto: Butterworth for The Institute for Research on Public Policy, 1978.

————. *Financing Canadian Government: A Quantitative Overview*. Toronto: Canadian Tax Foundation, 1979.

————. *Taxing Corporations*. Montreal: The Institute for Research on Public Policy, 1980.

Bird, R.M. et al. *The Growth of Public Employment in Canada*. Montreal: The Institute for Research on Public Policy, 1979.

Bird, R.M. and David K. Foot. "Bureaucratic Growth in Canada: Myths and Realities." *The Public Evaluation of Government Spending*, ed. by G.B. Doern and A.M. Maslove, 1979.

Block, Walter. *A Response to the Framework Document for Amending the Combines Investigation Act*. Vancouver: The Fraser Institute, 1982.

Blum, W.J. and Harry Kalven. *The Uneasy Case for Progressive Taxation*. Chicago: University of Chicago Press, 1953.

Boardman, A.E., C. Eckel and Aidan Vining. "The Advantages and Disadvantages of Mixed Enterprises." Paper presented at The Global Reach of Public Enterprises Conference, University of Illinois, November 3-5, 1982, (mimeo).

Borins, Sandford. "World War Two Crown Corporations: Their Wartime Role and Peacetime Privatization." *Canadian Public Administration*. Vol. 25, No. 3, 1982, pp.380-404.

Break, G.F. *Federal Lending and Economic Stability*. Washington, D.C.: The Brookings Institution, 1965.

Bregha, Francois. *Bob Blair's Pipeline*. Toronto: McClelland and Stewart, 1979.

Brooks, Neil. "Making Rich People Richer." *Saturday Night*, July 1981, pp.30–35.

Brown, Robert D. "A Critical Review of Tax Shelters: Loophole or Escape Hatch?" *Tax Policy Options in the 1980s*, Toronto: Canadian Tax Foundation, 1982, pp.102–158.

―――. "A Critical Review of Tax Shelters." In *Tax Policy Options in the 1980s*, ed. by Thirsk and Whalley, Toronto: Canadian Tax Foundation, 1982.

Buchanan, James M. et al. eds. *Toward a Theory of the Rent-Seeking Society*. College Station, Texas: Texas A & M University Press, 1980.

Canada. *Report on the Royal Commission on Taxation*. Ottawa: Queen's Printer, 1966.

Chilton, Kenneth. "A Decade of Rapid Growth in Federal Regulation." St. Louis, Washington University: Center for the Study of American Business, 1976 (unpublished).

Comptroller General of Canada. *Government of Canada Corporations in Which the Government Has an Interest*. Ottawa: Minister of Supply and Services Canada, 1980.

Courchene, Thomas J. "Towards a Protected Society: The Politicization of Economic Life." *Canadian Journal of Economics*, Vol. 18, No. 4, November 1980, pp.556–577.

Crane, David. *Controlling Interest: The Canadian Oil and Gas Stakes*. Toronto: McClelland and Stewart, 1982.

Department of Finance. *Economic Review*, April 1983. Ottawa: Minister of Supply and Services Canada, 1983.

Doern, G. Bruce, ed. *The Regulatory Process in Canada*. Toronto: Macmillan, 1978.

―――. *Spending Tax Dollars: Federal Expenditures, 1980-81*. Ottawa: School of Public Administration, Carleton University, 1980.

―――. *How Ottawa Spends Your Tax Dollars: Federal Priorities, 1981*. Toronto: Lorimer, 1981.

―――. *How Ottawa Spends, 1982*. Toronto: Lorimer, 1982.

―――. *How Ottawa Spends, 1983*. Toronto: Lorimer, 1983.

Doern, G. Bruce and Allan M. Maslove, eds. *The Public Evaluation of Government Spending*. Montreal: The Institute for Research on Public Policy, 1979.

Dominion Bureau of Statistics, *Government Transactions Related to the Na-*

tional Accounts, 1926-1951. Reference Paper No. 39. Ottawa: Queen's Printer, 1952.

Donner, Arthur. "The Canadian Environment: 1981-1986" in *Through a Glass Darkly: A Medium-Term Canadian Perspective.* Toronto: Royal Trust, 1981, pp.87–117.

Eckel, Catherine and Aidan Vining. "Toward a Positive Theory of Joint Enterprise." *Managing Public Enterprises,* ed. by W.T. Stanbury and Fred Thompson, New York: Praeger, 1982, pp.209–222.

Eckel, C. and T. Vermaelen. "The Effects of Partial Government Ownership on Stock Prices." University of British Columbia, Faculty of Commerce and Business Administration Working Paper No. 883, 1983 (unpublished).

Economic Council of Canada. *Responsible Regulation.* Ottawa: Minister of Supply and Services Canada, November 1979.

―――. *Reforming Regulation.* Ottawa: Minister of Supply and Services. Canada, 1981.

―――. *Financing Confederation: Today and Tomorrow.* Ottawa: Minister of Supply and Services, 1982a.

―――. *Intervention and Efficiency: A Study of Government Credit and Credit Guarantees to the Private Sector.* Ottawa: Minister of Supply and Services, 1982b.

Elford Craig and W. T. Stanbury. "Mixed Enterprises in Canada." (Unpublished paper, University of British Columbia, Faculty of Commerce and Business Administration, mimeo) 1984.

Fallis, George. "The Incidence of Tax Expenditures: A Framework for Analysis." *Canadian Taxation.* Winter, 1980, pp.228–231.

Fiekowsky, Seymour. "The Relation of Tax Expenditures to the Distribution of the 'Fiscal Burden.'" *Canadian Taxation,* Winter 1980, pp.211-219.

Firestone, O.J. *Canada's Economic Development, 1867-1953.* London: Bowes and Bowes, 1958, Ch.6.

Foot, David K., ed. *Public Employment and Compensation in Canada: Myths and Realities.* Toronto: Butterworth for The Institute for Research on Public Policy, 1978.

Foster, Peter. *The Blue-Eyed Sheiks.* Toronto: Totem Books, 1980.

―――. *The Sorcerer's Apprentices: Canada's Super Bureaucrats and the Energy Mess.* Toronto: Collins, 1982.

―――. "Battle of the Sectors," *Saturday Night,* March 1983, pp.23–32.

―――. *Other People's Money: The Banks, the Government and Dome.* Toronto: Totem Books, 1984.

Fournier, Pierre. "The National Asbestos Corporation of Quebec." in *Public Corporations and Public Policy in Canada*, ed. by Alan Tupper and G.B. Doern, Montreal: The Institute for Research on Public Policy, 1981, pp.353–564.

Gillespie, W. Irwin and Allan M. Maslove. "The 1980–81 Estimates: Trends, Issues and Choices," in *Spending Tax Dollars: Federal Expenditures, 1980–81:* ed. G. Bruce Doern (Ottawa: School of Public Administration, Carleton University, 1980), pp.23–48.

Gordon, Marsha. *Government in Business.* Montreal: C.D. Howe Research Institute, 1981.

Gordon, H. Scott. "The Demand and Supply of Government: What We Want and What We Get." Ottawa: Economic Council of Canada, Discussion Paper No. 79, 1977.

Government of Canada, Department of Finance. (1979) *Government of Canada Tax Expenditure Account.* Ottawa: December 1979.

———. *Government of Canada Tax Expenditure Account.* Ottawa, December 1980. (covers 1976–1980).

———. *Analysis of Federal Tax Expenditures for Individuals.* Ottawa, November 1981.

Gracey, Don "Public Enterprise in Canada," in *Public Enterprise and the Public Interest,* ed. by Andre Gelinas, Toronto: Institute of Public Administration of Canada, 1978, pp.25–47.

Gracey, D.P. "Federal Public Corporations in Canada" in K. Kernaghan *Public Administration in Canada*, ed. by K. Kernaghan, 4th edition, Toronto: Methuen Publications, 1982, pp.50–70.

Graham, Michael R. *Canadian Development Corporation.* Study No. 4 for the Royal Commission on Corporate Concentration, Ottawa: Minister of Supply and Services, 1976.

Gratwick, John. "Canadian National: Diversification and Public Responsibilities in Canada's Largest Crown Corporation." In *Managing Public Enterprises*, ed. by W.T. Stanbury and Fred Thompson, New York: Praeger, 1982, pp.237–249.

Green, Mark and Norman Waitzman. *Business War on the Law: An Analysis of the Benefits of Federal Health/Safety Enforcement.* Washington: The Corporate Accountability Research Group, 1979.

Green, Christopher. *Canadian Industrial Organization and Policy.* Toronto: McGraw-Hill Ryerson, 1980.

Hardin, Herschel. *A Nation Unaware: The Canadian Economic Culture.* Vancouver: J.J. Douglas, 1974.

Hartle, Douglas G. *Public Policy Decision Making and Regulation.* Montreal: The Institute for Research on Public Policy, 1979.

Hartwick, John M. *Public Expenditures in Federal States: A Comparison of Trends in Canada and the U.S., 1932–1963.* Ottawa: Department of Finance, 1967 (unpublished).

Hay Associates Canada Ltd. *Report to Opinion Leaders.* Toronto: Hay Associates, January 1983.

Hirschman, Alberta O. *Exit, Voice and Loyalty: Responses to Decline in Firms, Organizations and States.* Cambridge, Mass: Harvard University Press, 1970.

Hodgetts, J.E. and O.P. Dwivedi. "Growth of Government in Canada." *Canadian Public Administration.* Vol. 12, 1969, pp.224–38.

Hood, William and A.D. Scott. *Output, Labour and Capital in the Canadian Economy.* Ottawa: Queen's Printer, 1956.

Hughes, Jonathan R.T. *The Government Habit.* New York: Random House, 1977.

Hurley, Douglas. "The Social Environment, Social Trends and Consumer Attitudes and Behaviour." In *Through a Glass Darkly: A Medium-Term Canadian Perspective,* Toronto: Royal Trust, 1981, pp.31-62.

Kesselman, Jonathan R. "Non-business Dedications and Tax Expenditures in Canada: Aggregates and Distributions." *Canadian Tax Journal* Vol. 25, No. 2, March-April, 1977, pp.160–79.

Kirby, M.J.L. *Navigating Troubled Waters: Report of the Task Force on the Atlantic Fisheries.* Ottawa: Minister of Supply and Services Canada, 1983, 2 Vols.

Langford, John W. "The Identification and Classification of Federal Public Corporations: A Preface to Regime Building." *Canadian Public Administration,* Vol. 23(1), 1980, pp.76-104.

———. "Public Corporations in the 1980s: Moving from Rhetoric to Analysis." *Canadian Public Administration,* Vol. 25 (4), 1982, pp.619-37.

Langford, John W. and Kenneth Huffman. "The Uncharted Universe of Federal Public Corporations" in *Crown Corporations: The Calculus of Instrument Choice,* ed. by J.R.S. Prichard, Toronto: Butterworths, 1983, pp.219-301.

Langford, John W. and Neil Swainson. "Public and Quasi-Public Corporations in B.C." in *The Administrative State in Canada,* ed. by O.P. Dwivedi, Toronto: University of Toronto Press, 1982, pp.63-87.

Larkey, P.D., C. Stolp and M. Winer. "Theories of Government Size and Growth: A Literature Review." *Journal of Public Policy,* Vol. 1, No. 2, 1982.

Larkins, Dan. *$300 Billion in Loans: An Introduction to Federal Credit Programs*. Washington, D.C.: American Enterprise Institute, 1972.

LePan, Nicholas. "Measurement of the Revenue and Distributive Effects of Tax Expenditures." *Canadian Taxation*, Winter, 1980, pp. 220–224.

Lermer, George and W.T. Stanbury. "Measuring the Cost of Redistributing Income by Means of Direct Regulation." *Canadian Journal of Economics* (in press).

Lilley, William III, and James C. Miller III. "The New 'Social' Regulation." *The Public Interest*, Spring, 1977, pp.40–61.

Lipsey, Richard. "An Economist Looks at the Future of the Market Economy." Paper presented to the XV Annual Nobel Conference on the future of the market Economy, Gustafus Adolphus College, St. Peter, Minnesota, October 10, 1979.

Lyon, Jim. *Dome: The Rise and Fall of the House that Jack Built*. Toronto: Macmillan, 1983.

MacLean, Gordon. *Public Enterprises in Saskatchewan*. Regina: Crown Investments Corporation of Saskatchewan, 1981.

Maslove, Allan M. "The Other Side of Public Spending: Tax Expenditures in Canada" in *The Public Evaluation of Government Spending* ed. by G. Bruce Doern and Allan M. Maslove. Montreal: The Institute for Research on Public Policy, 1979.

———."The Distributive Effects of Tax Expenditures: A Suggested Methodology and an Example." *Canadian Taxation*, Winter 1980, pp.225–227.

———. *Public Policy, Tax Expenditures, and Distribution*. University of Carlton School of Public Administration, May 1981 (unpublished).

Maslove, Allan M. and Gene Swimmer. *Wage Controls in Canada, 1975-78*. Montreal: The Institute for Research on Public Policy, 1980.

Maxwell, Judith. "The Role of Government: Searching for a Framework." Montreal: C.D. Howe Research Institute, Staff Speeches No. 15, July 1977.

McLaughlin, Kevin and S.B. Proudfoot. "Giving by Not Taking: A Primer on Tax Expenditures." *Canadian Public Policy*, Vol. 7(2), 1981, pp.328–337.

Miller, James E. III. "Prepared Statement before the Subcommittee on Consumer Protection and Finance and the Subcommittee on Oversight, U.S. House of Representatives." Washington, D.C.: American Enterprise Institute, October 24, 1979 (mimeo).

Mintz, Jack. "Public-Private Mixed Enterprises: The Canadian Example." Kingston, Ont.: Queen's University, Department of Economics, Discussion Paper 325, 1979.

National Council on Welfare. *The Hidden Welfare System.* Ottawa: National Council on Welfare 1976.

Newman, Peter. *The Acquisitors.* Toronto: McClelland & Stewart, 1982.

Nutter, G. Warren. *Growth of Government in the West.* Washington: American Enterprise Institute for Public Policy Research, 1978.

Perry, David B. "Fiscal Figures: Corporation Tax Expenditures." *Canadian Tax Journal* Vol. 24, No. 5, September-October 1976, pp.528-33.

Perry, David B. "Changes in the Canadian Tax Structure." *Canadian Tax Journal*, Vol. 25, July-August, 1977, pp.441-445.

Posner, Richard A. "The Social Costs of Monopoly and Regulation." *Journal of Political Economy*, Vol. 83, No. 4, August 1975, pp.807-827.

Priest, Margot, W.T. Stanbury and Fred Thompson. "On the Definition of Economic Regulation" in *Government Regulation: Scope, Growth, Process*, ed. by W.T. Stanbury, Montreal: The Institute for Research on Public Policy, 1980, pp.1-16.

Priest, Margot and Aron Wohl. "The Growth of Federal and Provincial Regulation of Economic Activity, 1867-1978" in *Government Regulation: Scope, Growth, Process*, ed. by W.T. Stanbury, Montreal: The Institute for Research on Public Policy, 1980, pp.60-149.

Prichard, J.R.S. ed. *Crown Corporations: The Calculus of Instrument Choice.* Toronto: Butterworths, 1983.

Privy Council Office. *Crown Corporations: Direction, Control, Accountability.* Ottawa: Minister of Supply and Services Canada, 1977.

Reschenthaler, Gil, Bill Stanbury and Fred Thompson. "Whatever Happened to Deregulation?" *Policy Options*, Vol. 3, No. 3, 1982, pp.36-42.

Rosenfeld, B.D. "Canadian Government Expenditures, 1871-1966." Unpublished Ph.D dissertation, University of Pennsylvania, 1972.

Rosenfeld, B.D. "The Displacement Effect in the Growth of Canadian Government Expenditures." *Public Finance*, Vol. 28, No. 3-4, 1973, pp.302-314.

Royal Commission on Financial Management and Accountability. *Final Report.* Ottawa: Minister of Supply and Services, 1979.

Schumpeter, J.A. *History of Economic Analysis.* New York: Oxford University Press, 1954.

Shepherd, John. "Hidden Crown Corporations." *Policy Options*, Vol . 2, No. 2, 1981, pp.40-42.

Smith, Roger S. *Tax Expenditures: An Examination of Tax Incentives and Tax Preferences in the Canadian Federal Income Tax System.* Toronto: Canadian Tax Foundation, 1979.

Stanbury, W.T. "Changes in the Size and Structure of Government Expenditures in Canada, 1867-1968." Unpublished Ph.D dissertation, University of California at Berkeley, Department of Economics, 1972.

―――. "Changes in the Use of Governing Instruments by the Federal Government." Faculty of Commerce and Business Administration, University of British Columbia, August 1982 (unpublished).

―――. "Half a Loaf: Bill C29, Amendments to the Combines Investigation Act," *Canadian Business Law Journal,* (in press).

Stanbury, W.T. and Jane Fulton. "Suasion as a Governing Instrument" in Allan M. Maslove (ed.) *How Ottawa Spends, 1984: The New Agenda,* Toronto: Methuen, 1984, Ch. 9.

Stanbury, W.T. and Fred Thompson. "The Scope and Coverage of Regulation in Canada and the United States: Implications for the Demand for Reform" in *Government Regulation: Scope, Growth, Process,* ed. by W.T. Stanbury, Montreal: The Institute for Research on Public Policy, 1980, pp.17-67.

―――. "The Extent of Economic Regulation in the United States and Canada." Faculty of Commerce and Business Administration, University of British Columbia, 1981, (unpublished).

―――. eds. *Managing Public Enterprises.* New York: Praeger, 1982.

―――. *Regulatory Reform in Canada.* Montreal: The Institute for Research on Public Policy, 1982.

Stanbury, W.T. and Susan Burns. "The Department of Consumer and Corporate Affairs: Portrait of a Regulatory Department" in *How Ottawa Spends Your Tax Dollars, 1982,* ed. by G. Bruce Doern, Toronto: Lorimer, 1982, Ch.8.

Stanbury, W.T. and George Lermer. "Regulation and the Redistribution of Income and Wealth." *Canadian Public Administration,* Vol. 26(3), 1983, pp.387-401.

Stanbury, W.T., G.J. Gorn and C.B. Weinberg. "Federal Advertising Expenditures" in *How Ottawa Spends: The Liberals, the Opposition Parties and National Priorities,* ed. by G. Bruce Doern, Toronto: Lorimer, 1983, pp.133-172.

Standing Committee on Finance, Trade and Economic Affairs. *Bank Profits.* Minutes of Proceedings of the Standing Committeee, Issue 109, July 27, 1983.

Surrey, Stanley. *Pathways to Tax Reform.* Cambridge, Mass.: Harvard University Press, 1973.

Swedlove, Frank. "Business-government joint ventures in Canada." *Foreign Investment Review,* Spring 1978, pp.13-16..

Swimmer, Gene. "Six and Five." in Allan M. Maslove (ed.) *How Ottawa*

Spends 1984: The New Agenda, Toronto: Methuen, 1984, pp.240–281.

Tamagno, Edward. "Comparing Direct Spending and Tax Spending." *Canadian Taxation,* Winter, 1979, pp.42–45.

Treasury Board Secretariat. *Government-Owned and Controlled Corporations.* Ottawa: Financial Administration Branch, 1977.

Trebilcock, M.J. and J.R.S. Prichard. "Crown Corporations: The Calculus of Instrument Choice." *Crown Corporations in Canada: The Calculus of Instrument Choice,* ed. by J.R.S. Prichard, Toronto: Butterworths, 1983, pp.1–96.

Trebilcock, M.J. et al. *The Choice of Government Instrument.* Ottawa: Minister of Supply and Services, 1982.

Trebilcock, M.J., D.G. Hartle, J.R.S. Prichard and D.N. Dewees. *The Choice of Government Instrument.* Study for the Economic Council of Canada Regulation Reference, Ottawa: Minister of Supply and Services Canada, 1982.

Tullock, Gordon. *Economics of Income Redistribution.* The Hague: Kluwer-Nijhoff, 1983.

Tupper, Allan. "Public Enterprise as Social Welfare: The Case of the Cape Breton Development Corporation." *Canadian Public Policy,* Vol. 4, No. 4, 1978, pp. 530–546.

————. "The State in Business," *Canadian Public Administration,* Vol. 22, Spring 1979, pp. 124–150.

————."Pacific Western Airlines" in (eds.) *Public Corporations and Public Policy in Canada,* ed. by Allan Tupper and G. Bruce Doern. Montreal: The Institute for Research in Public Policy, 1981, pp.285–317.

Tupper, Allan and G. Bruce Doern, eds. *Public Corporations and Public Policy in Canada.* Montreal: The Institute for Research on Public Policy, 1981.

U.S. General Accounting Office. *Tax Expenditures: A Primer.* Washington D.C.: USGPO, 1979.

Vining, Aidan and Robert Botterell. "An Overview of the Origins, Growth, Size and Function of Provincial Crown Corporations" in *Crown Corporations: The Calculus of Instrument Choice,* ed. by J.R.S. Prichard, Toronto: Butterworths, 1983, pp.303–367.

Wallace, Marcia B. and Ronald J. Penoyer. "Directory of Federal Regulatory Agencies." Washington University, Center for the Study of American Business, as reprinted in *Cost of Government Regulations to the Consumer,* Hearings before the Subcommittee for Consumers of the Committee on Commerce, Science, and Transportation, United States Senate, 95th Congress, 2nd Session, Nov. 21, 22, 1978, pp.90–171.

Weidenbaum, Murray L. "The Case for Tax Loopholes." In *A New Tax Structure for the United States*, ed. by Donald H. Skadding, Indianapolis: Bobb-Merrill, 1978.

Weidenbaum, Murray L. and Robert De Fina. "The Cost of Federal Regulation." Washington, D.C.: American Enterprise Institute, 1978, Reprint No. 88.

Westell, Anthony. "Our Fading Political Culture." *Policy Options*, Vol. 3, No. 1, Jan./Feb. 1982, pp.8–11.

Woodside, Ken. "Tax Incentives vs. Subsidies: Political Considerations in Governmental Choice." *Canadian Public Policy*, Vol. 5, No. 2, 1979, pp.248–56.